EARTH-BASED PSYCHOLOGY

Path Awareness
from the Teachings of Don Juan,
Richard Feynman, and Lao Tse

Arnold Mindell, Ph.D.

Printed in the United States of America

Library of Congress Control Number: 2006937794

Mindell, Arnold
    Earth-Based Psychology: Path Awareness from the Teachings of Don
    Juan, Richard Feynman, and Lao Tse
    Bibliography
    Includes index

ISBN 10: 1-887078-75-4
ISBN 13: 978-1-887078-75-7

Book design by Anita Jones, Another Jones Graphics

Illustration and photo credits—cover: National Aeronautics and Space Administration; 4.2, 5.1: Susan Kocen; 5.5: Jeff Teasdale, from *Tao: The Chinese Philosophy of Time and Change* by Philip Rawson and Laszlo Legeza (New York: Thames & Hudson, 1979); 11.1: John Kahl, www.uwm.edu; 11.3: Susan Kocen; 15.5: reproduced from www.kashand.com with permission; 17.3: Western History/Genealogy Department, Denver Public Library, Denver, Colorado; 18.1: Charles Douglas, courtesy of the Canadian Museum of Nature, Ottawa, Canada; 19.1: *Spirit Mercurius,* Andevan Bronzeworks—www.andevan.com; 19.2: *Alchemy: The Secret Art* by Stanislas Klossowski de Rola (New York: Thames & Hudson, 1986).

Distributed to the trade by:
Independent Publishers Group
814 N. Franklin Street,
Chicago, IL 60624
Tel: (800) 888-4741
Fax: (312) 337-5985
www.ipgbook.com

To Amy, who walks real and timeless world paths with me.

CONTENTS

ACKNOWLEDGMENTS

Thanks to—

- Process-oriented psychology students and colleagues from around the world. You gave me courage to move forward with the writing of this book in its experimental stages.

- Richard Feynman for making clear that the material world is "the sum over histories." (Richard, did you know your ideas would be so helpful in describing the geometry of our human nature?) And thanks, too, to his teacher, John Wheeler of Princeton, and Wheeler's coauthor, Edwin Taylor of the Massachusetts Institute of Technology. Personal communications with Taylor and his way of following Feynman's primal sense of "least action" inspired me in many ways.

- Brian Josephson, physicist at the University of Cambridge, for pointing me to his paper, "The Pathological Disbelief," delivered to his Nobel Laureate colleagues at Lindau, Germany, June 30, 2004.

- The Los Alamos National Laboratory scientists (especially from the special materials department) who attended our first seminars on the quantum mind and who were so supportive of this work.

- C. G. Jung and Jungian sisters and brothers, for helping me understand that life is teleological and meaningful. And thanks to my Jungian teachers—Marie-Louise von Franz, Franz Riklin, and Barbara Hannah of the Jung Institute in Zurich. Without their early support, I would never have realized the importance of dreams. (Dear C. G., I believe your interest in mandalas may have been one of the forerunners behind my interest in the geometry of dreams.)

- Carlos Castaneda—or rather don Juan. You reminded me that the earth is sentient, has a heart, arms, and a mind that hold and guide us.

I am indebted to the work of physicist Fred Alan Wolf for exploring the domain where science and spirit are almost indistinguishable. Thanks to astronaut Story Musgrave for asking me, "What is gravity?"

All my work is based upon my past studies in theoretical and applied physics. Special thanks go to my teacher, Professor Walter Lowen, dean of the transdisciplinary systems program at SUNY in Binghamton, New York; to my many instructors at MIT; and to the E.T.H. in Zurich.

Margaret Ryan's sculpting has again been invaluable in editing this book. Thanks to Susan Kocen for the use of some of this book's pictures and also for transcribing the seminars from which this work arose. And thanks to Sharon Leeds of the University of Oregon Physics Department for checking some of my work. Many thanks especially to Lee Spark Jones of Lao Tse Press in Portland, for her patience and wisdom in parenting this book through to publication.

Thanks to the aboriginal groups we have worked with in Africa, Australia, and the Americas for their community consciousness and earth-based radiance. They remind me that we are all children of the earth, and from them I have learned so much. I now know there are many levels to racism, one of the most insidious and self-destructive inner effects of which is the unwitting repression of the dreaming earth by cosmopolitan cultures.

Amy Mindell, my partner in all things, helped me with every inch of this work, from the very first beginnings of elementary particles through its expressions in Taoism. Amy helped me bring sentient inner experience into a global context. Her singing, painting, dancing, and puppet making inspired much of what you will find here. She is as much shaman as scientist.

Every effort has been made to trace all present copyright holders of the material used in this book, whether companies or individuals. Any omission is unintentional and we will be pleased to correct any errors in future editions of this book.

PREFACE

The question motivating this book is this: *What inexplicable forces govern or direct our lives?* What moves us to take one direction one day, and another direction on the next day? Is the answer chance? Is it psychology, physics, or shamanism? Genetics, your dreams, outer events in the human world, or the cosmos?

To answer these questions, I liberally borrow from physics, psychology, and from my personal experience with earth-based, aboriginal beliefs and shamanism.

Earth-Based Psychology defines, explores, and applies a relatively new and fundamental concept: *path awareness*. To explain, experience, and understand our inherent direction-finding ability, I had to cross the conventional borders of various disciplines. Physics focuses mainly upon material experimental proof and is just beginning to explore subjective experience. Shamanism is mainly concerned with altered states of consciousness and community. The practice of psychology deals mainly with the emotional and functional problems of human life.

Because of the transdisciplinary nature of earth-based directional consciousness, I cannot do justice to quantum theory, shamanism, or even Taoism. Rather my aim is to bridge the gaps between these sciences and arts in order to define path awareness—that is, our innate ability to sense where to turn at a given moment. We will find analogies of path awareness in Richard Feynman's elementary particle physics, in Lao Tse's Taoism, and in Carlos Castaneda's form of shamanism expressed by his (real or imaginary) teacher, don Juan Matus. Above all, we shall find the predecessors of what I am calling *path awareness* in the ancient customs of our ancestors.

I invite you to travel with me on a path through this book. We shall move into thinking and feeling, using the rational mind as well as altered states of consciousness that sense the earth. We shall journey through the Way of Taoism, the possibility paths of elementary particle physics, and core elements of don Juan's shamanism. My goal is to develop directional consciousness or path awareness, show that it is basic to an earth-based psychology, and apply it to the solution of personal problems, and relationship, organizational, and world issues.

Path awareness is actually an ancient concept. Linked to the universe, our bodies sense direction in ways that merge our personal psychology with the real and imaginary nature of the earth around us. Aboriginal peoples have spoken about path awareness in terms of the gods of the four directions and the geometry of sand paintings. Einstein spoke of the mind of God and the geometry of space–time. Psychology, too, I hope, will soon speak more about the directional wisdom of the earth. Our psychology is intimately linked not only to disembodied dreams and feelings, but also to the nature of space and to the manner in which our bodies relate to this magical planet. In a way, psychology is an aspect of cosmology. *Earth-Based Psychology* will show how our deepest feelings can be expressed as mathematical patterns linked to earth-based directions.

Path awareness is the natural inheritance, the birthright of every human being. Path awareness is an updated form of earth-based spiritual paradigms. All of our aboriginal sisters and brothers, our real and mythic ancient histories, speak about moving according to the directions of a living planet, a sentient earth. Because of flashlights and maps, modern cultures mostly ignore dreamlike earth powers that are slowly slipping into the world of dreams and shamans. Instead we read fairy tales about story figures and science fiction heroes who move with the powers of darkness, through parallel universes, following allies only vaguely imagined by those of us following our daily programs. I want to bring all this down to earth and develop new methods of following the directional experience of the cosmos on earth.

My path

After my training at MIT in Cambridge and my Jungian studies in Zurich, I began meditating on the teachings of Carlos Castaneda's shaman, don Juan (discussed in my first book, *The Shaman's Body*). For years I worked as a therapist—at first as a Jungian trainer, then as a process-oriented therapist. I discovered how our dreams are mirrored in body symptoms and how to follow visible body signals to understand dreams. I wanted to show how *process* and *flow* are central to all psychologies and many spiritual traditions. Then my interest in physics returned and reappeared in *Quantum Mind*.

In *Earth-Based Psychology* I want to go further, honoring the work of my earlier teachers to develop new spinning and walking meditations that explore some of the mysteries of physics and the everyday problems of life. My methods will reveal new earth-based forms of inner work, relationship work, and community-making procedures. In particular, I will show how don Juan's teachings are connected to Feynman's "least action" formulation of quantum physics. Don Juan, a Yaqui Indian from northern Mexico, embodies the principle of least action—a principle that spans psychology and physics and appears in Taoism as "not-doing."

The manner in which I returned to Richard Feynman is mysterious. One day, while wondering about death and the world issues I meet daily in my work, something turned my head, and my eyes fell upon a little grey book sitting at the edge of a shelf in my home library. It was a little book I had not thought about since I had studied at MIT in the 1960s. The first words of the title read: *Richard Feynman, QED* (quantum electrodynamics). I asked myself, *How can the Nobel Prize-winning physicist Richard Feynman's thinking help me with my world of people and shamans? What on earth do elementary particles have to do with international events and the experiences I have in the middle of the night?* I could not resist: I was soon deeply involved reading Feynman's fascinating story of the paths of elementary particles.

Several hours later I emerged, realizing that his ideas were descriptions referring not only to particles, but to Aboriginal "songlines" among native Australians, and to the directional wisdom and orientation of all our ancestors. It took me another five years of thinking and working with people from all over the world to come to the conclusion that *what happens to elementary particles also happens to people.*

So to therapists: I hope you will read *Earth-Based Psychology* in spite of the physics in the first part of this book. I did my best to make directional awareness palpable to you. In Parts II, III, and IV, the discussions of path awareness will help you better understand the geometry or blueprint behind dream, body, relationship, and organizational processes.

To physical scientists: I hope you will be interested in thinking with me about endophysics, the experiential realm behind our physically based ideas and theories. For me, math describes physics; it is symbolic not only of the measurable universe, but also of what we don't know about our neighbors and ourselves.

The structure of this book

In Part I, "Path Awareness in Psychology, Taoism, and Physics," I try to make quantum electrodynamics at least intuitively reasonable, connect it with Taoism, aboriginal earth wisdom, and today's psychology, and develop new practices for individuals and communities. For more about physics, inner work, and worldwork, see the appendices.

In Part II, "The Universe's View of Body Symptoms," I show how to use new, earth-based walking meditations to heal body problems.

Part III, "Where Relationships Come From," explores entirely new approaches to relationships that are fun, geometrical, and mystical.

And in the final part, "Eldership and World Paths," you will find methods of "sitting in the fire" to process community issues based upon aboriginal spirituality.

PART I

Path Awareness in Psychology, Taoism, and Physics

*I consider science an integrating part of our endeavor to answer
the one great philosophical question which embraces all others . . .
who are we? And more than that: I consider this not only one of
the tasks, but the task of science, the only one that really counts.*
                                                —Erwin Schrödinger[1]

1

Lao Tse, Feynman, and Don Juan

*The key to everything was the firsthand knowledge that the earth is
a sentient being. . . . We living beings are perceivers . . . and we
perceive because some emanations inside man's cocoon become
aligned with some emanations outside. Alignment, therefore, is the
secret passageway, and the earth's boost is the key.*

—don Juan[1]

Earth-Based Psychology presents path-awareness methods to determine
where we are headed, where we are going, and the nature of our
momentary personal or community directions. One of my first and
greatest teachers in path awareness called herself a witch doctor. As the
center of a Kenyan tribal community, Nana (my name for her) and her
husband helped my wife and me through one of the most awesome
individual and community healing experiences we have ever had. After
creating a sand drawing of what Nana saw on the ground, our shaman-
ic healer went into trance state, danced, then fell to the ground. After
listening to the earth, Nana emerged from the trance and spoke words
she heard from what she called "a healing spirit." The result was that,
for years to come, I felt centered and inspired to follow the path I am
now on in psychology, shamanism, and physics.

Only a few years earlier, my analyst Dr. Franz Riklin—a nephew of
C. G. Jung and president of the Jung Institute in Zurich—modeled for

me how to live the shaman's potential in the streets of a Western city and as a Western psychiatrist. Riklin's amazing, intuitive ability to find the Way came to him, he said, "out of the air."

Until now my entire life has been devoted to making the perspective and path awareness of these two wonderful people available to others in the form of new methods of working with inner problems, body symptoms, relationships, and community issues. *Earth-Based Psychology* is the manifestation of this development, which I call *process-oriented psychology*. On these pages are integrated my scientific background with the shamanism and Taoism of finding guidance and divining the Way into the future. My goal is to find methods of easing the difficulties of everyday human life by bringing earth-based, aboriginal, directional wisdom to bear upon individual and world issues.

According to don Juan Matus—a Yaqui shaman in Mexico—to survive the mundane world filled with dreaming spirits, a warrior-shaman must live impeccably and move through altered states of consciousness and the *Nagual,* the world psychologists call the dream-world, or the unconscious. Because any path is just a path, according to don Juan, one must find and walk a unique "path of heart." It is the path that a very old person knows, the shaman said. It is your task to find that path and turn reality into magic.[2] It is the purpose of *Earth-Based Psychology* to help readers find that path with the help of not only shamanism, but also the math and metaphors of physics.

Richard Feynman and least action

Shamanism thrives in many cosmopolitan individuals as well as in aboriginal communities. Most of us have a bit of don Juan in us. Richard Feynman had a *lot* of don Juan in him. An American-born quantum physicist, Feynman won the Nobel Prize for his diagrams and explanations of how nearly invisible elementary particles of light and matter moved.[3] His intuitive diagrams, today called "the Feynman diagrams," aid quantum physicists in calculating and conceptualizing how particles sniff out all possible paths, so to speak, and take the most probable one, the one leading to "least action." I will show how the physicist's path of least action is very close to the shaman's "path of heart."

Together with the work of other physicists, Feynman's ideas created the standard theory of quantum electrodynamics (QED), the theory of light and matter. Still used today, the standard theory is the most accurate theory that physics has ever produced. How accurate? To borrow one of Feynman's metaphors, it would be like measuring the width of the United States between Los Angeles and New York—and being off by three hairs.

Feynman boiled the math of physics down into a series of diagrams that portrayed electrons as moving about in time and space. Quantum theory shows that if you add up all of an electron's various possibilities—all its possible stories, histories, and paths through force fields—you can calculate that electron's most likely behavior. This behavior follows the path of least action—that is, the least amount of time or the shortest distance for something to get done. A particle's seeming desire to follow the path of least action mirrors, metaphorically, the shaman's "path of heart."

Such quantum theory and shamanism are not about mere abstract experience. In later chapters I will introduce a walking meditation that uses your own body's instincts to find your paths of heart, your way of least action. This walking meditation, which we shall explore together, will give you a somatic understanding of quantum theory as well as of what don Juan calls "path of heart." We will use the resulting insights to work on inner problems, relationship challenges, or world situations.

The main limitation I see in my present theory and suggested practices is that they are based upon the aboriginal awareness ability we all apparently once had. Today, however, this kind of earth-based awareness is distant from the consciousness of most people. This awareness is like our capacity to be lucid while dreaming at night, or daydreaming during waking hours. Just as quantum theory is counterintuitive in many ways to the manner in which we understand everyday reality, shamanism and psychology also move beyond the normal thinking of your everyday mind. Earth-based body awareness perceives the world as a sentient being, as a real and dreamlike entity.

Feynman's absurd physics

One of the many things I loved about Feynman while I was studying at MIT was that he taught with his drums! Combining his expressive bongo playing with jokes made him a compelling and popular teacher. He loved painting, as well as physics, and is remembered for his outrageous statements as much as for his Nobel. "I can't explain why Nature behaves in this peculiar way . . . So I hope you can accept Nature as She is—Absurd . . . I am going to have fun telling you about this absurdity, because I find it delightful."[4]

Feynman is correct. Quantum theory is indeed absurd in that it is more dreamlike than real—and its dreamlikeness renders accurate results. Yet perhaps quantum physics is not so much absurd as amazing. Like the rest of mathematical physics, quantum theory is partially a projection of our dreams—the math is symbolic of what we do not quite know about ourselves: namely, the origins of our consciousness. To understand physics more fully, remember that *people discovered it.* Physics is about the magical quantum world in which things interact at distances without reason or force. It is the world in which the shaman moves, the world each of us meets every second of our lives, the realm we enter every night in dreams.

In many ways people are like elementary particles: we are always trying to sniff out various paths to find the easiest one and the one that feels best—the one with most heart, and the easiest one.

Path awareness creates least action

Since the 1970s Process Work, or process-oriented psychology, has been making the following point: *Within what we call problems are paths we haven't yet explored.* The momentary awareness of signals and feelings, images and motions, shows the way.

To find the magical paths of heart and of least action, you must develop your awareness, must become a better observer of what happens inside and outside. Notice exactly what people say and do as their evolving process sniffs out various paths and seeks least action. Name what they identify with and appreciate what they don't identify with.

There are many methods by which to follow the known and unknown processes. For example, we can note our conscious concerns and then follow our dreaming process.[5] Dreaming for couples includes becoming aware of the signals they don't realize they are sending each other—shaking your head implying no, for example, while saying yes to your partner.[6] Organizations as well as individuals need to listen to their gossip and enact it in a sort of psychodrama to discover more about the dreaming processes bubbling in their subterranean layers.[7] To extend and develop Jungian psychology, I showed that a focus upon nighttime dreaming is important but not always needed—for dreaming happens all day long in our feelings, gestures, body language, words, and signals. To notice these "awake dreaming" experiences is to notice our own particle energy sniffing out the best path. Over the course of time we go this way and that, exploring all directions before choosing the one closest to our personal nature—what Jung might have called the direction of our personal myth.

While physics helps us follow particles, psychology helps us follow the nature and patterns of people. If you are talking with a shy person, for example, who seems most comfortable looking at the ground, your least action might be looking at the ground as well. Instead of trying to carry on a face-to-face conversation, try focusing on the ground—on inner experience—for the time being. The shy person just might be relieved, smile, and eventually look up and tell you about an important experience. The Tao, the Way, the path can be seen in subtle, flickering pre-signals, pre-images, the sense of motion before movement has occurred.

These subtle, quantum-like signals lie in the nano-range of psychological experience. To notice these events, be aware of slight sensations or body tendencies. Simply ask your body where it wants to move, and notice where it tends to move, even before it has actually moved. Once you feel that tendency, try moving there deliberately. That experience might be as physically important to you as it is psychologically significant. *Tendencies precede real movements, just as dreams come before insights and actions.*

Why don't we use our body's wisdom more often? Perhaps our modern Western educational systems value only what we think with our everyday mind. Perhaps that is why body life, dreams, quantum physics, and shamanism seem weird to some of us. Nevertheless, if you have a problem, subtle signals are pointing you to a path waiting to be taken. Develop your awareness of the dreaming realm. Focus on problems, but also on awareness of the process. Learn path awareness. In the following pages I will use a new method based upon your body's sense of earth-based directions to show you what you already know about life. We will learn more about how aboriginal wisdom, dreams, and gravity can help resolve the problems, symptoms, and disappointments of your everyday life and work.

Dying to find the way

We are all dying to find the enchanted path of least action and most heart.

After hearing he was going to die, a client of mine lapsed into a comatose state.[8] After working with the subtle signals of that vegetative state, he suddenly awakened to tell a dream. When faced with the end of his life, he dreamed that he saw himself lost in a snowy landscape. He feared he could go no further in the snow and would drop of exhaustion. At that moment, he looked around himself in that dream landscape and found, to his great surprise, a path. Some human being had been there just before him and was showing him the way by making footsteps in the snow. He woke up and said, "There is a way!"

Seeing those footsteps is an example of path awareness. His own dreaming—his own body tendencies—were showing him the easiest path into the unknown future. We understood from his dream this lesson: Follow your tendencies, those impulses that precede actions even if you do not know the source of those tendencies. Follow the possibilities. Follow the path, step by step, as it moves into the future.

When the everyday self meets a problem, the dreaming process sniffs out the best path toward the problem's resolution. In a way my client was behaving like a shaman: when faced with the impossible, he went into an altered state of consciousness to find the way.

Perhaps we are all dying to find the right way. Near-death experiences frequently illuminate new paths. In Jung's autobiographical *Memories, Dreams, Reflections,* he described a heart attack and the resulting near-death experience of his dreamlike vision.[9] When his heart stopped, he found himself suddenly in outer space, and going still further: "I would know *what had been before me, why I had come into being, and where my life was flowing.* My life as I lived it had often seemed to me like a story that has no beginning and end. . . ." (italics mine).

Where is life flowing?

The purpose of *Earth-Based Psychology* is to help us find and experience what has been before us, why we have come into being, and where our lives are flowing. This flow has a geometry—the path is an arrow, a vector. It is, as Jung said, "a story that has no beginning and end."

Perhaps everyone and every particle in the universe is dying to know its story and sniff out its way, a forgotten direction.

▷ Things to Consider

- Don't focus your everyday mind only on problems; develop earth-based *path awareness.*

- The answers to problems and your next step in life can be found in the next moment. The physicist's path of least action may be similar to the shaman's path of heart.

- Perhaps everyone is dying to find their path beyond life or death.

CHAPTER 2

A First Principle: Awareness Is Nonlocal

I wonder why. I wonder why.
I wonder why I wonder.
I wonder why I wonder why I wonder.
I wonder why I wonder!
—Richard Feynman, as a student[1]

The student in me, too, wonders. Why do we wonder? Why are kids so curious? What makes us puzzle about the universe? Why do we constantly look in the mirror when we're already familiar with our appearances? What is consciousness? Is it biological, spiritual, psychological—or all of these? Why do we want to know who we are and where we are headed? What is this tendency to seek, to become aware of the path? Why are we always searching for the way, the easiest and best path? In this chapter I introduce the possibility that what we call our own awareness may precede existence—and that it actually belongs to the earth, or even to the whole universe.

Defining awareness

Path awareness is basic to our psychology and to the sciences. But what is path awareness? In other words, what is awareness of the Tao? Or, simply, what is awareness? Instead of defining awareness—which

11

many before me have tried—I will simply suggest that awareness is basic to everything we know. Awareness is basic to all of psychology and science. Our sense of awareness is connected to noticing, watching, knowing, mindfulness, realizing, wondering, and consciousness itself. When Feynman ponders, "I wonder why I wonder," therefore, he is identifying himself. That is, wondering or awareness is who we are. *Awareness is prior to any form of creation, manifestation, or consciousness.* The *a priori* existence of awareness and its resulting tendency to notice and wonder are psychology's basic principles. In fact, the *a priori* existence of awareness is not only a first principle in science, but it also appears in mythology.

Even after science has evolved during the last century, even after quantum theory, relativity, and depth psychology, still no one agrees on the nature of awareness or consciousness. Neither Einstein nor Heisenberg, neither Freud nor Jung agreed on fundamental principles, on the nature of consciousness, on the subatomic world, on the relativistic spaces of the universe. Why? Probably because it is difficult and perhaps impossible to know ourselves without a viewpoint outside of ourselves. Indeed, the very concept of awareness assumes the possibility of two or more interrelated but different frameworks, or different viewpoints: Something is aware of something different. If awareness is basic, it is a kind of field or medium, a kind of oneness that creates or produces two different frameworks—or two different observers, so to speak. In this way of thinking, awareness manifests itself in different forms of self-reflection and wonder. Awareness is an inherent tendency that precedes self-reflection, curiosity, and consciousness. *Sentient* awareness, furthermore, is awareness of things before they can be defined in terms of words and images.

Awareness and nonlocality

Three thousand years ago the ancient Chinese Taoists may have been more at ease speaking of the ungraspable. They did not speak about awareness, consciousness, or self-reflection, but rather of a Tao, or Way, that could be described, and another Tao that could not be described.

According to the basic *Tao Te Ching,* a sage simply knew the Way, the Tao—she simply had the kind of path awareness that could not be said, that was pre-verbal.

Yet you have this same awareness, too. Explore it with this experiment. Allow your body to give you a quick answer to the question, *What direction does your body want to go in right now?* If you don't get an immediate direction, try a few directions until your body tells you the direction it is headed. Then move in that direction until you know what that direction means for you. For example, your might feel directed to the north, south, west, or east. Or you may feel connected with a corner of the room because of its quietness. In some way you are yourself, yet at the same time you are that direction or spot on earth.

At some primal level we all are aware of directions before we can explain what they mean for us. We feel motivated to move in a certain direction before we even know exactly why. We feel best in certain spots and less well in others. Without knowing how, we are sentiently aware of tendencies to move before we even move. In a way, the direction that we take, the path that we can describe, is not the entire path. The *real* path was preceded by sentient awareness of the earth, an awareness we can barely speak of. In reality we are located in our bodies. But at the same time, we are also located, though nonlocally, at other places on earth and in the universe.

In a way, we *are* the directions, we *are* the area around ourselves. There is definitely something widespread, something nonlocal, about our most sentient awareness. In other words, what we call our awareness may not be entirely located in our own bodies. This nonlocality of awareness may be why researchers cannot find consciousness located in the brain. From the viewpoint of our experience, awareness is nonlocal; it is everywhere. Our awareness is not ours alone! This nonlocality of awareness is a first principle.

Nonlocal awareness may have been better developed in our ancestors. Needing to find their way around at night without maps or street lamps, they depended upon an awareness that they sensed was not located only in their bodies. The shaman don Juan spoke of awareness in terms of the "sentient earth," the planet on which we live. The old seers, he said, saw that "the earth is a gigantic sentient being subjected to the same forces we are."[2] The very earth possesses awareness; the very earth is a living being of which we are a part. Our lives and power are connected, don Juan said, to "aligning ourselves with its directions." By moving with the earth's sentient awareness, we align ourselves with the direction it intends for us—that is, with the Tao of the moment. Our sentient awareness belongs at the same time to the entire earth, to the universe in which we live.

The nonlocality of awareness may be why many aboriginal peoples identified themselves with the earth around them, with personal names like One Feather, Moving Cloud, Low Mountain. In particular, some Australian Aboriginal people of the Guugu Yimithirr tribe understand body parts as belonging to the earth's directions.[3] To the Guugu Yimithirr people (I'll speak more about them later), what I call my right hand is my northern, eastern, southern, or western hand, depending upon the position of my body on earth. That is, if the right side of a Guugu Yimithirr's body is to the north, then they call their right hand their northern hand. And that same hand becomes their southern hand if they turn halfway around.

In the upper area of Figure 2.1, we see a sketch of someone facing us. If she were a Guugu Yimithirr, she might identify her hand not just as the left hand, but as her northern hand.

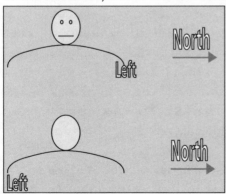

FIGURE 2.1 **Awareness and nonlocality.** The identity of what I would call my left hand is "really" the northern or southern hand according to my direction on earth.

In the lower half of the figure we see the same figure again, this time with her back to us. Now her left hand is her southern hand.

If, like the Guugu Yimithirr people, we identified our body parts with the directions of the earth—instead of identifying them with ourselves—we would tend to identify our body as part of the earth. Our self-awareness, then, would be nonlocal. We would consider ourselves part of the earth. We would believe that everything participates in who we are, in our consciousness.

In today's consensus reality, we are located in the spaces of our bodies at a given moment. But in our deepest experiences, in the world of our sentient awareness and of our dreaming mind, we are aspects of the earth. And we can go still further with this nonlocal aspect of awareness: In a sense we *are* the earth; we *are* the universe looking at itself. We do not become aware and conscious independently of what and who is around us. Our experiences are intimately connected with the world, with the universe itself.

John Wheeler's black holes

Such awareness may sound mysterious to our everyday mind; yet let us reassure those everyday minds that they are reflected in the bona fide science of physics. John Wheeler, one of the fathers of today's physics, was Richard Feynman's doctoral advisor and friend at Princeton and the inventor of the term *black holes*.[4] Wheeler is one of the most poetic and insightful physicists of the last hundred years. Although he avoided parapsychological topics, he did speak about a "self-reflecting universe." In

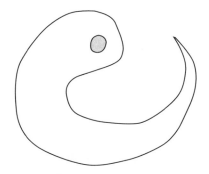

honor of Einstein's eightieth birthday, Wheeler gave him a sketch of the universe as obvious as it is bold: the universe, Wheeler suggested to Einstein, was a self-reflecting being.

The sketch (Figure 2.2) is of a gigantic, whale-like being facing at its own tail, its tail representing the earlier condition of the universe.

It is awareness that makes us look up at the night sky. Then the

FIGURE 2.2 **John Wheeler's universe looking at itself**

nonlocality of awareness breaks into parts as we stare at the universe. It is as if the universe looks through us at her own tail.

When we look up at the sky, we are looking backward in time, at our tail, for it takes starlight a long time (by human standards) to reach us.

When we look at the night sky, then, we look backward in time; we look at the history of the universe.

Just as don Juan said that the earth is sentient, Wheeler's sketch implies that the universe is a form of awareness, a self-reflecting and sentient being. At some level our awareness and the earth's are inseparable.

The first principle: Sentient awareness is nonlocal and pre-existent

Why is the universe curious to look at? Why does awareness exist, and what is it? Since we cannot experiment with the entire universe, we may never be able to answer such questions conclusively. Under these circumstances my approach to the unknown is pragmatic: I use theories that explain the most about individuals, couples, large organizations, particles, and planets. And the theory that explains much about physics, psychology, and spiritual traditions is this: *the universe is a sentient being.* The first principle is that this sentience is nonlocal, lies at the root of consciousness, and precedes all manifestations.

Because sentient awareness is experienced by us in part as a subtle body feeling, no one term will ever suffice to name it correctly. What I call sentient awareness is a kind of intelligence, a knowingness, a quantum mind.[5]

Sentient awareness, awareness, and consciousness

Sentient awareness may be only partially measurable, a nonlocal dreamlike ability that informs us where and when to move. In the experiment earlier in this chapter, you may have experienced sentient awareness of your direction. Sentient awareness reveals directional tendencies, such as the dreamlike sense of moving toward a specific spot.

Sentient awareness is nondualistic, the precursor to any awareness we measure, and consciousness we can use in everyday life. Sentient awareness is so subtle that we can hardly speak of it, although—when sentient awareness unfolds into something we can verbalize, and move with—I call it awareness. Then we are aware that we are moving. Awareness of movement—which is awareness of awareness—becomes consciousness as we reflect on the direction, purpose, or meaning of the movement. Then we can use that direc-tion to change our lives accordingly.

Awareness has various dimensions. At its deepest, at its essence, sentient awareness is a subtle feeling. It unfolds into what we notice as awareness of a feeling, motion, or nearly describable experience in the world of dreams. In everyday reality consciousness occurs when aware-ness reflects upon itself. Then we can easily say, "I am doing this or that." In other words, I am choosing to reserve *consciousness* for aware-ness of awareness, for everyday life. I see *sentient awareness* as the root of *awareness* and consciousness in us.

Sentient awareness is an *essence experience* of a nondualistic world. Sentient awareness is physical and spiritual, gravitational and psycholog-ical. Like the German word *spuren*—to sense, to find, to make a path—sentient awareness is close to the idea of the Tao, the Way. (Following chapters will more deeply explore sentient or path awareness.)

You can develop lucidity of sentient awareness and, in a sense, know things before they happen. Then, we might say, you know the Tao. Sentient awareness is the shaman's greatest gift. To use it you need lucidity to catch the most subtle experiences.

Awareness and the origins of the universe

It seems to me that, if John Wheeler were part of this discussion, he might well want to update his sketch. Just as don Juan speaks of the sentient earth, I believe Wheeler could well speak of the sentient universe. Figures 2.3 and 2.4 illustrate what happens if Wheeler's diagram reflects upon itself: it becomes suggestive of the great ultimate, the Tai Chi—the old Chinese idea of the creative power of the universe.

FIGURE 2.3 **Sentient awareness** gives rise to awareness and precedes consciousness and observation.

This correspondence between Wheeler's sketch and the Tai Chi may suggest that sentient awareness creates or sustains the universe.[6]

In the next chapter I explore how awareness can be seen in an apparently nearly empty vacuum—that is, at zero state—and in the creation of matter and, possibly, of the universe.

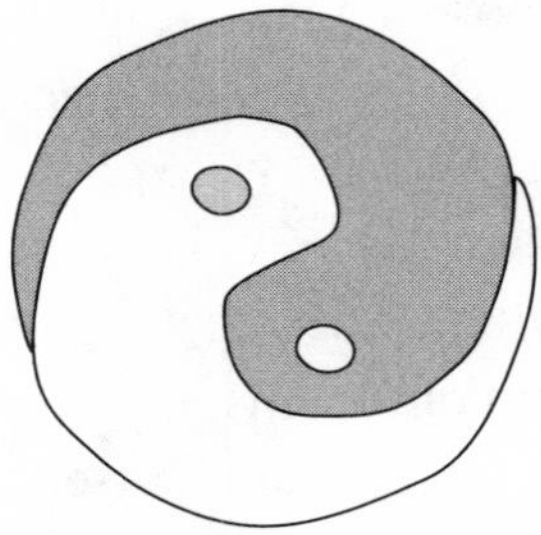

The Navajo universe

The idea that some form of sentient awareness (projected onto gods or other

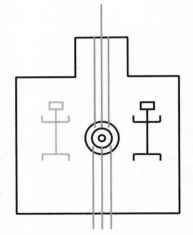

FIGURE 2.4 **The Great Ultimate,** or Tai Chi, generates the universe.

beings) created the universe forms the core of many creation myths. Like the equations of physics, creation myths of aboriginal peoples speak about the patterns of the universe. Aboriginal myths are like mathematical theories that pull together both inner and outer experience, both dreaming and more objective observation.

Most myths assume that some form of awareness preceded the visible universe. Creation myths, for example, often assume some primal form of sentient awareness. This awareness is symbolized by a being, person, animal, or god who is buried, sleeping, or emerging to create the universe. Often the gods awaken from sleep; sometimes humans emerge out of chaos. In some myths awareness emerges from the oceans; in others, from the earth or the air. Various intermediary stages occur until the world as we know it today appears. In the Judeo-Christian myth, for instance, God created light. If light symbolizes awareness, then awareness is preceded in this myth by sentient awareness—here represented by the Judeo-Christian God.

In the Navajo myth of the origin of the world, human beings—or First Peoples—emerged from beneath the first world. (The fourth world is where we live today.) As represented in Figure 2.5, the

FIGURE 2.5 **The Navaho first world** (the concentric circles), from which humans emerged

First Peoples came from the center of the circles, moving up through this first world along the straight rainbow path and through another three worlds, finally arriving at the surface of the earth.[7] Notice in the figure that on either side of the place of emergence, there are two beings (called "messenger flies") who are mirror images of one another.[8]

In this Navajo myth sentient awareness takes the form of humans emerging from a specific point in the earth. Awareness takes the form of a path surrounded by reflecting beings. We see again how sentient awareness arises, how it moves along paths, how it reflects itself to create consciousness and the everyday world.

Later in the book I will more deeply discuss this Navajo painting and the belief system behind it. My point here is that sentient awareness, symbolized by human beings beneath the earth, was and still is imagined to come from the earth herself. Add self-reflection, and sentient awareness creates, or unfolds into, the world.

Remember the personal-direction experiment you did at the beginning of this chapter? Before you realized in which direction your deepest self was drawn, the attraction was merely a nonverbal body experience buried in the earth, so to speak. You may have been only sentiently aware of it. But as it appeared to your awareness as a direction, and as your awareness reflected on itself, it became real and conscious. Then you could use that consciousness to adjust your life accordingly. Every moment is just this kind of chance—in a sense, a chance to re-create the world.

Creation in the Judeo–Christian–Islamic myth

Like aboriginal myths, the Bible also shows a kind of sentient awareness appearing in the form of a God who created the world through reflecting himself in human beings. Frescoed by Michelangelo on the ceiling of Rome's Sistine Chapel, the creation of Adam shows a God emerging from the heavens and, with a touch, giving a human being life (Figure 2.6).

Among other things, Michelangelo's painting symbolizes how sentient body awareness—God's subtle touch—that comes from the universe's awareness reflects and creates human existence.

Like the other artistic representations discussed in this chapter, this one too imagines or theorizes that consensus reality is preceded by nonlocal or universal sentient awareness. Both aboriginal beliefs

FIGURE 2.6 **The Creation of Adam,** a detail from Michelangelo's Sistine Chapel fresco

and modern religions suggest that we and everything else may have emerged from the earth—from the sentient awareness of the universe.

▷ Things to Consider

- It is plausible that sentient awareness precedes creation and manifestation in mythology and psychology, in spiritual traditions and physics.

- Don Juan said that the earth is a sentient being. Physicist John Wheeler also saw the universe as a gigantic, self-reflecting being. And the ancient Chinese Taoists referred to the magical source of all paths as the self-reflecting pattern of the Tai Chi.

- Sentient awareness is nonlocal; its origins are so subtle you can scarcely grasp them. Yet this awareness is so powerful that it creates everything. Perhaps even our everyday experiences are actually the universe reflecting on a part of herself.

CHAPTER 3

Path Awareness

Is the conscious mind subtly linked to a basic level of the universe?
—Stuart Hameroff, MD[1]

That nonlocal sentient awareness precedes all creation and manifestation is a core principle of shamanism, psychology, and other sciences. It is this principle also that has birthed all the various methods of process-oriented psychology. For what I call sentient awareness, Jung would have called the unconscious—that characteristic creative ingredient of everything that happens. Awareness training and awareness work can be applied to one's everyday reality by following signals, dreamlike subjective processes, and all those subtle experiences that are difficult if not impossible to formulate. Take the assumption of objectivity on which much of science currently rests. It is virtually invalidated in physics, for example, by theories about the primary role of the observer—that is, how the observer's actions actually change what is observed. Awareness concepts may be found in the self-reflecting mathematical patterns of quantum mechanics as well.

The principle of awareness as a nonlocal ingredient of creation is generally assumed to be true beyond anything that is presently known or measurable. The fundamental role of awareness in human development and functioning is axiomatic in shamanism, psychology, and physics. When in wondering about the universe's laws and patterns, we think like Einstein—that is, we believe that something like the mind of a god lies in the background—we are assuming that sentient awareness is axiomatic, or self-evident. Yet principles hold true only as long as they are useful. As events occur that support a principle, then that principle is deemed satisfactory. By that standard, therefore, if events prove that sentient awareness does *not* exist, then the principle of sentient awareness must be refined or replaced.

For now, let's say that the preceding existence of sentient awareness is the basic principle that produces awareness, self-reflection, and reality. In this chapter I discuss how this basic awareness principle underlies core patterns found in shamanism, psychology, and physics, and how path awareness is a great teacher.

Awareness as a mystical experience

Awareness may give rise to measurable experience that can be shared and mutually acknowledged, but its sentient roots remain mystical. In 1902 the pioneering American psychologist William James wrote *The Varieties of Religious Experience,* in which he posited that all mystical experience is—

- *Ineffable:* A nonverbal experience, difficult to describe.
- *Noetic:* Numinous, filled with a kind of knowingness.
- *Passive:* It seems to happens *to* us.
- *Transient:* It flickers in our experience and is difficult to hold on to.

These characteristics form a good starting point from which we can begin to understand the primal forms of awareness. Sentient awareness is mystical in that it is ineffable, notoriously difficult to describe. Sentient awareness is noetic in that it creates a kind of knowingness. It is passive in that the everyday mind must be reduced, "empty," or open and receptive to it. And sentient awareness is transient and difficult to sustain. In fact, after sentient awareness appears as awareness and consciousness, then consciousness seems to "forget" or marginalize its sentient beginnings.

I would add *nonlocality* to James's characteristics of mystical experience, because most of the mystical experiences I have personally experienced and seen in my clients involve a kind of interconnectedness with all things. Don Juan's "sentient earth" is a nonlocal characteristic of our sentient awareness. I relate sentient awareness to path awareness, in which *path* is a sense of inner direction and purpose, as well as the measure of the outer, literal meaning of direction—the hours and miles and such that define consensus reality for us.

Your body's path awareness is not only mystical and dreamlike, but also very real.

Path awareness and the Tao

It seems likely to me that the mystical, nonlocal characteristics of path awareness are what the ancient Taoists meant by *Tao*. According to the *Tao Te Ching* and the *I Ching,* the Tao is the mother of heaven and earth, the source of the gods. It is meant to represent an ultimate reality in which all things are located or occur. At the same time the Tao is a power, the source or energy behind the universe and the wisdom or order behind individual lives within that universe. The ineffable Tao cannot be described in words and is therefore variously translated as *way, path, right way,* or *meaning.* The Tao is a noetic path of awareness, transient and always changing and passive in the sense that one must be open to understand it.

We can learn more about path awareness by studying the structure of the Chinese pictogram for the Tao (Figure 3.1), which contains five basic elements: stillness, head, steps, path, and eye.

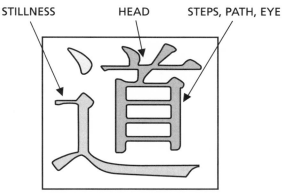

STILLNESS   HEAD   STEPS, PATH, EYE

FIGURE 3.1 **Tao pictogram**

The translation of ancient words such as *Tao* depends upon the translator's era, background, and culture. Still, judging from some of its basic elements—namely, *stillness, head,* and *eye*—it seems likely that the pictograph for Tao is connected to sentient awareness. The connection with *path* and *steps* makes a translation of *path awareness* even more likely.[2] Consequently, I translate Tao as *path awareness of both a real and ineffable way.*[3] For me, the Tao belongs to the physical and dreamlike nature of the earth.

Taoist awareness exercise

Your own experience can best elucidate the meaning of Tao and path awareness. Explore your own Tao or path awareness with this two-minute experiment. (It is an expanded version of the experiment you did in Chapter 2.)

1. Find a position that is comfortable and allows a little bit of movement. Focus on your body experience and be still, in both your body and your everyday mind. Notice your body.
2. While sitting still and not moving, ask yourself, "Given the chance, where would my body like to, or tend to, move?" Don't move yet—just ask the question. Sense your own tendencies, but don't go there yet.
3. Now let your body move slowly in the direction of the strongest tendency, and use your awareness to notice what happens. Just track the slow micromovements your body makes. Take a minute or two to notice what experiences you have while following your direction. Notice whatever is happening within you, even if you feel it is irrational. Keep moving in that direction until your body explains itself—until you sense the possible meaning of that direction.

How did your body know where to head? How do you explain to yourself your body's awareness? In your own terms, what is path awareness to you?

Path awareness is your greatest teacher

In stillness your body likely has its own mind and knows or sees the Tao—that is, the Way, or where you are headed. The Tao is, after all, a kind of directional awareness. The words *way* and *direction* refer to a mixture of real-world directions, dreamlike experiences, and ineffable or mystical experiences.

Your sentient awareness tendencies are pre-signals of sorts—a set of potential directions presented to you before you actually move anywhere. Awareness gives you a sense of your dreaming process; *path* awareness is potentially a great teacher. You can feel things happening before they happen. Your own awareness process, in fact, may be the best of all your teachers. There may not be one as illuminating as your own inner awareness process.

I say your sentient awareness is a teacher because if you submit to your path awareness, it carries you in the right direction with the least action—that is, the direction that affords you the least effort and resistance. Whenever you feel confused about what to do or where to go, allow your greatest teacher—your own inner awareness—to move you. It is always there, right near you, day and night. Just ask yourself, *In which direction is my body being guided by the earth?*

The ability to sense what is happening around us and at a distance gives us uncanny communication ability. You connect best with others when you connect with your deepest self and direction. Reminding others of their own inner teachers, furthermore, makes everyone both a learner and guru. (Elsewhere in this book I show how this teacher or principle also helps groups and organizations.[4])

Physics, zero-point awareness, and creation

Stillness is a central part of the Tao's pictogram (Figure 3.1). Within the framework of the path of awareness, stillness refers to temporarily reducing the busyness, the noise of your everyday mind so that subtler experiences and sentient awareness can appear. In this sense stillness is not emptiness, but rather an open space in which path awareness can arise. This open-space aspect of stillness is akin to quantum physicists' notion of a vacuum.

The quantum physics of a vacuum assures us that total emptiness is never present.[5] To our normal, everyday way of thinking, a complete vacuum means utter emptiness. In quantum theory, however, zero mass or energy is not possible. Heisenberg's uncertainty principle (named for the renowned German physicist of the last century who discovered it) indicates that a total vacuum cannot exist. To have a perfect vacuum, you would have to know where every piece of dust is in the box at any given moment. But because of an inherent uncertainty in nature, such knowledge is impossible. Complete certainty is no longer possible in the quantum world. Because there is a basic uncertainty about where everything is located and what it is doing at any given moment, even the best vacuum cleaner in the world would not be able to create absolute nothingness. Particles can seemingly appear out of "nothing."[6]

In other words, there is always a little something in the apparent vacuum. Zero energy or zero mass is an expression, not a possibility. Then what remains in a vacuum, in the supposedly empty space of a box? Physicists think of what remains in the box in terms of particles and explain their behavior in terms of waves.[7] Yet how can we be sure these waves or particles are present? Answer: quantum physics self-reflects to produce probabilities and measurable results in everyday reality. No one knows why waves self-reflect—in the math of physics, they just do.

Though physicists cannot explain how or why quantum waves self-reflect (as we cannot explain why awareness self-reflects to produce consciousness), some physicists have speculated that this sudden creation of particles popping out of nothing may exemplify how the universe began from apparent nothingness. Cambridge University's Stephen Hawking, the popular astrophysicist known for his advances in cosmology and for the study of black holes, said that those self-reflecting quantum waves may have "tickled the universe into being" by perturbing itself and igniting the big bang.[8]

Hawking's phrase expresses precisely what I know to be true about human beings: If you don't know the way, just wait. Relax. Dream. Go to sleep. Meditate until emptiness occurs. It is then that sentient awareness tends to re-create reality and set us on new paths, again and again. Things pop up—awareness and yet another beginning of a new consciousness occurs.

The Casimir force

A vacuum, then, is governed by the uncertainty principle and by self-reflection. Furthermore, it can produce a measurable pressure—a "force of nothing." Here is how. Quantum physicists speak about waves, reflections, and fluctuations in the stillness of the zero-point energy of a "vacuum" (see Figure 3.2). Before quantum theory was discovered and discussed, people thought that if you placed two small mirrors near each another in a vacuum box, nothing much would happen to them because there is nothing in that box to move them around.

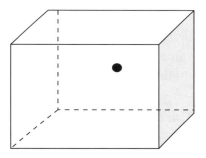

FIGURE 3.2 **Physics of the zero-state vacuum.** There will always be an unpredictably minute amount of energy and resulting pressure in the box.

In the middle of the last century, however, the Dutch theoretical physicist Hendrik Casimir speculated that those two small theoretical mirrors in a vacuum box would be attracted to each other. And only a decade ago this quantum theory was actually proven by experiment to be true. The particles or quantum waves in the box essentially push the two small reflecting surfaces together. If the mirrors are close enough to keep small waves in and larger waves out, a minuscule pressure—the *Casimir force*—pushes the mirrors together (see Figure 3.3).

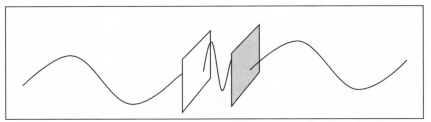

FIGURE 3.3 **The Casimir force: the force of almost nothing.** Casimir suspected, corrrectly, that two mirrors placed in a vacuum would keep out waves that did not fit in. These waves create a measurable force pressing the mirrors together. Some physicists call this *the force of nothing.*

And if those two theoretical mirrors in the box are precisely the proper distance from each other, a kind of "cavity resonance" occurs that creates "vacuum pressure." In other words, even in what physicists call a "zero-point energy field," even in a vacuum at low temperatures, there is a potential Casimir force.[9]

The force of path awareness

Now picture not mirrors and empty boxes, but imagine resonating with your deepest self in your empty mind. The Casimir force of nothing, which nonetheless produces vacuum pressure, becomes a metaphor for how, when we resonate with our deepest self, a pressure or force is produced that carries us. When our everyday mind is relaxed and in that state we reflect upon the minutest impulse, we may become aware that awareness is not just teacher, but also a somatic force attempting to move us. You know the phenomenon: Every now and then at night during sleep, a dream will literally push you out of bed in a certain direction. Everyone knows that once we feel or know something, that something often moves or tickles or bugs us, and thereby pushes us along. For centuries, people have meditated in order to open up to their spontaneous creativity. In a way, the Casimir force of nothing is simply another form of the creative power we sense in meditation.

As the reflecting mirrors inside the box suggest a person's self-reflecting awareness, so the Casimir force in that box can be a metaphor for the perturbations and tiny pressures always present in our universe. These minute pressures I call the *force of silence,* or *force of awareness.*

The beginning of the universe was an itch

Let's return for a moment to Stephen Hawking's idea that the universe tickled itself into existence. Although I know of no evidence that Hawking studied ancient Chinese mythology, his speculation that self-reflecting quantum waves may have tickled the universe into being by perturbing itself and igniting the big bang is nonetheless close to how the Chinese of the second century B.C.E. viewed their world. In his book *To Become a God: Cosmology, Sacrifice, and Self-Divinization in Early China,* Harvard's Michael J. Puett reports on diverse ideas about the origin of the cosmos.[10] An ancient passage from Puett's book suggests that in the beginning there was "only figure without form." Then two spirits arose and "aligned Heaven, they oriented earth," and the chi energy gave birth to insects and people.[11]

In other words, the oneness energy ("only figure without form") becomes two powers aligning and orienting everything—and in the process, people and bugs became the first beings! Or one could say it a bit differently: that with people came bugs—tiny perturbations that "bug" us, little pressures that irritate us and make us reflect. According to early Chinese mythology, very close to the beginning was "the bug," a little something that caught our attention by pestering us.

We all know the experience of being bugged by something, be it an itch, a tickle, a song running through the mind repeatedly, a worry. We might even rephrase Hawking's idea that the universe tickled itself into existence by saying that the universe bugged itself awake. I don't insist Hawking was thinking of this when he wrote the phrase, but I do want to emphasize that a little something is always trying to catch our attention: there is always a quantum wave tickling us, a disturbance in our body, a person or flea that bugs us, that tries to move us from the experience of awareness to consciousness. In English we speak of being bugged and pestered by something until it is made conscious and useful; a similar idea exists in the Japanese language, in which the mental pesterer is also called a bug, but more—it is assigned consciousness.[12] Indeed, the bug is a form of sentient awareness, an example of awareness pressure that creates consciousness by pressing reflection to occur.[13]

Empty mind, bug-mind dreamwork

Who knows if the universe tickled or bugged itself into being? We can say with much more certainty, however, that we are often bugged by something trying to reach our everyday consciousness. You can test this "bug theory" with the following inner work. As you do it, notice what has been bugging your body. A barely perceptible bug may prove to contain the wisdom of dreams. Are you ready? Let's begin . . .

1. Empty your mind. Sit as quietly as you can for a moment, until your everyday mind is relaxed. Wait until you have an empty mind, or what is called "beginner's mind." Now use your lucid attention and explore that emptiness. Notice what you sense, notice the tiniest thing that touches or bugs your body. If there are several, let your inner life determine which bug to focus on.

2. Now catch that bug and name it. Was it a sensation? What does that bug or sensation want? What direction is it bugging you in? Submit to it and follow that bug; let it move you until it tells you its direction and message. What is that bug doing there and what does it *really* want? Keep following and asking the bug until it gives you a clear explanation of itself.

3. How is the bug trying to redirect you and create or re-create your world? Recall a recent dream and notice if the new direction and world the bug is trying to create are somehow in that dream.

When a student of mine did this exercise, she felt a pressure inside her stomach. There was a bug there that cried "LET ME OUT, I WANT TO *PLAY!*" It surprised her to remember that in a recent dream, she learned from a child—you guessed it—how to play!

The post-Copernican universe

Sentient awareness is a teacher of the Way, appearing as a tiny force that bugs you until you become conscious of it. Zero states are creative; they renew everyday life. More often than not, however, the world of supposedly real things, of time and space, occupies our attention. In such consensus reality, what we can measure becomes the center of things.

Yet physicists since Copernicus have known that the universe does not revolve around our consensus reality. There is no stable, unmoving earth that is the center of the universe. Until now, however, most of us have lived in a pre-Copernican universe in which our everyday consciousness is centrally focused on time and space.

A truly post-Copernican universe would be more deeply democratic, placing equal importance upon everyday physical reality as well as the first principle of awareness. In a post-Copernican world of subtle, "zero-point" sentient awareness, path awareness would be as important as our normal focus. Remember the bug! This subtle awareness is not our everyday reality, but rather an aspect of our quantum mind. The universe does not orbit around our conscious mind and its observations, but around the mystical aspects of awareness, paths, bugs, as well as around the reality (and illusion) of time and space. What I call my mind is actually linked to the universe's sentient nature—as is your mind.

▷ Things to Consider

- Principles are guides; accept them as long as they are useful.

- Path awareness is axiomatic; it appears as the Tao that can't be said.

- Sentient awareness is ineffable, noetic, transient, and an effective teacher.

- Your body's path awareness is mystical and dreamlike as well as "real."

- Awareness pressure appears as the Casimir force in zero-point vacuum theory, bugging us into consciousness.

- The universe may orbit around a new paradigm that includes mystical aspects of awareness, paths, and bugs.

CHAPTER 4
Parallel Worlds

Don Juan says there is this parallel world existing around us,
a force of energy that we don't let in because we are too busy with
upholding what the social order dictates. Dreaming is one of
the main techniques for perceiving this parallel world.
—Florinda Donner[1]

Our conscious or everyday mind is only a small part of who we are. This chapter discusses how our everyday mind is but one of many parallel worlds—a concept that will help us later in the book as we explore and experience the geometry of path awareness and apply it to relationships and organizations.

Where we are so far

Sentient awareness is the ground, or the essence level, of all experience. It appears as the Tao that cannot be said, and then as tendencies toward paths and directions that *can* be verbalized. Sentient awareness appears in the math of physics as quantum waves or particles that "tickle" themselves into existence. Both myths and math imply that these waves "bug" themselves, creating awareness pressure—what physicists call the Casimir force. In many ways, physics is an apt metaphor for psychology, just as math may be a metaphor for mythic structures and actions.[2]

The vacuum field, then, is a metaphor of the "almost empty mind" operating at zero-point energy, tickling itself into creating elementary particles and possibly the rest of the universe. Math, myth, psychology, and shamanism are analogous not only to physics, but also to "endophysics"—innerworld patterns and experiences of the measurable, "real" world of "exophysics."

Psychology and physics are brought ever nearer each other by the concepts of sentient awareness and by the directional wisdom of the quantum mind behind dreams and quantum physics. In fact, to *combine* psychology and physics, I suggest that both sciences be viewed as aspects of a more encompassing social and physical one-world science, a unified science including at least today's psychology, physics, and shamanism.

Wonder

Sentient awareness gives us our first principle of human functioning: All experience arises out of or is preceded by sentient awareness. From sentience also come other methods, skills, and principles—the experience of wonder and curiosity, for instance, and the ideas of process as teacher and of path awareness. How you formulate these derived terms depends upon who you are, your culture, your state of mind, the times you live in. Some use cultural or religious frameworks; others, biology, sociology, or physics. Others think in terms of the universe as a self-reflecting organism; still others, of self-reflecting quantum waves. Sentient awareness contains within it the curiosity to seek awareness of itself. Most of us routinely experience sentient awareness as simply *wondering* about things.

Wonder is a grand therapeutic tool. When you've exhausted all other means of helping someone, you will seldom go wrong by wondering with them, "What is that? Where did this come from?" Wonder has an incredible ability to elicit information and encourage self-reflection.

Wonder follows the sentient awareness process that seeks to become aware of itself.

Nearly all psychological methods use sentient awareness and its expression as self-reflection and wonder. The Rogerian therapist uses such phrases as "What I hear you saying is—" and "You're feeling like—," reflecting the client's statements back to the client instead of analyzing or diagnosing. Gestalt therapy is based upon awareness techniques or reflection methods—the "empty chair," for example—to bring out parts of the self. Freud used associational methods, and Jung explored the amplification of dream images.

Bugs and flirts in physics

When you are lucid, you can sometimes recognize that what your mind settles on was actually flirting with you, so to speak, attracting you to your thought or wonderment before you consciously settled there. Your attention was caught, was grabbed. Similarly, the universe flirts with us, bugging us continuously with little things before we even dream about them. *Bugs or flirts are pieces of the universe trying to reach awareness and consciousness.*

The idea of flirts occurred to me while studying quantum waves. One interpretation of these waves suggests that before an observation can take place, quantum waves move back and forth between observer and object, between past and future.[3] You could call it an exchange of flirts. Former NASA physicist John Cramer, now at the University of Washington, first proposed that quantum waves could be understood as a kind of communication—"offer waves" moving forward in time, while "echo waves" returned backward in time.[4]

This "transactional" interpretation of quantum physics mirrors what we know about ourselves—namely, that experiences of sentient awareness try to catch our attention before we have even realized we wanted to consider or look at them. Before you can observe some-thing—that is, before consciousness occurs—these waves must first self-reflect. Before we speak with one another, sentient awareness connects us. Realizing sentient connections as the ground of relationships is essential, for otherwise we are under the impression (in everyday reali-ty, at least) that the other is "out there," apart from us, distinct from us—instead of being part of the awareness field in which we all live. Unless we become aware of this sentient connection, we will experi-ence other people as being only "out there" and bugging us. (In later chapters we will explore more about bugs, arguments, and conflicts.)

This reciprocal and timeless interaction process has not ceased to interest me, even after writing a pair of books about it (*Quantum Mind* and *The Quantum Mind and Healing*). I recall my Jungian studies in Zurich with Dr. Marie-Louise von Franz. During our study of syn-chronicity, she became fascinated by the ancient Aztec understanding of time as going both forward and backward.[5] Today I perceive a simi-larity between this Aztec concept and physicist John Cramer's transac-tional interpretation of quantum physics. Consider the doubled-head-ed serpent, a design from fifteenth-century Aztec jewelry that sits in the British Museum (Figure 4.1).[6] In Mesoamerican cultures (occupying present-day Mexico and Central America), skin-shedding serpents were revered as religious symbols of timeless rebirth and renewal. Von Franz points out that this two-headed serpent symbolizes the double aspects of time, moving forward to the future and backward to the beginning.

FIGURE 4.1 **Double-headed Aztec serpent.** Replica of a piece of jewelry (15th century)

The very shape of the serpent suggests to me self-reflecting waves and the dual nature of quantum waves, communicating forward and backward in time. Remember that Cramer's interpretation of quantum physics is based upon the transactions across time. The math of quantum physics makes us think that the future can connect with the present, and the present with the future.

Most dream therapists will recognize such a reversibility of time. What you may experience as your "future self" appears in dreams and communicates with what you experience as your "present self," giving your *present* self some subtle guidance about how to be *now*. It is as if parallel worlds of the future and present and past are trying to connect to one another. Their connection can create new aspects of awareness and consciousness.

Nonlocality and projection

Sentient awareness, then, operates like quantum waves: tiny, evanescent "pre-signals" quickly appear and disappear, flirting with us. Sometimes they seem to catch our attention, as if we have flirted with them first. These flirts are hardly measurable or visible. Likewise, we cannot see quantum waves, we don't see possibilities (as Heisenberg called quantum waves)—we see only actualities. Thus the exact location and timing of flirts are impossible to ascertain, just as Heisenberg stated that the position and momentum of a quantum wave cannot be pinpointed simultaneously. When something catches your attention, its origins in time cannot be located exactly. We don't know for sure if it is coming from the past or the future, from this place or that place. Only when we become aware of it do we begin to think, "Ah, that flirt or idea is coming from that thing or that other person." Consider my wife and myself on opposite ends of the Aztec serpent (Figure 4.2). If I am on one side of the serpent and Amy is on the other, who is flirting with whom? Am I reacting to her, or is she reacting to me? Who did what first?

FIGURE 4.2 **Flirting and nonlocality.** Who did what first?

The idea of projection should be updated as a consensus-reality term that involves nonlocality—that is, when I look at or think of Amy, she is part of me, and I may be part of her. At the same time, nonlocality makes my thoughts and feelings part of the universe! In dreaming— that is to say, in an experience of sentient awareness, in the world of the dual-headed serpent—we cannot speak of projection as belonging only to me or to Amy; there is rather a oneness of awareness in the background. Thus on one level projection refers to something coming from one person going out to another; on another level projection refers to a sense of connection, a dreaming together. From the view of sentient awareness, there is a nonlocal field between us even though we experience this field in our awareness and everyday consciousness as images, projections, and the "other." Yet, from the sentient viewpoint, no person or thing is doing anything. Events just happen between us. When awareness first arises, it arises not from Amy or me, but from the universe, the serpent. Sentient awareness, then, is spread out in the whole universe. It is like a vibration of the vacuum field or, as some Native peoples say, of the "Great Spirit."

What psychologists call *viewpoints* and what physicists call *observation* are rooted in projection and sentient awareness. Projection belongs to the universe's natural patterns—as Einstein would say, to "the mind of God," the quantum mind.[7] Regardless of the name you give the dreamlike space of nonlocality, from the viewpoint of sentient awareness it is relatedness to all things.[8]

Several years ago two Aboriginal Australian men asked me to help them with a conflict that had arisen between them. They introduced themselves to me, thanked me for helping them, and described their conflict. Then they told me, "We are going to work on our problem." I prepared myself for a real confrontation: "Okay, guys, let's get into it," I said. But they only looked at each other, closed their eyes, and sank into themselves. After five minutes they returned out of their inner reverie, said "Thank you" to the other, and that was that. They used a belief system and gained access to something between them, and in so doing solved or at least reduced their problem. For these Aboriginal men, nonlocality is no mere theory, but a way of life.

Lucidity and parallel world experiments

Let's explore the subtle and delicate nonlocal nature of sentient awareness with the following experiment. Feel and dream the following exercise.

1. First, simply raise your hand to your cheek—a common motion you do many times a day.
2. What did you notice when you did this? Describe what happened.
3. Now repeat the gesture—but this time in slow motion, and with greater attention to what you're doing. As you're slowly moving your hand toward your check, heed two or three of the slightest feelings and sensations that arise. Be as lucid as you can, use your sentient awareness, and trust your experiences even if they seem irrational.
4. Finally, recall one or two of the sensations, feelings, moods, or irrational ideas you noticed. Make a note about a few of them.

Parallel worlds

The first time you raised your hand to your cheek, you simply did the action. The second time, you used your lucidity (Figure 4.3). What's the difference between the first and the second experiment?

The first time, you used your ordinary mind and simply moved without much awareness. The second time, I asked you to move slowly and focus more, using your lucid or sentient awareness—and it's during this second, slow-motion time that people typically notice two or three separate experiences arising. Some notice sensations; others remember events from the past.

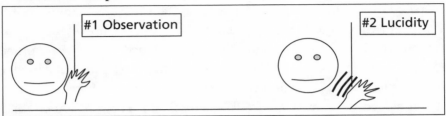

FIGURE 4.3 **Observation and lucidity.** The first experiment was about observation; the second, about lucidity.

Whatever you call experiences or memories, those two or three experiences, thoughts, or feelings are flirt-like—they are subtle and normally go unnoticed. For example, one person told me that as she slowly moved her hand towards her cheek, the first thing she noticed was a memory. She remembered having her teeth pulled out when she was a child, and consequently acquiring a terror of dentists. She said she was not taking good care of her teeth now, and that if she took that dental flirt seriously, she would care for her cheeks and mouth more. Then after that first "dental" experience, she proceeded with the experiment, moving her hand further toward her cheek and told me about a second experience that occurred to her. This time, she felt the sense of a loving touch on her cheek.

Flirts are parallel worlds

The dentist and the loving touch were two different experiences to this woman.[9] I call them *parallel worlds*. In your experiment, the parallel worlds were the various experiences that occurred as you moved your hand lucidly. Having a sore mouth is one world. The loving touch is another.

Parallel worlds are flirts—those quick, evanescent experiences that appear with sentient awareness. They are like dream fragments, the beginnings of stories that at first seem unrelated to one another. Parallel worlds can seem bizarre and shocking to you. But then doesn't every-thing you know about yourself and life have various sides, different possibilities? You may hope for a certain world that holds a good out-come for you—but you may fear other, parallel worlds in which unpleasant or undesirable outcomes occur.

Although the idea of parallel worlds or universes is ancient,[10] it has been gaining a measure of popularity in mainstream American media. Former President Bill Clinton complained in his autobiography about parallel worlds: in one world he was president, in another he was a purely sexual being caught in a scandal. In the previous century par-allel worlds found expression in the two lives of Superman (and of a host of other superheroes). Around the same time the idea of parallel universes—where past events are still present, or where different ver-sions of our history unfold—and of "multiverses" showed up in science as well as in science fiction.

My first contact with parallel worlds was not through comics but physics. Scientists speak about the parallel worlds of particles, atoms, and even the entire universe. In the middle of the last century, Hugh Everett earned a doctorate from Princeton using the concept of parallel worlds to reinterpret quantum theory.[11] The physicist began with the idea that a piece of matter such as an atom has many possible states. He assumed that each of these exists as a parallel world before observa-tions. All parallel worlds exist simultaneously in the quantum world as possible ways in which an atom can behave and is behaving. Simply said, such worlds describe various ways in which an atom can "vibrate."

Everett's point was that in the quantum realm, all worlds coexist. The overall or universal state of matter is the sum of these worlds. Imagine an elementary piece of matter, like an atom, vibrating in par-allel worlds (Figure 4.4). In one world the vibration is vertical; in the other, horizontal. The sum of these two worlds then becomes the basic pattern or quantum wave function of the atom.[12] The idea is that par-allel worlds are separate, are more or less independent, and are nonlo-cal and everywhere! What we see in everyday reality, on the other hand, is the most probable, or the "square" pattern.[13]

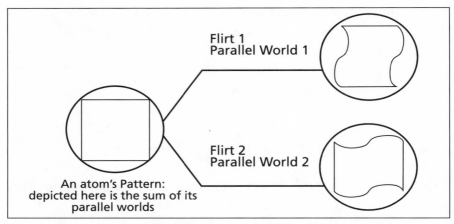

FIGURE 4.4 **An atom's parallel worlds**

As a therapist I am very aware of parallel worlds. Even so, I do not know why we have them. Perhaps nature loves diversity, loves seeing things from different viewpoints. Perhaps she is deeply democratic and insists that everything have many possibilities, all of which are important. That may be why dreams do not give us one simple answer to a problem on our everyday minds, but usually many answers, a variety of dream fragments. Each of these fragments or worlds is not only possible, but a significant part of who we are. Each dream fragment is also a direction. A dream's interpretation may be the sum of these many directions.

Each flirt you notice is part of a story happening in a parallel world. Flirts happen so quickly that you usually don't notice the states or stories they speak about. But with attention you can explore and understand them. You may dream of a monster during one part of the night, for example, then in the next hour about your cooking, then about the stars. At first these separate worlds of the monster, your cooking, and the stars seem independent and unconnected. The "rules" of monsters, cooking, and stars seem so different! Yet after unfolding your dream fragments—that is, expanding upon them—you can see that their sum is a meaning or significance. This significance is the thread connecting stray thoughts and feelings throughout the night and day.

The thread or meaning of the dream is the sum of all fragments. If you reflect upon this meaning or experience, you can make conscious changes in your daily life. The basic problem therapists continuously deal with is that everyone tends to identify with some worlds, but considers other worlds to be bad or not good. With a larger and more open mind, you can add up all the worlds, "superpose" them—as a mathematician would say—so that you realize the larger meaning and direction of life.

Observed, observer, and the big U

In everyday reality we speak of observations or dream fragments. What we notice during the day or night, however, arises from a more sentient perspective, a parallel world. This world, as well as all other worlds, depends upon the state you are in when you are looking at it. In dreams we see this state of mind as what Jung called "dream ego."

This dream ego is not a fixed state, but an ever-changing primary process we identify with in everyday reality. If you are feeling doubtful, supportive and affirming people catch your attention. If you are falsely optimistic, pessimism often reveals itself. The parallel worlds that appear depend upon your everyday mind. This mind itself is a parallel world and an ever-changing process, the primary process with which we identify.

So in a sense, parallel worlds see each other and are constantly in flux. Furthermore, because of nonlocality, we can no longer be entirely certain about who is the observed and who is the observer. The words *observer* and *observed* are, after all, only conventions created by consensus reality. From the viewpoint of the larger dreaming mind, what we call an observer and an observed are parallel worlds. In the same manner, the ideas of the dreamer and the dreamed are parallel worlds—and, because of nonlocality, are exchangeable. We have no absolute way of knowing whether you dreamed a dream, or whether the dream is dreaming you.

Together with all the other worlds, the dreamer and dreamed, the observer and the observed add up to the total you, an experience I refer to as the *big U*. Just as the quantum wave or basic pattern of an atom includes all its possible states, your big U has all your parts in it as well. The big U is the thread connecting all your dream fragments. It is the sum of all your parallel worlds and contains the major direction of your life. As the sum of many parallel worlds, you life adds up to the big U, the core of who you are.

The problem is that that in everyday reality, all we identify with is the primary process, the "dream ego"—the little u, so to speak.

Florinda Donner says all this very poetically. There are parallel worlds around us, she writes, but we ignore their powers because we are too busy with consensus reality. Let us add to this that the total sum of these earth-based worlds, the big U, is the shaman's central and most powerful tool. In later chapters we shall apply this tool to bodywork, relationships, and organizations.

▷ Things to Consider

- Sentient awareness is the ground of wonder, flirts, nonlocality, projections, and parallel worlds.

- Lucidity is needed to notice parallel worlds.

- Psychology has much to learn from physics, but then physics has much to learn from the psychology of nonlocal, parallel worlds.

- The observer and observed are two of your many parallel worlds; their sum is one of life's main tools and central experiences, the big U.

CHAPTER 5

The Big U, Feelings, and Directions

We living beings are perceivers . . . and we perceive because some
emanations inside man's cocoon become aligned with some
emanations outside. Alignment, therefore, is the secret
passageway, and the earth's boost is the key.
—don Juan[1]

In the last chapter we discussed how flirts or bugs are parallel worlds. We explored how even the most mundane action—such as placing your hand on your cheek—is actually the experience of parallel worlds, seen from the viewpoint of sentient awareness. As the sentient essence of an experience arises in our awareness, it breaks into differentiable, parallel worlds—separable possibilities (*quantized* possibilities, to use the quantum mechanics term for this phenomenon), like the fragments of a dream. Now we'll look at how these worlds are organized by their overall sum—the big U—just as dream workers have shown how the meaning of a dream lies behind its fragments.

Superposition

To make path awareness more practical in psychology and to bring it closer to the mathematical and physical sciences, allow me to add a technical term to the discussion now and then. Such terms describe the quantum mathematical structure of all matter and are central to understanding ourselves as individuals, couples, communities, and worlds.

Literally, *superposition* is the placing of something on top of something else. In geology superposition means that in a regular series of sedimentary rock layers, the oldest layers are at the bottom, and the youngest are at the top. Superposition in psychology means that there are various layers in us. As in geology, our ancient history (dreamlike, timeless layers beneath our identities) is on the bottom, and our recent history can be imagined to be on the top. Superposition says that when various states or parallel worlds in the physical or quantum realm of a system are layered upon one another, they create the system's overall pattern or quantum wave. In psychology as well, an overall or general pattern or state of mind at any given moment can be partially understood as the sum or superposition of dream fragments or parallel worlds. We are the sum of all our various possible states at any given moment—as, for example, our general mood upon awakening in the morning is the sum of the dream fragments from the previous night.

Or think of superposition like this: imagine that each of our various possible states is represented by a sheet of plastic, transparent paper. If variously colored sheets are placed upon one another in front of a source of light, the resulting color would be analogous to our overall state of mind. This overall state is the sum of various "parallel worlds." In many ways we are like light, a superposition or sum of many different colors.

Let's make superposition more visually explicit: Pretend that last night you had a dream fragment about an African shaman; in another part of the night, you dreamed about George W. Bush. There are your two parallel worlds.

When you awaken, you wonder, "How do these dream fragments, these parallel worlds, go together?"

If the dreamer were an artist, she might combine them with a superpositional sketch. As you can see, in Figure 5.1 the combination

FIGURE 5.1 **Superposition of a native shaman and George W. Bush**

figure at the right contains various elements of both parallel worlds. This is the dream's big U, a superposition of the shaman and George Bush. You could imagine this sum of dream fragments, this composite, this superposition to be a Native American chief—that is, both a shaman and a war leader. The interpretation, furthermore, might be the recognition that you are actually a chief who follows the Great Spirit. If we followed your moment-to-moment process, we might see first the president emerging, then the shaman, then a deep sense of the chief or big U—someone experienced at organizing the entire process, at some moments exercising the dreaming powers of a shaman, at other moments leading your clan to war.

Our dreaming processes not only show us our parts, but they also imply a complete picture of things, all operating at the same time, sometimes in harmony with one another, sometimes not. And the right interpretation of the dream is usually the one that works best in a given moment—that feels best and uses all the parts, all the fragments. The big U is a pattern, an interpretation, and an experience of the essence and sum of all the parts. Getting to know that U is crucial. It inspires you, carries you, and (as I will explain later) makes life a path of least resistance, or least action.

Superposition of feelings as directions

There are many ways of doing dreamwork: You can act out dream figures (as in Gestalt or psychodrama), talk to dream parts (as in Jung's
active imagination), even dance the figures, noticing how they arise at
every moment.[2] (Later in this chapter I will suggest a new, noncognitive method of dreamwork based upon the superposition of dream
parts using their "directions.")

The idea that dreams or dream fragments are connected with directions is ancient. Native American spirituality is based, in part, upon
respecting and worshiping the earth's grandmothers and grandfathers—
that is, the four directions. In the northern hemisphere, the east is often
connected with light and wisdom, the west with insight, the south with
love or abundance, and the north with cool detachment. The idea that
feelings and dreams have directions is as ancient as mythology itself.
Even today we associate feelings with directions. We speak of life going
down, up, forward, or backward. "Where are you headed today?" we ask,
talking about feelings as often as geographical location.

Remember the body-direction exercise from Chapter 2? Recall and
re-experience how your feelings are connected to directions. Then ask
yourself about the deepest part of yourself. At this moment where do
you imagine sensing or feeling the deepest part of yourself in your
body? In your head or in your chest? Or your abdomen? Wherever it is
located in your body, ask yourself where this feeling is headed, what
direction is this feeling associated with in the room or in the space you
are now in. Or is your deepest feeling connected with a location outside
the immediate and enclosed space you may be occupying now—somewhere else on earth? And if so, toward which direction is your feeling
connected—north or south, east, or west?

If you are in connection with the sentient earth, you can notice at
any moment that the earth calls you to one direction or another.
Although your everyday mind may think this is impossible, with sentient awareness you develop path awareness and notice each of the feelings of the space and directions around you.

Arrow or vector addition

Here's a new kind of walking meditation based upon body feelings and earth directions. I'll show how feelings can be directions, how they superpose as if they were arrows to create the big U (the central and guiding pattern of the moment). Thus, all your feelings are directions, and adding them gives us a picture of the whole of you.[3]

As we've seen, superposition is a special kind of addition. Normal addition works with simple quantities: Two apples plus one apple make three apples. Superposition, however, can add waves—or arrows that show the strength and other qualities of waves. Arrows or vectors like *2 feet straight ahead plus 1 foot to the right* are described by their lengths as well as their directions or angles.

A vector is simply an arrow (the Latin word *vectus* means *carrier*) with a given length (or magnitude) and direction. For example, the force with which you pull something is a vector. The force has a quantity (such as 10 pounds of weight) and a direction or angle (such as 45 degrees). Vectors are useful in explaining the forces acting on sailing vessels, whether canoes in ponds or liners in midocean. There are mainly two forces acting on a sailboat, for example: the force and direction of a current, and the force and direction of the wind (see Figure 5.2). The boat's resulting direction is the sum of the current and of the wind.

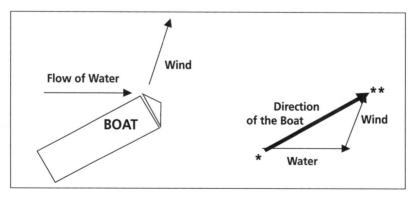

FIGURE 5.2 The boat's direction is the sum of wind and water arrows.

You can see how the boat's resulting direction is the vector sum, or superposition, of the forces acting on it—in this case, the current and the wind. (The right-hand side of Figure 5.2 shows how to add or super-pose the current arrow, starting at the point marked by the *, and the wind arrow, beginning at the end of the current arrow and ending at point **. The resulting Boat direction and vector goes from point * to point **). The graphical nature of vectors is one reason science makes such common use of them: They help explain things clearly. Quantum physicists like Richard Feynman used similar diagrams to understand the real and imaginary directions of elementary particles moving about in quantum realm spaces (more about that later in the book).

For the moment I will use vectors (directions, arrows) to graphi-cally represent subtle body feelings and earth directions. For me, vec-tors are real—after all, they indicate a literal north, south, east, and west. At the same time they are imaginary, as in your dreamlike sense of where your feelings are headed.[4] Directions are organized partially by physical forces such as gravity and magnetism, and partially by spiritual, earth-based experiences such as the grandparents that Native Americans have imagined as the four directions. (It is in this latter sense that I particularly appreciate vectors, especially in light of the word's root meaning, *carrier:* as a spiritual force, vectors carry us.)

So: the direction you are headed is the sum of your parallel worlds. The superposition of any two or more vectors (or worlds, forces, arrows—whatever you choose to call them)—can occur by drawing one vector, then—starting at the end point of that one—drawing another. To create a sum, draw a line from the starting point of the first arrow to the end of the final arrow. Later in this chapter we will use this new dreamwork method.

Parallel worlds are dreamlike earth directions

Until relatively recently, our ancestors had no flashlights or maps to guide them, surviving only with their intuition or body wisdom. I indicated in Chapter 2 how the Guugu Yimithirr people of Australia can sense direction even blindfolded and turned around in a room without light.[5] Aboriginal intuition does not stop there: Some Australian groups feel the earth's "songlines"—earth-based experiences expressed as songs and mythic stories.[6] Songlines are experienced as directions or vibrations believed to have been sung originally by mythic ancestors who created the physical characteristics of earth, the myriad forms of life, and the codes governing conduct and relationships among humans. For Aboriginal Australian peoples, vectors or directions are personal forms of nonlocal community and earth wisdom operating in dreamtime. Songlines are paths through the landscape; they are symbolic markers that organize the land and give it spiritual meaning. These paths connect dreamtime with the present time and space.

This worldview of the Australian Aborigines is an example of sacred geography—a way of ordering space that imbues the landscape with spiritual and dreamlike meaning. Although many people today still have a sense of the earth's directions, the continuous use of maps and lights has sent some of our original directional sense—once needed for survival—into the background of awareness. Still, even city dwellers have retained an impulse for the significance of directions. East has traditionally been a sacred orientation for both Christianity and Islam. Such sacred directions in Ireland, England, Scotland, and Wales were called *ley lines,* or *dragon lines.* Along the alignment known as the St. Michael ley line, many sanctuaries were created thousands of years ago. One of the longest in all of Britain, the St. Michael is the longest line one can draw across southern England, running from southwest to northeast (see Figure 5.3).[7]

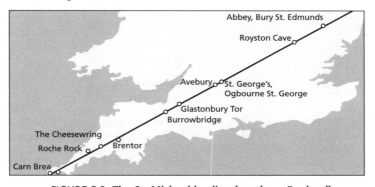

FIGURE 5.3 **The St. Michael ley line (southern England)**

In one way or another, we human beings are probably like the rest of the animal and mineral kingdom: We all have a sense of path awareness. We sense magnetic and gravitational fields; we sense the dreamtime as if we had an inner psychospiritual compass. Because the magnetism and gravity of the earth are connected with the rest of the universe, our so-called earth-based sense of direction is linked to the whole universe. The experiences of ourselves and our bodies belong not only to us, but to the whole planet, the entire universe.

The endophysics of space–time in Taoism

The earth, then, is the solid substance on which we stand (exophysics) *and* the mythic power that affects us with or without our noticing (endophysics). The earth has both concrete and dreamlike characteristics.

According to the authors of the *Tao Te Ching* and *I Ching*—one of the divination practices in the world—to find the Way or the Tao you have to notice the time—i.e., the quality—of the moment. Such time is expressed in the *I Ching* by a hexagram (Figure 5.4), created from doubling trigrams. When one trigram is placed upon another one, the Tao appears as a hexagram—a superposition of six lines. The *I Ching* uses the sum of the hexagram's structure—the sum of all its lines—to give the hexagram its meaning. In fact, the gestalt of the hexagram gives the individual lines its meaning.

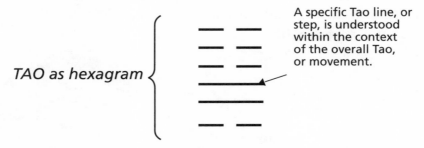

FIGURE 5.4 **Tao as hexagram.** The Tao expressed here as Hexagram 46 in the *I Ching* is called *Pushing upwards*. This is a superposition, or layering, of the upper trigram, ☷ representing the earth, atop the lower trigram, ☴ representing the sun. The overall meaning is *growing*, or *pushing upwards*.

It fascinates me that the ancient Chinese originally associated these trigrams from which hexagrams are composed with spatial directions and characteristics of the seasons (Figure 5.5). These directional characteristics were linked with Chinese mythology, or the endophysics of space.[8] The hexagrams of the *I Ching*, which may be five thousand years old or older, still show with riveting clarity the nature of our directional and superpositional psychology.

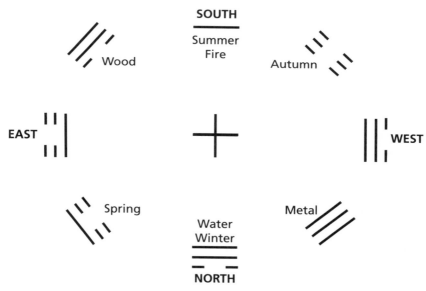

FIGURE 5.5 **Top:** Directions, seasons, and elements of the *I Ching* hexagrams. **Bottom:** The cardinal directions from a 13th-century text, in which north, east, south, and west are pictured on a talisman to nullify the effects of curses.

Dreamwork with directions

Our indigenous sisters and brothers—indeed, everyone's ancestors, including the ancient Chinese, Aboriginal Australians, and Native American peoples—had a path awareness that was a mixture of real and imaginary directions, associated with the organizing powers of the universe. Path awareness and vectors, however, offer us a new form of dreamwork.

This new dreamwork is a walking meditation based upon the directions of your everyday life as one parallel world and the figures of your dreams as other parallel worlds.[9] We shall experiment with how your ordinary self and dream figures are characterized by directions and vectors. Then to do the dreamwork—that is, to interpret the dream in terms of your everyday life—we shall explore how to add your everyday self and a part of a dream to find your big U, which is the direction of your life in the moment; perhaps it is your overall direction. To discover the U, the superposition, and the meaning of your dreams, I shall suggest relaxing and opening up to your path awareness. If this is new to your everyday mind, just relax and let your body show you the way.

To keep things simple, we'll work here with a short dream, a dream fragment, or an image from part of a dream—although this method can be expanded to include as many dream fragments and images as you like. Furthermore, for the sake of simplicity, try to find the directions associated with your dream figures on the horizontal surface of the earth. (Finding *vertical*, or heavenly directions—that is, the sense of depth—can be important, but it is usually easier to begin by finding the directions on the apparent plane of earth. Yet vertical directions often have their horizontal equivalents—for example, a particular heavenly quality may also be found in a certain place or direction on earth. After you become more familiar with vectors, using all directions will be easier. (For more details about vector walking, see Appendix 9.)

Let's begin.

1. Describe your everyday self in a few words; call this *#1*. A high school teacher doing this exercise described her everyday self as "A nervous teacher," and called that *#1*.

2. Now recall and write down a recent dream or dream fragment. If you can't remember one, write down an older dream that intrigues you. Then select and name one part of your dream (if there are many parts to choose from, choose just the one part that pops into your mind right now). Call this *#2*. (Later on you can add other parts of your dream.) The same high school teacher remembered only one dream fragment from the previous night—something about going to a doctor who laughed and said she was healthy. For *#2*, then, she wrote "Laughing doctor."

3. Time to put feet to your experiences *#1* and *#2*. You'll need two small pieces of paper and a little floor space. (If you can't walk, or if your space is too constricted to walk in, simply use your pencil and

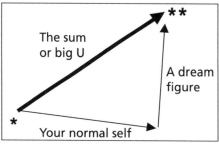

FIGURE 5.6 **Dreamwork vectors**

paper.) Mark a starting point on the floor with one of your pieces of paper. In Figure 5.6 that point is marked with a *.

4. Recall your self-description *#1*. When you are ready, ask your body and the earth to show you which direction on earth is associated with your normal self. A direction in the room you're in (or a direction on the sheet of paper you're writing on) or some general earth direction may appear to be the direction of your ordinary self. Standing at the starting point (the *), let your body turn until you sense a specific direction.

5. Letting yourself be turned by the direction of your normal self, walk a few steps in that direction. The direction may seem reasonable, or it may seem totally strange to you.[10] Perhaps it will be a part of the room that is associated with your self-description *#1*. Or maybe one of the four cardinal directions will attract you. Walk on in that direction—the direction of your ordinary self. Be aware that your direction may be very different from that portrayed in Figure 5.6. Trust

your body to know the direction and how many steps to take there. (If you cannot easily walk, at least feel your upper body move in a particular direction—then trace that direction, with a pencil on paper.)

6. Now, there where you stand at the end point of arrow *#1*, recall *#2*—remember, feel, and sense the direction of one of your dream figures. Let your body sample various directions. When you feel the earth associate a direction with your dream figure, take a few steps in that direction—and call that vector *#2*. Use your path awareness to let the dream figure move you as many steps as your body requires. Finally, at the far end point of vector *#2*, mark the spot (**, in Figure 5.6) on the floor with a piece of paper. Did moving along that second vector give you insights into the nature of the dream figure?

7. Now you are ready to superpose your everyday self and your dream figure. Return to *, your original starting point. Spot the piece of paper you just laid down at **, and begin to move slowly and sentiently toward it. Feel this path as you move. Walk that big U path a few times until feelings and ideas emerge or catch your attention. These experiences are important characteristics of this direction or path for you. They may seem irrational to your everyday mind, but let them emerge. *Re-walk the big U path until its feeling and meaning are clear to you.* Make a note about these feelings and meanings.

8. Finally, *interpret your dream* in the new way by asking yourself what meaning this U path has for you. How can you use that meaning or direction in everyday life? How does it help with your problems? In what way are each of the paths, #1 and #2, both important paths from the viewpoint of the final path? This is your dreamwork. Make notes about any insights you may have received.

When the high school teacher walked her vectors, she wondered at first about the irrational nature of it. Could she trust what her body was telling her about direction and steps and paths? Yet she put her hesitations aside and finally walked the first two paths, and the big U. Then she understood. The feeling that emerged in her while on the U path pointed to her need to follow her most sensitive self as a teacher. She had forgotten about this sensitivity, she told me later. She had been pushing herself at teaching until she felt unwell, and then became anxious about her ill health, instead of sensitively feeling her way along in her career. This insight resolved her anxiety. She realized she had forgotten to base her work on her sensitivity. She recalled that her dream doctor was laughing because there was nothing wrong with her! She said that being more sensitive made her feel well.

Each person's experience and directions are very different. You must follow your own body, your own directions, develop your own path awareness by trusting the earth and your body's wisdom. The big U will probably add up to something very significant for you. It will include but likely be beyond your everyday self and even your dream image. Adding vectors is one way to understand the geometry of dreams.

All the parts of our dreams, our psychology, and perhaps our whole lifetime are tied up with specific directions. We need to get aligned with these big U directions, their meanings, and their earth-based experiences. Don Juan said it simply:

> We living beings are perceivers . . . and we perceive because some emanations inside man's cocoon become aligned with some emanations outside. Alignment, therefore, is the secret passageway, and the earth's boost is the key.

▷ Things to Consider

- Every material object has quantum states and parallel worlds. Likewise, every motion we make is filled with parallel worlds.

- The sense of parallel worlds as earth-based feelings, arrows, or vectors is very old. Feelings can be experienced as earth-based directions. Superposition of parallel worlds belongs to your psychology and relationship to the earth.

- Using earth-based awareness of feelings as vectors, you can create a new kind of walking meditation that can reveal the meaning and geometry of your dreams.

CHAPTER 6

Why Dreams Become Real

Warrior-travelers can count on one being on which they can focus all their love, all their care: this marvelous Earth, the mother, the matrix, the epicenter of everything we are and everything we do; the very being to which all of us return; the very being that allows warrior-travelers to leave on their definitive journey.

—don Juan[1]

The sentient earth, sentient awareness, is perhaps our greatest teacher, and we can find it in most states of consciousness. This idea was brought home to me again, thanks to an e-mail from a German man. Matthias Turtenwald was climbing the steps of a tower with his three children in order to watch a sunset. He picked up one child who had become frightened at the height, and somehow they toppled over the banister together, to the ground 28 feet below. The father's head smashed into the concrete; the child fell on his body and was spared major injury. Matthias was not expected to live—if he did survive, his family was told, it would be in a vegetative comatose state. A friend of his, however, apparently read my *Coma: Key to Awakening—Working with the Dreambody near Death* and applied the methods to the injured man.[2] The friend assumed that some level of awareness was present; she spoke to him and breathed with him, watching his minimal cues carefully for feedback. Against all odds, and to everyone's surprise, in a few days he slowly came back to everyday consciousness. He eventually wrote about his experiences.[3]

Matthias's struggle and success at surviving and regaining consciousness were undoubtedly due to many factors. I retell it here to remind us that *awareness is available in nearly any state of consciousness.* Perhaps it is always present. All of us have had the experience of wondering, *What do I have to hold onto when nothing is really working, and I need help right now but don't have it?*

We all have our own answers to this question. An answer I have suggested and described in previous chapters is, for me, a first principle: Train your inner focus, sense your sentient awareness, and use it—for it has the ability to produce consciousness. Awareness is present in one form or another in all states of consciousness as long as we are alive. Finally, in the immediately preceding chapter I encouraged you to find the direction of your big U, for—because it includes all your parts—your awareness of it can be used as a guide.

Coma work is a quintessential example of applying awareness principles. In a comatose state helpers can see only tiny movements or changes—the movement of an eyebrow, for example, or the slight jitter of a hand. Yet by heeding these miniscule movements and reflecting to the comatose person what the helper is noticing, changes are created in the comatose state.

Heeding the little things is a matter of psychology. It is a metaphor for zero-state physics even as it is a spiritual act or belief, a feeling, a "metaskill."[4] Paying attention to small, nearly imperceptible things is really a basic life skill. Develop your awareness to focus on nanolike, tiny, almost invisible things—on their colors, motions (however slight), their smells and sounds.

Where we are so far

The next time you have a question about your life, ask it—and *remember what you notice* immediately after asking yourself the question. The smallest things can be your teachers—that is, if you notice them. The basic principle of *sentient awareness* is a great teacher—it unfolds into parallel worlds, which when superposed give us a sense of the big U. In this way our feelings connect to the world, to its various directions, and to our aboriginal roots. I explored how to add together the various flirts and parallel world experiences. The resulting montage becomes a superposition, a felt sense of meaning—a new noncognitive form of dreamwork.

Let's review the details of that dreamwork method. Any method is right for a dreamer when she says, "Yes, *that's* what the dream is about!" That *yes!* is our goal. Directional, or vectored, dreamwork has the potential of helping you feel on track. The U is the sum of parallel worlds, the various directions of your dreams, the larger background direction inclusive of all your possibilities. The big U doesn't merely advance your primary processes and help you solve your everyday problems (although that is important, too). The U is *inclusive*. The U says, "This direction you normally take is needed, yet so are other directions that you don't know as well—for they are parts of you, too." This sense of inclusiveness is a kind of spiritual experience that governs the deep background not only to all of us, but even to all particles in the universe.

The various subvectors, or parallel worlds, that add up to the big U are very different from each other. These subvectors represent your inner diversity. Because parallel worlds remain relatively independent of one another, it can be challenging to integrate various subvectors into your everyday self—which itself is a parallel world!

The differences within you, the conflicts between your inner parts or directions—these are due to nature's insistence. And they all add up to your big U.

Think of it in numerical terms (see Figure 6.1). Say your big U is the number 4. If one of your directions (or subvectors) was -6, then in order to arrive at your big U of 4 you'd need a second direction: a +10. Granted, -6 and +10 seem headed in opposite directions, yet both are necessary for you to be you—or for U to be 4! (Your big U of 4, by the way, embraces many polarities—you can arrive at 4 with a -3 and +7, with a +68 and -64, etc.)

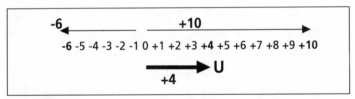

FIGURE 6.1 In a way, +4 "needs" -6 and +10 to be itself.

Again, the various subvectors represent your diversity. In this simple case, -6 and +10 are very different from one another. They are different not only from each other, but from your big U of 4. This variety of viewpoints, however, is essential to awareness, which thrives on differences and relativity. In other words, our inner conflicts show us that there are different ways of looking at things—even within ourselves. Relativity is inherent in awareness concepts because awareness (you could say) is an equal-opportunity phenomenon: It respects and values *all* states. The U-vector level of awareness is a kind of intelligence that says, *I see the tension or the fight, but I am on both sides! I am their elder. I am the parent of their conflict and also of their resolution.*

How do dreams enter reality?

Earlier in this book I noted that awareness self-reflects to produce everyday reality. Yet how does this occur? What is the process? This is significant, for the arising of consciousness and reality from sentient awareness is fundamental to everything we do. A similar question has troubled physicists and philosophers at least since the advent of quantum mechanics in the early twentieth century: How do quantum waves enter reality? Do these waves or their parallel worlds—that is, their possibilities—disappear or collapse when they are observed? How does one possibility (or quantum state) become a reality, and what happens to the others when this occurs? (The current assumption in physics suggests that the other parallel worlds collapse.)

The corresponding question in psychology is this: How do our dreams, our myth, how does the deepest part of us—how do we enter reality? One could respond, "Who cares? All my parts somehow add up, and one way or another I become conscious." Yet discovering the answer to this question is crucial if we are to understand the relationship of personal experience to the rest of the world and the universe. Physicists wonder how the universe came into being. Spiritual beliefs speak of divine beings. And at one point or another, everyone wonders, *Who am I, really? How did I get here?*

The basic rule in quantum theory

I am suggesting that sentient awareness is connected with nonlocal quantum phenomena. Quantum physics noticed that the math that describes reality best is characterized by a mathematical rule for how reality occurs. No one understands where this rule came from; all physicists know is what the rule says: simply, that the universe can be described by quantum waves or arrows, and their superposition—what we have been calling the big U vector. The rule says that this vector self-reflects to create a probabilistic description of reality. Allow me to briefly summarize the math.[5]

Quantum waves are described by what mathematicians call vectors—complex numbers, which are a combination of real numbers (1, 2, 3, etc.) and imaginary numbers (i1, i2, i3, etc.). Imaginary numbers were invented because of the need for square roots of negative numbers—an impossibility with real numbers. Imaginary numbers are kind of like the essence of real numbers. They resemble, in fact, the Holy Ghost, wrote the late-seventeenth-century philosopher and mathematician Gottfried Wilhelm Leibnitz.[6] In short, real things can be described by quantum waves—or vectors, or complex numbers—which are partly real, partly imaginary.

Quantum waves describing a particle become real and measurable through the process mathematicians call *conjugation*. Conjugation is a form of reflection in which a quantum wave or complex number—such as a + *ib*—is reflected to become a real measurable number. Figure 6.2 maps complex numbers, including real numbers (–a and +a) and imaginary numbers (*ib*). Specifically, this figure locates the complex number a+*ib*. You can also see its *conjugate*, a-*ib*, below the real number axis. a+*ib* and a-*ib* reflect one another across the real-number line.

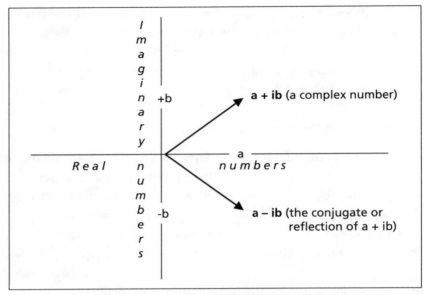

FIGURE 6.2 **Complex and conjugate numbers**

Conjugating a complex number (which is essentially squaring it) creates a real number.[7] In other words, the result of conjugating a quantum wave gives us a real number that, according to the rules of quantum mechanics, tells us the probability of finding the particle that this wave or vector describes in everyday, measurable reality.[8]

Physicists know that the rules of quantum theory work, but not why they work. Therapists have noticed that the basic part of the human being, our deepest psychology, seeks to know itself and realize itself. Why does the U vector (or complex number) tend to self-reflect to give us the probability that an event can be measured in everyday reality? There is no one answer. So instead of searching for *the* answer, I call self-reflection an aspect of the sentient-awareness principle (sentient awareness implying differences and multiple viewpoints). Self-reflection lies behind what we all agree is real, or consensus reality.

Recall for a moment Wheeler's whale (Chapter 2, Figure 2.2) and his gift to Einstein. In psychological or anthropomorphic terms, the quantum wave self-reflects because the universe wonders about itself, seeks to know itself. Wonder itself wonders; awareness seeks awareness of itself; we wonder and wonder. Awareness self-reflects. In its most primal beginnings, sentient awareness is awareness of something that has not yet been defined. Awareness implies duality: One thing is aware of something else. This duality is the core of self-reflection—which is, in a way, a derived property of the awareness principle.

This tendency of the universe to self-reflect answers the question *How do dreams enter reality?* Self-reflection happens, things flirt with you, you barely notice them, or you pretend to not notice them. So they flirt again, and again, constantly catching your attention—and yet you forget them. We all do. You tend to have the same problems, are constantly pondering about the same people, thinking about yourself again and again, asking the same questions, self-reflecting until you finally discover an answer that feels real and understandable. In that moment you are freed from the ruts, the people, the problems bogging you down. Something bugs your body, but you forget it until it recurs and finally appears as a symptom. Then, as if you did not know, you say (we *all* say), "Where did *that* come from?" As long as we identify with only everyday consciousness, we marginalize the sentient aspects of awareness.

If awareness self-reflects in everyday life, it must be ubiquitous, must be obvious to everyone. And it is. We find awareness and self-reflection principles in physics. Remember the physicist John Cramer's transactional interpretation of quantum theory (Chapter 4)? Before reality is manifested, the quantum wave of an object self-reflects. Before the particles (or people) can speak with one another, their quantum waves, their sentient awareness, flirts and bugs them to form a connection in a world beyond time and space.

When we awaken in the morning, we often forget our nighttime experiences. We rise from bed, put our feet on the floor, look around at our room and the world beyond our window, and call it all *reality*. Then almost without realizing it, we continue daydreaming or rather projecting what we dreamed about onto the world around us. Until CLICK!, with luck we eventually self-reflect. We realize that we share or have projected a piece of ourselves onto the people and objects around us. For something to become conscious and enter reality—for a quantum wave to become an object, for a flirt to become a projection and finally a piece of our consciousness—our most primal awareness potential must reflect and reflect again upon itself.

Happy birthday, universe!

Self-reflection of the awareness principle is widespread. You find it just about everywhere, and not only in quantum physics or psychology. Music, in fact, may hold the best example. Lyrics tend to repeat themselves throughout a song. Take, for example, the Happy Birthday song (with "Auld Lang Syne" and "For He's a Jolly Good Fellow,") one of the three most popular songs in the English language.[9]

> *Happy birthday to you,*
> *Happy birthday to you,*
> *Happy birthday, dear Amy,*
> *Happy birthday to you.*

A simple, sung "Happy birthday!" conveys the message clearly; the addition of the person's name in line three hones the message. So why the redundancy? Why repeat the line four times?

Probably because repetition is necessary for our feelings to become conscious, for us to understand things deeply. My guess is that if they are going to sink in, if they are going to become conscious, then pieces of awareness, bugs and flirts, parallel worlds, and vectors must self-amplify and self-reflect until you get it. *It's your birthday!*

It is self-reflection that makes dreams become real. Sufi teacher and musician Hazrat Inayat Khan writes in his *Mysticism of Sound and Music*, "The effect of this repetition is that the word is reflected upon the universal Spirit, and the universal mechanism then begins to repeat it automatically. In other words: what man repeats, God then begins to repeat, until it is materialized and has become a reality in all planes of existence."[10]

Khan brings God—that is, the nonlocality of the universe—into the picture. We can imagine the universe trying to make a point with our everyday mind when awareness self-reflects. In this sense, consciousness is the result of a repetitive sequence of sentient events, during which something about the universe is trying to reach our everyday human consciousness.[11]

Self-reflecting and nonlocality

Self-reflection has a mystical as well as a pragmatic aspect. Recall the last time you watched a love scene or fight scene in the movies or on TV—what happened with your body? What occurred in you during the heroine or hero's action? Why did your heart begin to pound? It wasn't *you* in the scene of romance of combat—so why did you react as if it was?

Because of nonlocality. You know you're not in the movie, yet you experience the nonlocality of what you view on the screen. You're probably seated, on your couch or in a theater seat—yet something in you rejects the fact that you're there, while the movie is *out there*. Something draws you into experiencing the onscreen love or danger. Part of the truth, of course, is that you are indeed seated *here* while the action is happening *there*. Another part of the truth, however, is that you are both in the chair *and* in the movie. You are both real *and* dreamlike. Nor is it that you are merely entangled in the dream world. You *are* the other in the incredible reality of dreaming, where things repeat themselves and drive you to become aware and conscious of them. You sense events, you experience directions—yet you simultaneously *are* the events and directions and paths. In short, the normal concept of everyday reality depreciates and undervalues the turmoil and creative madness that brews life into being.

Nonlocality in relationships and therapy

When I work with someone in therapy, I notice when a parallel world of this person catches my attention (perhaps when the person "bugs" me). By reflecting on this parallel world, I try to bring it to consciousness for the person and for myself. Here's why. It's commonly believed that what you notice about other people belongs only to them; that you help others by experiencing their parallel worlds, which are distinct from *your* world; that the discussion is about *them*, not you. Yet nonlocality means that one-to-one work, like therapy, is about you, too—in fact, is global, about everyone and everything. Working on yourself alone or with others is one way the universe gets to know itself. If you are stuck on some problem, the entire world around you is stuck as well.

All of this has been known since the time of the earliest mystics, and now even quantum theory proves nonlocality. But without repetition we forget; we think everything is personal. Repetition helps us remember and get the point: that the universe is the center of consciousness. In a way psychology is not primarily a modern science about people, but an ageless story about how our consciousness arises from the universe.

Don Juan says it best:

> *Warrior-travelers can count on one being on which they can focus all their love, all their care: this marvelous Earth, the mother, the matrix, the epicenter of everything we are and everything we do; the very being to which all of us return; the very being that allows warrior-travelers to leave on their definitive journey.*

▷ Things to Consider

- The basic rule in quantum theory and psychology: *Dreams enter reality via repetition*. Working on yourself is the universe working on Herself.

- Happy birthday to you!

- Your best teacher is a nonlocal one.

- Psychology is an aspect of the earth and of cosmology.

CHAPTER 7

The Quantum Compass

He who loves practice without theory is like the sailor who
boards ship without a rudder and compass and
never knows where he may cast.
—Leonardo da Vinci[1]

The universe and all its parts, including people, are characterized by what I call a *quantum compass*. This is what I will explore in this chapter, with help from anthropology and with metaphors from quantum physics. A quantum compass is the origin of human directional senses; this compass is as necessary for psychological orientation as a magnetic compass is necessary for geographical orientation. It is responsible for the sudden turns we make at given moments in life; it explains why things appear when they do.

Whatever we say about spatial direction is intimately connected with our sense of time, and our sense of direction or "being turned." Simply put, we are organized by this internal "compass," our directional indicator.

Sleeping in the shuttle

After I spoke several years ago to the Science and Consciousness Forum in Tucson, former NASA astronaut Story Musgrave posed some intriguing questions for me.[2] Why, he asked, did he sleep on the ceiling of the earth-orbiting, zero-gravity space shuttle, while other members of the shuttle crew slept on the floor?

"What is gravity?" Story asked. "If the spacecraft is neither accelerating nor decelerating, but hanging between the moon and the earth in a zero-gravity orbit, then what orients you? Where is up? What is down?" (Figure 7.1)

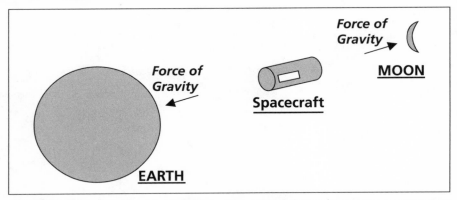

FIGURE 7.1 **The relativity of up and down.** In a zero-gravity environment—as astronauts live in while in orbit or en route to the moon—what is up? What is down?

My first thought, I admit, was that we therapists have enough problems on earth to deal with; the last thing we need is psychological problems in a zero-gravity environment. But the effect of gravitational changes on our feelings is something with which more of us will eventually have to deal, considering the increasing accessibility of space travel. We need to learn more about what organizes us both on and off the earth, in life and near death. What happens to us when our normal directional horizontal and vertical senses are missing? To understand what organizes us when gravity and its effects are minimized, we need to know more about our directional sense. What organizes us when we are sleeping, when we are dreaming, when we are unconscious? Is there some power that guides us on a moment-to-moment basis in everyday life?

The nature of light

To understand more completely what draws and turns us about, let's think about the properties of parallel worlds as they appear in the quantum world, starting with properties of light. The science of physics tells us that light can be represented by particles (photons) or waves. We know a particle of light is present if a single photon triggers a beep on a photon meter.[3] The paths of these elementary particles may be understood as paths through space and time. (It is necessary to remember that these photons are neither waves nor particles as we know them in everyday reality. In this context, *particles* and *waves* are merely consensus-reality names for the mathematical properties of quantum theory.)

Turn on a flashlight, and the beam of light goes where you direct it. Although most of the photons go forward, there are other possibilities: some particles of light may even go "backward" (Figure 7.2); photon counters placed behind a light source have measured such errant particles, which I call *backlight*. For themselves, physicists have no term for any of the many possible directions of light except where it is directed —its "most probable" direction.

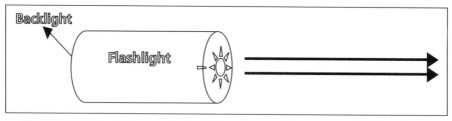

FIGURE 7.2 Although most of a flashlight's light travels the direction it is pointed, some light actually goes backward.

Backward is an unlikely direction for light; in truth, the amount of energy flowing backward is so little that a photon meter is required to detect it.

Just as all the possibilities of an object—all of its parallel worlds— add up to its quantum wave function, so all of light's possible directions add up to its quantum wave function— the most likely essence of the directional vector. In the case of our flashlight, the most likely,

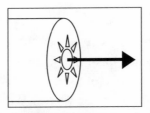

FIGURE 7.3 **Light's normal or expected direction**

expected, or normal direction is where it's pointed (Figure 7.3).

If all the vectors traveled more or less in the same direction—as they do from a laser—the light would be even more coherent; the forward vector would be very strong. Our flashlight is an ordinary one, however, whose possibilities or parallel-world vectors are more readily scattered.

Yet light has more than just these two directions. All the possible flashlight vectors (A in Figure 7.4) are needed for the final sum, U (B in Figure 7.4). Notice that the backlight direction is needed, too. Without each possible direction, the most likely direction of light could not occur. Think of backlight as a cat's tail—it helps maintain the balance of the overall entity. The backlight, however, is only one of the many components that add up to make the whole U.

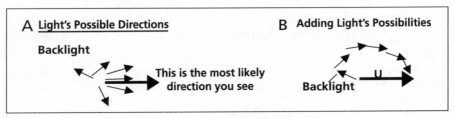

FIGURE 7.4 **Light's quantum possibilities**

Backlight in psychology

These concepts not only define physics, but serve as metaphors for psychology and shamanism. Thinking in terms of vectors and paths helps us to understand not the nature of light, but our own inner diversity, our many possible directions (as we have already explored in Chapter 5). The math of physics helps to describe the world of dreams and our sense of direction. Just as the quantum possibilities and vectors symbolize parallel worlds—all of which are needed—so our various dream parts and parallel worlds are also needed to create who we are and who we are most likely to be—namely, our basic selves, our own big U.

Therapists are familiar with backlight—not, like physicists, in a photonic sense, but in a psychological sense. Unlike light, people complain when everything is not going in the same direction as their normal identities or primary processes are. We lament when something inhibits us, or when we are forced to regress. The vector of our primary process is always at odds with other vectors, and especially with backlight.[4]

Everyone is confronted by backlight. Anything you feel contradicts your primary direction, path, or process typically bugs you. When something deviates from the most probable norm, humans (unlike photons) complain about it and pathologize it. Nature may insist on backlight as part of the overall equation, but we humans insist that it is evil or wrong or sick. From the viewpoint of nature, however, backlight is simply part of a many-sided universe. Light, after all, goes both backward and forward at the same moment, even if the final addition goes forward.

Double signals are backlight

You know the phenomenon: during a conversation with someone, some facial signals are smiling, and some are frowning. It's a mixed message—a double signal.

A double signal is simply a secondary expression (of face, of gesture, of voice) that is different from, or even contradicts, the more obvious primary expression that we identify with (Figure 7.5). We do not convey only one expression, but many—perhaps an infinity of them— although only a few seem to be significant. The double signal is one of the most pronounced of many signals and processes that a person emits.[5]

You are a combination of possibilities. If, as in Figure 7.5, your primary process is a smile and your secondary one a frown, your big U will be a combination of at least those two processes. In this way your face is like a flashlight: Some photons beam a smile, and backlight emits a frown. Who we are is the superposition of these two (and many other) processes. What we seem to remember about one another, however, is neither our signals nor double signals, but rather the big U—the deep process in the background, the overall direction in life.

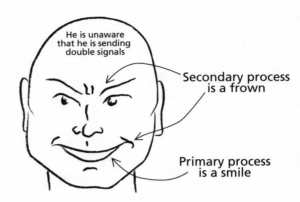

He is unaware that he is sending double signals

Secondary process is a frown

Primary process is a smile

FIGURE 7.5 Frowning is a double signal on a smiling face.

Pathology and backlight

When I watch a video of myself lecturing, I can see a typical double signal: I tend to look down at the floor when I speak. One message is direct: I am speaking to the audience—that is, I am standing up in front, talking directly to the audience. Another message, however, implies that I am *not* speaking directly to them at all, but rather speaking to the floor! When I studied my own behavior, I realized that I speak to the ground during lectures because *I'm speaking to the ground*. I eventually realized that I am actually speaking to the earth; I am speaking to something deep. So now, when I become conscious of looking down in public, I don't necessarily "correct" it, but I try to value that vector, that direction. I may continue speaking to the earth, but—while I speak to the earth as well as to my audience—I slow down my speaking and make it easier for them to understand and listen to me.

We need the entire process, not just part of it. We get attached to our primary process—such as giving a lecture—and forget subvectors and dream worlds. This is to be expected, for our primary processes usually work against the other worlds. Still, to add up to your complete self—your big U—you need many directions.

The everyday mind is a kind of allopath (the term literally means *against the disease*). The allopath says, "I want to direct things; other directors are wrong." Your little u (your everyday mind, as opposed to your complete self, or big U) moralizes and condemns other vectors—this vector is good, that one is bad. From the viewpoint of the big U, however—from the viewpoint of the sum of all paths—*all* paths are crucial. The inclusive nature or eldership of the big U is needed if we are to have compassion for inner and outer diversity.[6] The big U is deeply democratic and values all paths. The big U feels that all levels, all parts, and all paths in the physical and psychological universe have equal importance.

The quantum compass

Your directional nature at least partially determines which paths you travel, and for how long. It can determine which path appears at a given time; your directional nature can compel you to follow a specific vector. Have you noticed those times in your life when you suddenly switched from your normal, predictable behavior and did something new? Why did you wait so many years before making such a change? How do some people, in making their changes, even step out of time and space? What creates the turning points in our lives?

Part of the answer to all these questions is the *quantum compass*.

The idea of the quantum compass first occurred to me when I studied Richard Feynman's description of quantum electrodynamics, a part of the standard theory of particle physics.[7] Feynman spoke of elementary particles "sniffing" along *all* paths. They don't merely choose the most likely path, but try each one. Feynman wrote that the paths (vectors of light particles, in this case) were oriented by a "quantum stopwatch." Feynman's exotic quantum stopwatch is not numbered like a typical clock, but with both real and imaginary numbers.[8] The clock's speed is partly determined by the frequency or color of light, and partly by its rate of movement from one point to another in a given medium.

Like other quantum concepts, Feynman's clock metaphor is as imaginary as it is real. Remember that the reason physicists use math and its associated concepts is not because they understand them, not because they are supposedly real, but because they work. They produce results that we see in overt consensus reality. No one really knows exactly why quantum theory works. It simply does.

I imagine Feynman's clock as a compass (Figure 7.6). First, elementary particles move about in complex mathematical "space"—that is, in a space of both real and imaginary numbers. The idea of a compass, furthermore, aptly fits the idea of space (our real sense of earth) and relates to our psychology (our imaginary sense of the earth).

FIGURE 7.6
Quantum compass
Feynman's quantum stopwatch changes direction according to the vibration (or frequency) of the vectors.

Aboriginal experience of space and time

Some of us have forgotten that our time sense was originally connected to space. With no artificial light, with no mechanical timepieces, we simply watched the earth and our place on it. Dark followed light followed dark. Stars wheeled predictably over us. What we now call *time* was originally linked to trees' shadows, as the sun moved through the sky. Then came the sundial (Figure 7.7).

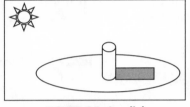

FIGURE 7.7 **Sundial**

This kind of time was connected to the spatial behavior of the earth, sun, and universe. Humans then moved with special, sentient, earth-based awareness. They identified their bodies with the earth, feeling the ley lines or songlines as their dreaming bodies connected to the dreamlike nature of the earth. Today most of us are oblivious of our earth-based sense, in part because consensus reality does not support it. Our reality favors digital clocks over body sensing. Nevertheless, our sense of direction still exists.[9]

Time seems to be a modern abstraction, a concept derived from the experience of movements and changes in space.[10] Astrologers and shamans have always told us that our particular nature is reflected in constellations, whose spatial orientation determines how we should go about our day. In other words, we are affected not just by what is happening on earth, but by what is happening in the entire universe as well.

The quantum compass and forgotten dreams

For all the foregoing reasons—and because of my experience with Aboriginal peoples—I interpret Feynman's quantum watch as a quantum compass that helps us reconnect with the earth.

To feel the quantum compass with your body, try this exercise:

1. Focus your awareness. It's okay to be practical: Think about a problem in your life during this season. What is it? Or what is one of them?

2. Now use your quantum compass—that is, follow your body and its relationship to the earth. Follow your sentient awareness. Let your body turn you about until you know in what direction that problem is leading you. Trust your body, even if your everyday mind is skeptical. (If you must, just pretend you still have access to your indigenous mind.) When you find the direction, jot it down on a slip of paper.

3. Imagine you had a dream last night that you cannot quite remember; also imagine that it is important to you to remember that dream. Imagine or feel where this vague dream might be located in your body. Now feel the earth. Let the earth tell you which direction corresponds to this body feeling. Take your time—explore your various directions, noticing which one is pulling you. Turn your body in that direction and take a few steps there. Move along the lines of your forgotten dream.

4. What direction does this dream go in? Face and move in that direction, and let the vague dream speak to you. Let the earth tell you the meaning of the dream you had and the direction you walked. What is the meaning of your forgotten dream? And how does this direction help with the direction of your problems?

During some work in Australia, my wife and I were working on conflict problems. One of the people I met there was an Aboriginal woman, for whom sensing direction was easy (as you might imagine).

She told me she had been asked to give a talk about Aboriginal problems. "I can't do that," she said. "The listeners are mainstream Australians, and they might not understand." I asked her what direction on earth she associated with this problem. She said the direction of the talk went eastwards, which for her meant the hectic life of the big city of Sydney. When I asked her what she had dreamed, she replied that she could not remember. "If you had a dream and could remember it," I then asked, "what direction would this dream go in?"

"Westwards," she replied instantly—that is, toward central Australia, toward Aboriginal land, toward the earth. Tears came to her eyes as she turned and walked a few steps in that direction. She mumbled, "Home, home . . ." And before I could question her further, she turned to me.[11]

"I know how to speak to the people in the city." She would not speak about problems, she said. She would talk about the earth, her home.

Earth wisdom is deep and obvious. If you relate to the earth—if you sense its compass—you cannot be lost for long.

▷ Things to Consider

- Light goes in many directions, most of which we don't see.

- Feynman's quantum watch is a metaphor for events in particle physics.

- Modern time concepts may come from the experience of spatial changes.

- With a quantum compass you can never be disoriented for long.

CHAPTER 8

Mythic Paths

I find that teaching and the students keep life going, and I would never accept any position in which somebody has invented a happy situation for me where I don't have to teach. Never.
—Richard Feynman[1]

What creates and keeps life going, I call the big U. Physicist Richard Feynman said that his main path was teaching—an obvious truth to those who knew and learned from him. You may not have remembered all the details of his lectures, but you would never forget his ability to play and his enthusiasm about teaching. It was clear that teaching gave him life.

The path of heart, don Juan would have called that U. Lao Tse would have named it the Tao. Jung would have said it is your personal myth. For the power of one's main path goes by many names: the Great Spirit, Mother Earth, God, Jesus, Allah, Yahweh, the daemon. In their book *The Mythic Path,* psychologists David Feinstein and Stanley Krippner call it just that. Psychologist James Hillman calls it the "soul's code" in a book of that name. Abraham Maslow referred to the "self-actualized" person. Still others call it enlightenment.

The science of the universe, the world of quantum waves, and the earth-based, personal you—in order to remain true to all these, I refer to this main path as the big U, the sum of all your other paths. In this chapter I will show how the big U is connected to uncertainty, to myth, and to David Bohm's "pilot wave."

The psychology of uncertainty

As real as you may feel your big U to be—as certain as you are that you are moved along your path by a subtle yet undeniable force—you may never be able to "prove" or measure that force. It is ineffable. It is transient. It requires training and practice and especially repetition. Like the sand paintings that structure the universe in Tibetan or Navaho traditions, you must blow away the vectors and create another blueprint again and again. Yet with all the building up and blowing away, what seems certain to you in a meditative state can seem doubtful, unprovable, and uncertain in the light of everyday reality.

There is no solution to this doubt. Uncertainty is part of the very nature of parallel worlds, of different viewpoints, of awareness and its inherent relativity and duality. For it is relativity that characterizes our personal world, our organizations, the very universe. On the one hand, we have visions we cannot prove but which make life worthwhile. On the other hand, we live in a concrete world of clocks and meter sticks. We sense the quantum compass, we sense something deep in the earth, and we discover parts of ourselves we did not know—and then we return to our everyday minds as if we never heard of the world of dreams. In the thirteenth century the Council of Avignon officially condemned the enchanted world of magic, and praying to water nixies became a sin. But nothing can truly erase animism, as the flood of animated cartoon figures on TV proves.

Modern psychology, too, is typically divided between mind and matter. The world of ideas and dreams was once perceived by psychology to have no connection with body and earth experiences. Even today, if people think of innerwork at all, most imagine meditation or merely talking to oneself. The innerwork I am describing, however, is not just thinking or talking; nor is it merely feeling your body. This new innerwork is a mixture of earth-based, sentient, body experience. The new meditative practice I am suggesting follows the quantum com-pass—that is, your sentient sense of direction and wisdom that leads to insights and practical conclusions.

The split between parallel worlds seems to be the psychological and anthropological background to the physics of the uncertainty prin-ciple. In 1927 the German physicist Werner Heisenberg formulated the quantum mechanical version of uncertainty—which, he said, is a nat-ural law. Measuring precisely how fast a particle is traveling creates uncertainty about its exact location. Heisenberg said that it is impossi-ble to simultaneously know the exact *location* and *momentum* of a par-ticle, such as an electron. Sometimes called the *indeterminacy principle*, the theory tells us that the more you know about one quantity of a par-ticle makes the measurement of its associated property less exact.[2] At the end of his 1927 paper explaining the character of uncertainty, Heisenberg said simply, "We cannot know, *as a matter of principle*, the present in all its details."[3]

In the most general sense, location and momentum or motion are two parallel worlds. If you know where you are (that is, a specific point or location), you lose track of the flow. By the same token, if you are aware of being in the flow of your process, you can easily lose track of where you are. Focusing precisely on one world eventually makes you uncertain because you lose touch with other worlds. Without an overview, there seems to be a fundamental conflict between the move-ment of process and the fixity of states. When you dream you feel alive, but if you try to measure those dreams in terms acceptable to consen-sus reality, you can become uncertain.

Uncertainty is painful; it is sometimes even connected to depres-sion and anxiety. Using only your rational mind can make you feel dis-oriented, even abandoned at some elementary level, or at least uncertain and anxious. To the contrary, the deepest and irrational mind (irrational according to the everyday self, that is) doesn't doubt; it simply *is*, and in that is-ness is a sense of connection to the whole of the universe. Nonetheless, the uncertainty of the rational mind is not solely "bad," for it bugs you and motivates you to relativize the conflict between view-points, with the overarching experience of the big U.

Uncertainty is not only psychologically unsettling and destructive. Uncertainty inspires some to pray and others to dream and connect to something more inclusive and relativistic.

Heisenberg realized this motivating potential of uncertainty because, according to him, physics is part of a historical process in which consciousness widens. Through the openness of physics "to all kinds of concepts, it raises the hope that in the final state of unification, many different cultural traditions may live together and may combine different human endeavors into a new kind of balance between thought and deep feeling, between activity and meditation."[3] We will use what Heisenberg refers to as "thought and deep feeling" in understanding the big U as the mathematical structure of your personal myth.

Personal myths

Luckily, a secretary of Jung's gave me a copy of his unpublished *Kinder Traueme*, a seminar he gave at the University of Zurich in the 1920s in which he spoke of early childhood dreams as manifesting patterns that last a whole lifetime. He remarked that you could predict future professions from childhood dreams.

After working with hundreds of people on their earliest childhood memories and childhood dreams, it seems to me that these childhood dreams are examples of personal myths. I found that these dreams predict not only our professional futures, but the kinds of relationships we will have, the nature of our chronic symptoms, and even near-death experiences.[5] In *Coma* I discuss how even the visions of the last moments of life may be organized by your childhood dreams or earliest memories.[6]

The power that wakes you in the morning and re-creates who you are . . . the constant repetition of deep underlying themes throughout your life . . . the tendency to sum things up and make sense from the chaos of nighttime dreams—all these seem to be characteristic of the organizing structure of the big U. "There is a tendency inside us to become what we are potentially," said Abraham Maslow. We are inclined toward becoming everything that we are capable of becoming. What is this tendency? Perhaps it is what Zen calls the face that we had before we were born.

Pilot waves

If David Bohm were alive today, I am certain that the quantum physicist would have called this U the wave function. In particle physics, the wave function is the organizing mathematical factor behind a particle's possible worlds, its various subvectors. The wave function describes relatively simple objects, such as an electron—and in principle the entire universe. Building on the work of Louis de Broglie, Bohm spoke of this wave function in terms of "pilot waves."[7] In line with Einstein and de Broglie, Bohm felt that a particle was guided by this fundamental pattern.

He imagined this wave as a radar wave informing a boat at sea how and where to go (Figure 8.1). His pilot wave (or vector) of a particle (or boat) is the sum of many other vectors, or parallel worlds, including what in Chapter 7 is called its backlight.

FIGURE 8.1
A boat's pilot wave (dark line)
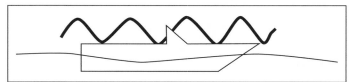

Bohm added an important sense to the wave function. He believed the pilot wave was a kind of intelligence that kept the boat on course. At any given moment, he said, there is a chance that the boat may take one direction or another, but its overall direction and course are guided by its pilot wave, which is nonlocal and fills the entire universe.

Bohm and Debroglie's pilot wave is a mathematical structure of the big U or personal myth. Like the pilot wave, the big U is also both real and imaginary, both local and nonlocal, both wavelike and vector-like. The big U is the underlying pattern of dreams (as I have discussed in previous chapters). This big U expresses itself in many ways. It can appear as a story, dream, vibration, or direction; and it is composed (in principle) of parallel worlds and dream figures or fragments.

For example, the mathematical structure of the big U or personal myth can be perceived as the sum of three subvectors (1, 2,
and 3 in Figure 8.2). These three vectors represent parallel worlds, dream fragments, or
parts. Later in this chapter I will show how to

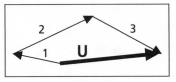

FIGURE 8.2 **The pilot wave's vector**

make such diagrams useful and applicable to your personal life. Although
for simplicity the representation here shows only three parallel worlds, in
principle there are an infinite number of possible worlds and parts.

We change over time; the various subvectors of our lives (such as
the three in this diagram) change according to our personal experiences, outer situations, and factors in the universe we may be unaware
of. If you dreamed of a lion chasing you as a child, chances are that that
lion's power as well as its sensitivity to other powers will characterize
much of your life.

Your mythic pilot wave

Let's test this theory and explore your big U. In the following exercise
trust your own awareness to reveal aspects of your personal myth and
life direction. Let's begin.

- **Ask yourself about a problem that is on your mind today.**
  Name it and write it in your journal. You may want to write
  down a dream or memory from childhood that comes to mind
  just now. Whatever you choose to write down, it may take
  some time, unless you are close to your problems.

  *[I'll speak about myself. My biggest problem today is how to finish
  this book. An early dream that occurs to me just now is of a bear
  moving around my father's car.]*

  Now let's travel some of life's paths. Your response to these
  four questions will give you a sense of the directions that characterize your life.

1. **What has been the most difficult part of your life until
   now?** Note that problem in your journal. (You'll need those
   notes in a few moments.)

[Just now I remember my time at MIT as the most difficult period of my life—an intense year of hard studying. At another time my response may be earlier relationships that were most difficult. But right now, MIT comes to mind first.]

2. **What has been one of the best parts and directions of your life?** If there are many, choose just one and note it down.

    [It was wonderful to meet Professor Ben Thomson of Antioch College, who became one of my favorite teachers—especially because he introduced me to another student of his, who became my wife!]

3. **What is the usual or normal way you go through life?** Again, make a note.

    [In general, recently I have been studying something, then trying to experience it.]

4. **What is the most accidental part of your life that comes to mind just now?** Again, there may not be one answer to that question. But choose the one you think of just now. Note it in writing.

    [The most accidental thing that comes to my mind is a Santo Daime ceremony and Ayahuasca experience my wife and I had with the indigenous peoples of the Amazon near Manaus in Brazil. The warmth of the people and the depth of the visions I had there were wonderful and unexpected.]

- **Now find some space in the room around you.** With your notes in hand, look at the answers to the preceding questions, feel your body, and let the earth and your quantum compass tell you where to turn and how many steps to take.

- **Walk the directions that your body associates with the experiences you jotted down above.** First, mark a * on a slip of paper and place it at your beginning point. Then feel the various vectors, 1 through 4, and walk them, noticing how many steps your body tells you to take for each. In detail this means naming, feeling and letting the earth direct your body to take a few steps along vector 1, your worst life path. At the end of that path, feel, turn, and then walk vector 2, your best path. Then walk vector 3, the normal you. Finally walk vector 4, your most accidental path. When you arrive at the end of your fourth vector, mark a ** on a second slip of paper, and place it there at your ending point. (Figure 8.3 represents my own walking meditation. Your directions and experiences will be different, of course.)

Now you are ready for the U line. Return to your starting point at *. From there, walk a straight line directly to the end point **. As you walk, feel the meaning and sense the name of that big U path. As you walk that U-vector, use your sentient awareness and dream. Funny things can happen inside of you when you walk in the various directions; all sorts of feelings and thoughts may come up. Just notice them and write them down; they are crucial information about your pilot wave, your personal myth. Take your time with this last part.

Once you have the meaning and name of this path, walk it again. While walking this path, consider the question or problem you identified at the beginning of the exercise. Walking the U-vector may well stimulate all sorts of insights—for U is a story line. So while you are walking that final vector, let yourself create a brief story.

[Figure 8.3 illustrates my walking meditation. The most difficult part of my life (path 1) was an intense period at MIT, which is east of my starting point in Oregon. My best part (path 2) was meeting Ben Thompson and Amy. When thinking of them, I felt something turn me to Kenya! As I walked in that direction, I realized that it was in Kenya where I had many shamanistic experiences with Amy. Ben, too, was very mediumistic.

*I pondered the normal part of myself (path 3), which is study and reading—and I could feel something turning me north. Why north? Perhaps because a favorite scientist of mine, John Cramer, lived in Seattle. And finally path 4, the most accidental path: it was my Ayahuasca experience in Manaus, Brazil, the location of that surprising event in my life. I took a few steps toward Manaus on path 4 and marked the end point **.]*

After I walked my big U a few times, exploring the superposition, strange feelings arose in me. I realized that I was walking again in the direction of Kenya! I recalled the people I met there. I could see the shamans; I remembered how the elders had so warmly welcomed us

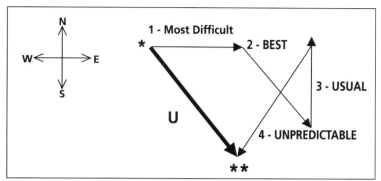

FIGURE 8.3 **Finding my mythic path.** To find my big U, I walked the various directions, starting at * and ending at **. I found my mythic path by walking directly from point * to **.

into their community. I was touched that they initiated and called us Africans, though we are obviously light-skinned Caucasians.

While walking this U path, I felt again the generosity of these people and their ability to bridge worlds. I recalled the importance and warmth of community. In a split second I realized the answer to my original question: how to finish this book. For me, life in this form of the U path involves welcoming all worlds. I realized that even though I personally want to stress the shamanistic and community angles of the work, I also really want to explore the common ground between earth powers and modern science.

The toughest part of writing this book is reflected in path 1—trying to bridge the worlds between MIT and psychology. In my twenties I had to drop one field to study the other. But from the perspective of my big U, the quantum nature of that magical earth beneath us, of shamanistic experiences, is one and the same thing. In this way, my path is to try to create community between the aboriginal and scientific sides of myself—and, I hope, between others as well.

Path questions

When you walk these vectors and directions, your experiences will be very different from mine. Trust your own experience. Questions may come up as you walk these vectors: How many steps should you take, and in what direction? The only answer is that your body will know. Each direction has its own feelings, its own frequency, its own vibe. The direction itself might seem to move you. Therefore, follow your body in deciding how many steps to take.

Another common question concerns your myth. Is your big U really *your* myth? Following the process of many people over the years has shown me that the version of the U path and imagery *today* relates to your present situation best. Tomorrow the images might change, but the sense will be similar. Your sense of the best and worst paths, the usual and most unusual ones, changes as well. But the overall pattern, your big U, seems to remain more or less the same.

Some ask if there is significance to the order in which they walk these vectors. Must they walk them in the order as I've listed them, or will any order do? Deep democracy does not give one path more significance than any other—be it in vector math, particle physics, or psychology. The order in which you walk the various vectors is irrelevant as far as the total answer is concerned, the big U. From the larger U viewpoint, all paths have equal *a priori* value as far as the order they are walked is concerned.

Can one use other questions and vectors to find the big U as well? Of course. I formulated these four basic questions in terms of the worst and best, the most usual and most accidental experiences, to give you a basic sense of the various polarities that structure life. You could add any other number of possible vectors that seem difficult or wonderful. I choose these four because they are very common and fit most people. In principle, the most accurate answer—that is, the most accurate big U—might come from adding together all your life's experiences!

The point is, each of us explores all our paths in time. Each path is needed, especially our backlight! We need the diversity. Richard Feynman said it this way: Nature insists that every particle in the universe explore each and every one of its paths.

Your myth is characteristic of you. It was present in your childhood and in all the twists and turns of your life. The U's quantum compass gives you many turns of fate, many zigzags. In a way the details of your life are due to chance, to the times and place you live in, to the motions of the stars. But your overall direction may have determined just how much of each of these zigzags was allowed at any given time, just as a potter decides how much clay, water, and spinning are needed for her pot. If one ingredient is changed, the others are reorganized to add up to U.

▷ **Things to Consider**

- Uncertainty comes from identifying with only one world, either the real world of the everyday mind *or* the world of dreams.

- Accept the one-sidedness of the everyday mind. If its limitations bother you, seek the solace of a more encompassing view.

- Your myth is an earth-based direction composed of many parallel worlds and many turns of fate.

- Your big U, not you, pilots the ship.

CHAPTER 9

Time? The Shaman's Choice

A warrior is always joyful because his love is unalterable and his beloved,
the earth embraces him and bestows upon him inconceivable gifts.

—don Juan[1]

People have myths; particles have pilot waves. Both people and particles have uncertainty. And both seem to have sentient awareness. That
is probably why psychology seems to connect to particle physics in
many ways. In this chapter we'll explore *moods*, especially how they
resemble physical force fields, such as magnetism. Both moods and
fields share three possible characteristics: They can foster creation,
annihilation, or detachment. The latter is the shaman's choice; with it
she can follow the big U outside time and space.

   Until now, we have focused upon how sentient awareness re-
enchants the universe. The more sensitive you are, the more you notice
your own path as well as various paths or parallel worlds. The less you
are aware of your path, the more you feel lost or pushed around by fate.
Over time, all paths must add up to the big U so that in principle, *all*
paths are needed, even the ones we don't prefer. The universe has within it the formula for consciousness: Repeat and reflect upon parallel
worlds until they become consensus reality. (Remember "Happy
Birthday"—it must be sung many times!)

91

Fields are moods, figures, hidden paths

When you are troubled, when you stand before impasses or moments of transition, your path awareness can connect you to the earth's dreaming and show you the way. I have called that earth power, as it manifests in your personal life, the quantum compass. When you have questions, walk your various paths and find a big U line. Follow the earth. Each time you have a problem, you have the chance of re-creating your everyday life by getting closer to the big U. Use your sentient awareness and move with the twists and turns, until the path, meaning, and images emerge. Remember deep democracy; all paths are equally important. Their sum, your process, is your best teacher.

Life without a sense of the dreaming is governed by an almost intolerable uncertainty: day-to-day paths, this way and that, swinging between uncertainty or its opposite, success, between stress and excitement. On paper these paths seem linear and clear, like arrows on the ground. But in the reality of our everyday mind—that is, in consensus reality—we are often in a fog, moving through vague or fierce moods, like a small airplane in the midst of thick clouds. Before you get clear about what is happening, before you can even say that you are troubled by something, vague moods of anxiety, depression, euphoria, or irritability prevail.

What are moods? Usually thought of as the business of therapists and psychiatrists, moods are also where shamans often find spirit figures, allies, and ghosts. Behind moods lie virtual realities that can both kill and create. Physicists don't usually study moods; they seem more interested in what they call fields: an area or region within which some force exerts its influence at each and every point. Such fields (like gravity or electromagnetism) seem to move objects about at a distance. Instead of terrifying figures, particle physicists imagine invisible and almost immeasurable particles in the midst of fields undergoing creation and annihilation. Just as scary ghosts and figures seem to pop out of almost nothing in your mind, matter and antimatter particles pop out of nothing in fields. These particles annihilate their counterparts, just as you get knocked out by the figures behind your moods. Moods and fields have much in common. Here is a comparison.

PSYCHOLOGY	——	PHYSICS
Moods (like depression)	——	**Fields** (like electromagnetism)
You (like your normal self)	——	**Matter** (like an electron)
Dream figures (like a critic)	——	**Antimatter** (like a positron)
Creation (of inner figures)	——	**Creation** (of new particles)
Annihilation (altered state in which your normal self is temporarily knocked out)	——	**Annihilation** (a particle collides with its antiparticle, destroying both and releasing energy and other particles)

For example, behind a heavy or depressed mood, some critical figure might be lurking. Behind a sunny mood may be an excited child. The point is that behind both fields and moods are virtual, dreamlike figures and their potential directions or paths. If you are out of touch with these figures, they can knock you out or even annihilate you in dreams. This may mean that an altered state of consciousness prevails in everyday life. On the other hand, if you know and can flow with the dream figures behind your moods and fields, you feel more creative.

In the standard theory of particle physics, force fields can be replaced by their virtual particles, which are imagined to carry their field's forces. Physicist Richard Feynman, a main developer of the standard theory (in the form of quantum electrodynamics and its developments in terms of quantum chromodynamics), studied electric and magnetic fields. He did not believe much in fields. Who needs a macroscopic field like a magnetic or electric field? In a way he was like a shaman who says there is no such thing as a bad mood! Instead, he might have argued, there is a dream figure spooking you in the background. He called such figures *virtual particles*. What people thought of as an electromagnetic field between two charged pieces of metal was to him a force-carrying virtual particle, such as a photon (see Figure 9.1).

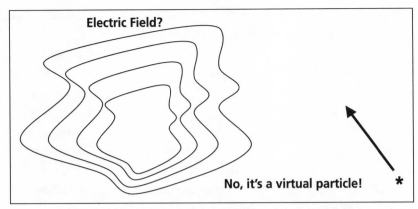

Electric Field?

No, it's a virtual particle!   *

FIGURE 9.1 Fields can be replaced by virtual particles.

Paths behind moods

Because this mathematical theory of quantum physics proves so useful in explaining experimental results, people believe it. Quantum field theory also gives us a hint about dream worlds in psychology. Let your own experience explain it all to you, using the following inner experiment.

Take a moment and feel the atmosphere around you. Play with the idea that the atmosphere can be described as a weather system, that is, as a sunny sky or as cloudy and overcast. Feel that atmosphere around you for a minute and when you can feel it, use one of your hands to express that atmosphere. Make a gesture that somehow expresses that atmosphere. What kind of person or persons might be making this gesture? (You see, virtual figures can be behind atmospheres or moods.)

Now that you have made a hand gesture and noticed a dream-like figure, ask yourself which direction in space this particular hand gesture goes toward or feels drawn toward. What direction in space does this hand gesture go in? When you are ready, walk in that direction in your imagination; just feel yourself walking in the direction of your atmosphere figure. Maybe some meaningful experience will come out of that for you. What does that direction mean to you? My guess is that this atmosphere, the hand gesture, and the dream figure's direction may clarify recent dreams, ideas, and feelings you have had.

Moods can be annihilating

Moods or atmospheres and fields can be represented by dreamlike figures or parts. These figures or parts can be wonderful or annihilating. Consider a sour critic. Remember the last time you had to present something to a group of people? Just thinking about those people may have made you feel ill at ease. If you used your awareness, you may have noticed an uncomfortable field in the air even before you got to the room. Perhaps something you might call your inner critic was around, or perhaps you imagined that one of the real people in that group was against you. In any case, by the time you finally got to that group, you may have felt a bit paranoid; the looks and sounds of some of the people seemed scary to you, even annihilating. Perhaps one of the critical-looking people drove you crazy, bugged you, knocked you out. A few minutes later you emerged from the field and wondered what happened!

All this can be pictured by field theory. The story line of the picture in Figure 9.2 is about the presentation you just considered. You enter the field or room at the lower left and emerge at the upper right. As you enter, the critic pops up. The critic is part real and part imaginary. You feel knocked out and shortly thereafter exit the room.

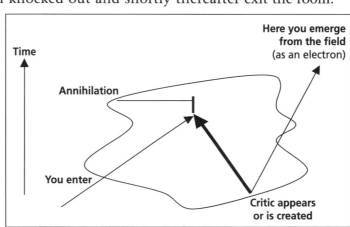

FIGURE 9.2
Moods, fields, creation, and annihilation

Paths through quantum fields

Now let's think about some of the basic patterns in Richard Feynman's quantum theory of fields. My summary of Feynman's quantum field theory is this: As noted, one or all of three processes can occur to a particle or a thing or a person or shaman in a field: creation, annihilation, or what I have called *detachment.*[2]

Feynman realized that we cannot know exactly what happens when a particle enters a field. We can only know that it leaves the area with a new direction, or rather, an altered original direction. He said we know that an electron, a material particle, enters into an electromagnetic field and is moved about by that field. However, because no one can track the exact path of the particle in a field, all we can say for sure is that afterward, the electron changed directions. Because we don't know for sure what happens in that field, why not examine the mathematical patterns of physics and make some guesses about what might happen? After all, these patterns tell us what happens at the beginning and end of the process; perhaps they can also describe the middle. Feynman guessed that several different processes might occur.

In one scenario an electron enters into the field on the lower left (Figure 9.3). At the same moment at the lower right, an electron–positron (or matter–antimatter) pair is created out of nothing. How do we know? The math predicted this possibility and it turns out to be experimentally significant. There is no one accepted totally satisfactory

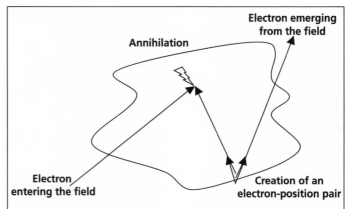

FIGURE 9.3
Electron path
through a field,
including pair
creation

Electron emerging
from the field

Annihilation

Electron
entering the field

Creation of an
electron-position pair

explanation. For a moment in the midst of the field, we have the original electron as well as a second electron created with its antimatter opposite, a positron.

This is not quite as crazy as it sounds. Make a cartoon of what happens to yourself in a field (Figure 9.4). In the beginning of making a presentation, there is just you (electron entering at lower left). Then for a moment, something pops out of your head and suddenly there you are with two other figures (the electron–positron pair): There is the original you, a dream version of you, and a dream version of some critic who does not like you! The dream critic is a kind of antimatter opposite, a kind of not-you.

FIGURE 9.4 Creation of another you and an opposite out of nothing!

In physics the matter–antimatter pair, the electron and positron, lives for a short time. The positron annihilates the original electron. This annihilation produces a lot of energy. Shortly thereafter, the second electron leaves the field (the original was just annihilated) and emerges from the field to go on its way in a direction that is slightly altered from its original direction (see Figure 9.3). The existence of antimatter and the alteration of the original electron have been validated empirically.

But QED (quantum electrodynamics) predicts even more. Feynman explained that there was another possible process in the background. In the first scenario there is an electron–positron created out of nothing (Figure 9.3). The antimatter particle lives long enough to annihilate the original entering electron. However, in another possible scenario permitted by the equations of physics, the original electron moves fluidly through space but back and forth through time! (Figure 9.5) In this scenario there is no electron–positron or matter–antimatter pair creation!

This time-reversal scene is extraordinary. It is one of the solutions to the math of quantum physics and implies that the original electron does not have to get annihilated. In fact, there is no spontaneous electron–positron pair creation at all. Instead, in the new scene, the original

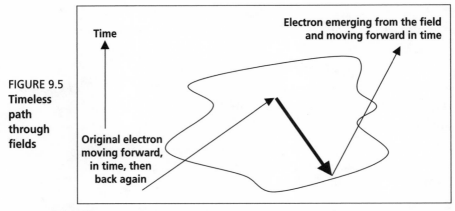

FIGURE 9.5
Timeless
path
through
fields

electron detaches from time. Instead of moving forward, as everything is supposed to in consensus reality, the equations say that the electron might follow a time-reversing path. No one has yet tested this possibility of a timeless path through fields because no one knows how to measure things going backward in time!

Until recently physicists neglected this "beyond time" possibility. Now it is becoming more popular to think about such things.[3] Still, most physicists are not interested in such mathematical possibilities as time reversal. After all, though math helps understand observable reality, that same math suggests many imaginary situations in the quantum world that have never been seen in consensus reality. Moving backward in time is one of those as-yet unobserved situations.

The shaman's choice

However unreasonable the mathematical possibilities may seem for today's consensus reality, psychologists and shamans must often move out of time to deal with events occurring at the border of space and time. How often have you wandered back into the past in your imagination and returned again shortly thereafter? How many times have you thought about your personal history?

In Feynman's notion of detachment from time, the original electron moves free of time (Figure 9.6). The psychological analogy to this detachment occurs when you relax and forget your identity and move forward and backward in history. When you do this consciously, you become a kind of shape-shifting shaman. If you no longer feel obliged to follow the dictates of time and social reality but follow your sense of some force, stressor, pressure, or mood, you temporarily relax the identity you have spent your life developing. Then you can let the field move you about. You use your sentient awareness, notice tiny things, move with flirts, leave your ordinary self-identity, and *reverse yourself,* so to speak, moving with the dreamlike processes. You ride with experience beyond what people call time into the spaces of dreaming.

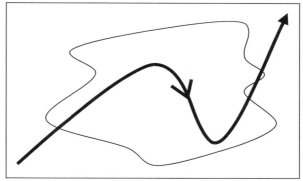

FIGURE 9.6
The path of the shaman (or electron) free of time

In this way, when you enter tense or otherwise weird situations, you can let go of your everyday identity and flow the way the earth directs you, using your quantum compass. Of course, you can always insist upon your everyday way of doing things and, at all costs, stick to time going forward. However, if you repress moods and feelings too long, you will probably begin to curse everyday life or at least do a lot of complaining about stress or the impossibility of it all. The more you stick to moving forward in time, the more those moods get to you—and the more you begin fearing death and annihilation. Forward movement in time is threatened by moods as they turn into relationship problems or medical fears.

But what is this fluid movement in and out of time between paths with opposing directions? What could allow you, or the shaman in you, to move first in the direction of your everyday self, the little u, and then switch directions so to speak and travel backward in the direction of something that is threatening to attack you, in the direction of backlight? The only way I know that you can have such detachment, and encompass or embrace the essence of what is attacking you, is to have a big U attitude. That means to move with your deepest self—your pilot wave—through both supportive and apparently opposing tendencies, seeing them all as useful. That is the easiest way to go through moods and fields.

Chronic fatigue

I am reminded of a client of some years ago, who proudly told me that her normal path involved thinking and working hard. She complained, however, about being tired all the time. In fact, the reason she was coming to see me was that she suffered from ongoing chronic fatigue. She complained bitterly of its many symptoms.

In our first session together I suggested that she remember her deepest self, whatever that meant to her, and use her most sentient body awareness to explore her problems. At first she was afraid of the moody field around her illness. She said that she had never given in to her fatigue. But over the course of several weeks, and with my encouragement, she asked her body what its deepest and best direction might be. Having found that earth-based direction (the big U), which she said was magical, she felt more centered temporarily to let go of her fear and explore her feelings of fatigue. She began to feel and follow her body, and said that she felt herself being pulled downward by some force. She kneeled before a window in my office. Quite unexpectedly, she lifted her arms into the air and found herself standing up and almost crying as she exclaimed that she felt she was a bird, flying freely, leaving her home. She smiled and perked up and said she felt like a child again. Turning to me, she explained that it would feel wonderful to live so freely and independently in everyday reality!

As she emerged from the field of that chronic fatigue, she explained to me that centering herself in the magical direction allowed her to trust her body and go with it, into that kneeling position. She then said she realized that her everyday life was not quite right for her.

Too much time stress! She was no longer interested in working at her job, or even being a mother or a partner. In fact, she said that she had been contemplating suicide. Now, the happy experience of being a child again surprised her. The experience of flying like a bird gave her great relief. Several sessions later it turned out that she wanted to develop a new attitude towards her job and her husband and child. This new attitude was related to following her body more, dreaming and flying in everything she did!

Using the vocabulary of the present chapter, we can say that she found a more detached attitude by centering herself in her big U experience. By centering herself and using her field awareness, her chronic fatigue, which had been threatening to annihilate her, became a path down to the earth and backward in time to childhood. From there she came back to the present, flying like a bird, leaving (at least at that time) the field of chronic fatigue. Her symptoms produced exhausting moods—backlight (antimatter!) experiences that stole her energy. She had felt chronic fatigue was against her (Figure 9.2). Centering herself and going into and with her experience helped her step out of everyday time, and flow with experience. In a way, during our session, she moved backward in time and then forward again into the future. From the larger viewpoint (Figure 9.5), the field of her chronic fatigue was an opportunity, not just a problem.

Everyone and everything has potential detachment and fluidity of the big U. Everyone occasionally temporarily steps out of time and explores various directions. Perhaps everybody has the shaman's potential, the choice to step out of time and move with oppositional experiences instead of being only downed by them. Don Juan said that if we choose to live only in ordinary reality, we will eventually curse life. My suggestion is to use your awareness when you meet strong fields, find your big U, and temporarily step out of time. Then you can let the flow of sentient experience move you backward and forward through all possible directions to re-create your world.

▷ **Things to Consider**

- People and particles have a lot in common.

- Physical fields and psychological moods contain virtual figures and paths.

- Atmospheres have the power to annihilate us. But with the big U, they may also lead to new forms of experience and creativity.

CHAPTER 10

Zigzagging and Process Wisdom

Great straightness seems twisted.
—Lao Tse[1]

Shamans move forward or backward in time and history, make changes, and shape-shift into new forms of being. If you want to do the same, you need to detach from your ordinary consensus-reality (CR) identity and relax into a slightly altered, dreamlike state of mind. To swing with the various oppositional tendencies in life, you need to allow creativity to occur; remember the first moments of awakening in the morning, remember that sense of dreaminess. You already have a lot of experience letting go; every night before you go to sleep you let the organizing power of your dreaming mind, the big U, pilot you along. It has the inclusiveness needed to detach from the substates and yet appreciate any and all of your internal directions—including the ones that disturb you, the ones that go forward and also backward in time. From the U's viewpoint, there is something "okay" about them all. The big U is not simply wisdom. Rather, it is a superpositional kind of intelligence that seeks to know itself through the diversity of your parallel worlds. I call actively participating with this intelligence "zigzagging" or "process wisdom."

Zigzagging and free associations

Zigzagging is process wisdom; it comes from a sense of freedom and an awareness of, or interest in, following whatever path is coming up. It seems to be such a basic need that if ignored, it causes many to seek substances to "loosen up." Alcohol and other substances allow us to dream while awake (Figure 10.1). The way in which you walk when drunk is one way of saying "yes" to many directions.

FIGURE 10.1 **Zigzagging on alcohol**

Free association, one of Freud's great psychoanalytic methods, was a way of zigzagging. In general, free association involves a spontaneous, uncensored expression of thoughts, which allows deep experiences to emerge. When I was a teenager and could not recuperate from a fever, my doctor sent me to get help. He thought I had a psychological problem. My helper turned out to be a Freudian analyst. He had a grand leather couch, and he told me to go lie down and relax. So I went and lay down on the Freudian couch and put my head back, and he said this delightful thing: "Just say whatever comes to mind when I say a given word. Just let yourself freely associate." Wow, that was really great. If you have not tried it, you should. One reason that free association became so popular may have been because it frees us to start zigzagging, saying things that we would normally leave for the night to dream about. Freely associating is a verbal version of zigzagging and path awareness: moving back and forth between various directions until we see the overall path. In my case, relating to that Freudian analyst and zigzagging through all of my associations helped my fever go away.

Brainstorming and Picasso

Zigzagging lies behind brainstorming. Apparently Alex F. Osborn, who was born in New York City in 1888, came up with the idea of brainstorming sessions after he noticed that some of the junior people in his advertising agency weren't speaking up at meetings.[2] He felt there were four aspects to brainstorming:

- Defer judgment; no idea should be rejected.
- The crazier the idea, the better.
- The more ideas, the better.
- Create new ideas as well as improving and incorporating the ideas of others.[3]

I would like to reformulate these four characteristics in relation to zigzagging (which is crucial to individual and team creativity), and then add a fifth:

- Use your awareness; notice and then record and explore every experience, feeling, and idea that emerges alone or when working with others.
- The craziest ideas that are far from normal life, like backlight, are often the best and bring the newest information.
- The more ideas and paths, the more complete the process.
- Your brainstorming process is nonlocal; whatever you think in response to some problem—including the thoughts you associate with others—is needed in the solution.
- The most exciting or emotional zigzag that occurs in brainstorming can be one of discovering what is needed for the next step. At first the zigzagging of brainstorming seems as random as a conversation among diverse friends who have not spoken together for a while. Only retrospectively may it appear reasonable and important.

Zigzagging is essential in any creative understanding. Picasso was a great zigzagger. I discovered this one day when my wife Amy showed me a film about Picasso, *The Mystery of Picasso* (see Figure 10.2). The film studies the artist's creative process by viewing the reverse side of the paper on which Picasso painted. All in all, the camera allows you to see 23 different ink paintings bleeding through the paper.[4]

Often he would start at the left on the bottom of a piece of paper and then spontaneously move his brush to the upper right corner of the paper. Then his brush would suddenly appear in another part of the page, and so forth. I tried to sketch this sequence with my computer by showing the evolution of a picture from the reader's top left to the right and then continuing on the next line below (Figure 10.2).

I am no Picasso, but you can hopefully get the idea of zigzagging from my line drawing. I tried to draw a line and then move to the other side of a given picture without knowing exactly what I would be drawing.

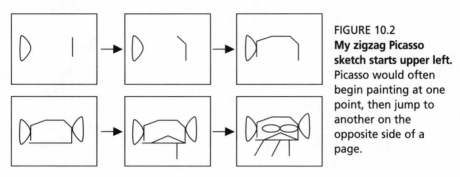

FIGURE 10.2
My zigzag Picasso sketch starts upper left. Picasso would often begin painting at one point, then jump to another on the opposite side of a page.

People and particles are zigzaggers

Both humans and elementary particles zigzag. Feynman said it beautifully: "Particles must explore all paths." To add up to the overall direction or picture in everyday reality, a particle must explore all its various directions. For you to see the book or computer screen in front of you, particles of light must bounce off the book or be emitted from the computer screen. Do these particles of light come directly to you? No. Some light comes directly to you where you are sitting, but some of the light arrives by way of Tokyo or Moscow or the moon. For you to view a book or your computer, the possibility waves of light travel everywhere in the universe to finally add up so that you can view your book or computer. Nature sniffs all possible paths (and takes the easiest, as we shall see in future chapters), though we humans focus on and believe only the most usual ones and try to forget all the other hallucinations or seemingly false perceptions. From the viewpoint of process wisdom, however, there are no false perceptions—only parallel worlds.

Process wisdom is like the "crazy wisdom" of Chögyam Trungpa (founder of Naropa University in Boulder, Colorado, USA). In his book *Crazy Wisdom* he describes the open-minded, almost innocent state of mind needed to value all that happens. He equates the necessary quality of mind with the early morning, with a fresh, sparkling, and completely awake attitude. His book links crazy wisdom with the life of Padmasambhava, the revered Indian teacher who brought Buddhism to Tibet. One of Trungpa's suggestions is to note the existence of all our paths.

Right now or before you go to bed tonight, explore your own crazy wisdom or zigzagging and process wisdom. Take your pencil and put its point on a piece of paper, and let the pencil draw a bunch of zigzagging lines. The resulting figure may tell you about what you will dream tonight (Figure 10.3). From your own sketch you might be able to guess, feel, and see the possible significance of the overall direction and the meaning of the type of motion emerging from your pencil.

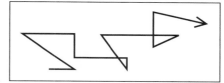

FIGURE 10.3 **Example of a bedtime zigzag to predict dreams**

Creativity and zigzag exercise

Let's apply process wisdom to questions you may have about one of your larger projects. This project can be anything you are working on right now. We will explore its various paths to create a final picture, to find the big U that will help guide you in this project.

First choose and discuss a job or creative project or life task—a current one, or a future one you anticipate—that you would like to know more about. Identify one central question you have about it. Write that question down. Describe in detail, sentiently feel, and then let your body walk the following five questions, one after another, as we have done in previous chapters.

1. **The typical way** you approach the job/project (e.g., depressed, avoiding, pushing, studying). Make notes and draw a direction, like this: →

2. **An accidental or crazy part** of that project—however you define that. Make notes and draw a direction, like this: ←

3. **The most troublesome aspect** (backlight) path; in some cases this might even be the same as 1 or 2. Make notes and draw a direction, like this: ↑

4. **A best part** of the project. Make notes and draw a direction, like this: ↓

The direction that you feel in response to a given question may follow your sense of north, south, east, and west. Or it may simply follow a direction you do not fully understand, until you actually move there. For example, the corner of the room may have specific feeling associations for you. The point is to follow your directional wisdom, your quantum compass, as it turns you for whatever reason towards one direction or another. Let your body and its relationship to the earth lead you. The results may surprise you.

With a process-wisdom/zigzag empty mind, and beginning at your starting point *, let your body tell you the direction and how many steps to walk for each of the vectors (1–4, above). As always, the space you walk in and the earth around you determine where and how much to move. First, feel and walk your typical way; then, an accidental way; and so forth. At the end of path 4, mark a ** on the floor.

5. **Now find your big U.** Return to your starting point, *, and walk sentiently to your ending point, **. As you walk that big U, notice your experiences and let them create a story. The completed story may have an answer to your original questions.

Amy's musical U

I did this exercise with my wife Amy in our living room. She was work-ing on a musical, she said, but didn't know how to bring into it the many voices and stories she wanted to. So her opening question was "How should I go about bringing all the parts of my project together?" We began working on this together.

Amy's typical way of working on her project, she said, was to pon-der it and explore various musical possibilities. Feeling the various directions around her, she marched like a soldier toward the north. "There is something serious about my normal methods," she said.

The most accidental part of her project, she said with a huge smile, was the utter surprise of first hearing music coming out of the ground—of the ground singing to her—while in eastern Oregon. So she walked toward the east (Figure 10.4).

Finding the most troublesome part of the project took Amy a few minutes of meditation. "Oh!" she finally exclaimed. "The worst part was losing all the notes I had taken on some of the musical pieces! How horrible that was!" And with that, she felt the various directions and walked toward central Canada, which she said was a very cool, remote place, where only animals lived.

Her best part was the experience of the artistic possibilities in the project: "You can dance, sing, tell stories, and all that!" she explained. Then, feeling the earth, she moved toward the east, almost dancing. "East again," she said, "but this time to New York!" She was shocked by her own answer, but then after thinking for a moment, said, "Greenwich Village. That's creativity!" She moved as far as she could go in the living room and stopped at the wall, marking the end point **.

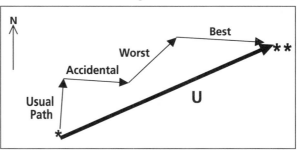

FIGURE 10.4 **Amy's zigzags**

When I asked Amy to go back to the beginning point and sentiently explore the big U path, she started at * and slowly walked to **. She did that several times. She walked sentiently and experienced images, feelings, and rhythms along that line. She made a gesture and a sound that portrayed the U's experience. "The path of this U is extremely unknown," she observed. After walking that final line several more times, she grinned widely. "Aha! I am going to Greenland. I feel like I am a little girl playing, skating." And a Joni Mitchell song came to her:

FIGURE 10.5 **Joni Mitchell on ice**—the big U of Amy's project.

I wish I had a river I could skate away on / I wish I had a river so long, I would teach my feet to fly.

Amy said she imagined that Joni Mitchell composed and sang (Figure 10.5) when she was trying to free herself from conventional social concerns.[5] And with that, Amy began to glide and skate. "That makes me want to cry," she said with tears in her eyes. "Greenland. The wilderness, the trees and vastness are my friends. This land and its immense freedom is the story of my big U."

I read back to Amy her original question: How should I go about bringing all the parts of my project together again? In answer, Amy sang that Joni Mitchell song again, put her arms out, and proclaimed she would "embrace all of nature. Let nature make the music She wants, not what others think."

Amy explained that from the viewpoint of this path, this river, and its music, even the act of losing all her music was perfect. Nature was telling her that it will do the work, not she. Her pilot wave zigzags through serious thinking, the art of Greenwich Village, losing all her papers, and hearing music from the ground. She said she was all of these directions but felt most closely associated with the "river to skate away on." From the viewpoint of Amy's river, all the paths were needed.

Becoming a brush

In a way, every life, every project has its own mind. When you are in touch with the mind's direction, you don't really do things; rather you are a kind of paintbrush the big U uses to paint with. This pilot wave organizes and uses the

FIGURE 10.6 **Which way?**

electrifying, terrible, and amazing parts of life. So whenever you have a question about which way to go (Figure 10.6), try them all; find and relax into the big U to move onwards.

Life is amazing. Normally we don't see the picture trying to emerge from the dots and dashes of individual days and nights. The larger picture takes time to emerge for any one person's lifetime. There are many twists and turns, but in a way, one straight line. This is what Lao Tse must have meant when he said:

Great straightness seems twisted.

▷ Things to Consider

- Nature explores all paths; she brainstorms and paints like Picasso.

- Every beam of light has already zigzagged just about everywhere, before adding up to what you see.

- "Which path should I take?" When the question arises, try all the paths that occur to you. Let them add up to the big U and go on.

- Develop your big U's "crazy wisdom." From its viewpoint, from the deep vision of a project, or the myth of your life, all possible paths are important.

CHAPTER 11

The Physics and Aikido of Least Action

When it blows there is only wind.

When it rains there is only rain.

When the clouds pass the sun shines through.

If you open yourself to insight you are at one with insight.

And you can use it completely.

If you open yourself to loss, you are at one with loss and

you accept it completely.

—Lao Tse[1]

Path awareness means using your sentient awareness to notice and follow the various zigzags of life. The average cosmopolitan little u has mostly everyday awareness of time and space and tends to marginalize tiny feelings and the sense of the earth. However, the big U has most access to sentient awareness. It follows zigzags most easily. It's like whistling while you work. Just working without awareness is tiring. Focusing on the music of the big U, however, produces "least action." When you are in touch with the overarching pattern, the pilot wave or big U of the situation, you can use your quantum compass best. Every zigzag path then becomes an aspect of your overall mythic path, the big U. When you lose your sentient ability, the usual result is identifying only with one path, with the little u and with time, which often results in stress, symptoms, or social anxiety or even the threat of death.

Then you can take the shaman's choice of "alternative death" and step out of the limited forward movement of time to move forward and backward in time with zigzagging and process wisdom.

Causality and awareness

To the adult living in a cosmopolitan setting anywhere in the world, life is stressful. When things don't go the way we want, we get depressed or begin to push. We use power, then, to change ourselves or others, just as whole countries build militaries to defeat their opponents. In this frame of mind, we are attached to a belief in causality: that is, we believe in time, and that everything that happens must be the effect of a preceding cause. The opposite of a causality mentality is sentient awareness—mindfulness of even the slightest things, which allows you to adjust to them. The difference between the causality mentality and sentient awareness can be understood in terms of a ball. From one viewpoint, the ball's motion is simply due to the "laws" of causality, to the force that threw it. A sentient-awareness explanation of the ball's movement would claim, in contrast, that the ball, just like the particles studied by physicists, used some primal form of awareness to "sniff out" all paths and choose the one that "feels" best and requires "least action." The ball follows the principle of sentient-awareness that leads to least action. *Awareness* and *least action* may be linked to purpose and teleology (which I discuss in the next chapter).

From the previous chapters we know that sentient awareness precedes anything we know about mind or matter. It seems to be present in pure emptiness, the zero-state vacuum field. Everything else that we know about the universe appears to be a derivative of this awareness, unfolding diversely into various levels and worlds, each equally important. *Sentient awareness notices the equal validity of all parallel worlds.* I called that *democracy*. It's a mathematical characteristic of vectors in physics and a central principle in psychology: everything is needed, all levels and parts, even backlight!

If we follow sentient awareness, we—

- Value all paths and self-reflections.
- Create many possibilities through brainstorming and crazy wisdom.
- Explore flirts, and all earth directions.
- Can "sum them" as the story line behind our work, our relationships, our group, life itself.

Least action

Using awareness leads you to an understanding of various paths and the sense of the big U's inclusiveness. When you have access to, and can feel, the big U, your everyday mind relaxes and you feel carried; there is less of a sense of cause-and-effect pushing and more of the sense of least effort, least action.

Least action is one of the most basic and general principles of science. Least action governs the motions of bodies in everyday classical physics, of particles in quantum physics, and of stars in relativity. The principle applies to just about everything in the visible physical world, including the paths a ball takes as it moves through the air, the path a photon of light takes as it moves through glass, the way a stream of water meanders down a mountain, and the way lightning seeks the fastest path to the ground (Figure 11.1).[2]

FIGURE 11.1 Electricity tries many ways and chooses least action.

The quantum wave function or pilot wave (the sum of all vectors or parallel worlds) is the root of least action for the motion of an everyday object. We should expect the big U, which is patterned after those quantum waves, to also be the root of least action for what we do in everyday life. In Chapter 13, I will show how the big U's least action is even behind the way we dream.

Most of us have heard that throwing a ball follows Newton's basic principle that a force will produce acceleration of the ball:

force = mass x *acceleration*

But the amazing thing is that you can find Newton's principle—and even the law that energy must always remain constant in a closed system—in the principle of least action. This principle determines how the ball or particle will move. *Least action says that there is one single journey the ball can take* (Figure 11.2). Nature tells us that for a given amount of time for the throw, the ball could take a number of possible paths. The principle of least action tells us, however, that the ball "sniffs" (or has a kind of awareness for) and chooses from all the available paths the one that involves the least action (the dark line in Figure 11.2).

FIGURE 11.2 The thrown grey ball has many possible paths, but only the dark path has least action.

As I mentioned earlier in this chapter, you can think about that ball in at least two ways. You may think of the ball as being accelerated because it was thrown, or you can think in terms of awareness, that given the time to go from one place to another, the ball "chooses" a path with the least action.

This idea is somewhat analogous to the physiological notion that the energy we use to move is closely balanced with our potential energy. To save energy, your body works with the energy available to it. You may use more energy than you have at a given moment, but if you do, you pay for it the next day. Something in us balances and tries to use our energy in a way that creates the sense of least effort. (For a more technical explanation of least action, see Appendix 11.)

Leibniz's least action: *vis viva*

We can all be thankful to Gottfried Wilhelm Leibniz (1646–1716) for the principle of least action. One of the first "modern" physicists and mathematicians, Leibniz lived at the time of Newton, a time when scientists were more overt about their interests in both the qualitative and quantitative characteristics of matter. For Leibniz and others of his time, matter was real in the sense of being quantitatively measurable, but it was also alive and enchanted, animated and dreamlike. He studied the stars and life on earth and intuited that nature was trying to preserve the inherent life force—*vis viva*—in things. (He defined v*is viva* as a mathematical quantity—mass times velocity squared—which is double of what today we call kinetic energy.)

Though his mathematical reasoning was not quite correct in terms of today's physics, he intuited that nature's "sentient awareness" knew just how much energy and action to use. As such, his ideas are a precursor to what we today call the least action and conservation of energy principles, which were discovered at least 100 years after his death.

I can easily imagine Leibniz as if he were sitting with us today. I imagine him observing *and* feeling events. He marveled at the way in which rocks fall down a hillside, pulling other rocks along. He felt what it was like to catch a ball. He felt the force of the ball push against his hand and watched how it moved. He called that subjective experience of the ball's motions a living force. He watched birds fly and fish swim. For him and others of his time, the earth was still something sacred. Matter was not just inert but *animated*, full of the spirits. And so for him and other earlier scientists, least action was a kind of least effort, an inherent sense that there is an easiest way through even the most difficult situations. It seems to me that this sense lies behind today's principles of relativity, quantum physics, and classical mechanics.

Aikido embodies least action

Much of our psychology and technology is driven by a concept very close to the intuitive idea of least action. We are constantly trying to make things easier. Today's computers are not fast enough; they must be faster. We use a remote control rather than get up and move a few feet to push a button on the TV itself. In fact, we have gone so far with least action that some of us need to remember to exercise!

Least action appears in the martial arts as well. Master Morihei Ueshiba, the originator of aikido practice, described aikido as involving "the union of spirit, mind and body in *aiki*," meaning "harmony with life-force."[3] From his experience of ancient Eastern traditions of the samurai, Taoism, and Buddhism, he developed a martial art based upon his sense of kinship with the universe involving *ai* (harmony), *ki* (energy), and *do* (the way). Furthermore, Ueshiba says that the *Budo*, or best attitude, is in combat generally considered to reduce the chatter of the everyday mind and the predilection of *doing* things, so that the universe can take over allowing a form of least action. In a way, *Budo* speaks of least action: that is, you should adjust your kinetic or movement behavior to the potential energies given to you by the universe.

To get through the most difficult times, Ueshiba suggests the use of awareness as the least action. He and his disciples pragmatically demonstrate the usefulness of awareness by a simple exercise: Stick one of your arms out straight, then ask a friend to bend it. If your friend is strong enough, she should be able to bend your arm. But it is suggested that if you meditate on the principle behind your action, that is, on straightness, your friend will have more trouble bending your arm! Try it. You need less action, less kinetic activity if you are closely linked to your straightness. In a way, you do better with less. Aikido masters show how even very old people can send their attackers flying into the air in a form of least action![4]

Martial arts on the subway

My brother Carl told me a story of a spiritual master and martial artist riding with his disciples on a train in Tokyo. A bully swaggered into the compartment and said to all, "Move away!" The huge man grabbed somebody and threw him in the corner. People got scared and ran to another part of the train—everyone, that is, but the martial arts master. He did not move. He remained sitting in the corner as the big bully came swaggering over to him. "Move away!" the bully commanded.

The master happened to have a bottle of sake with him, and so he pulled it out at that moment and casually though politely asked, "Hey, man, you want a glass?" The bully hesitated, growled, but then to the surprise of everyone said, "Yeah," and sat down next to the master, shared some sake, and started a conversation.

That master was engaging the least-action principle. He did not fight, he did not berate the bully's horrid treatment of others, and he almost accepted the "backlight" situation by joining it in his own way. I imagine the master was not relating directly to the situation but rather to the universe, to what I have been calling the big U.

Move your chair with least action

I am no martial artist, but I remember my own big U that I have found from walking various exercises in this book. My big U experience was symbolized by a green dragon, very much like the song "Puff the Magic Dragon," made famous by Peter, Paul, and Mary.

I decided to explore my big U and notice if and how least action occurred when I did an ordinary task such as picking up a chair (Figure 11.3). First I picked up a chair with normal effort and in a normal state of mind—that is, with my little u, which meant using a lot of my strength and straining my back in the process. So I set the chair down as quickly as possible

Then I began singing to myself:

> *Puff, the magic dragon,*
> *Lived by the sea*
> *And frolicked in the autumn mist*
> *In a land called Honah Lee.*

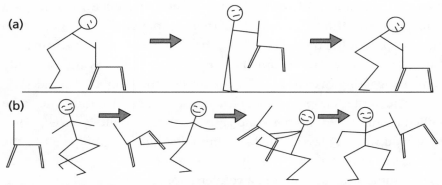

FIGURE 11.3 **Top:** Lifting a chair with effort. **Bottom:** Lifting a chair with least action.

And I lifted the same chair again. This time, however, I remembered my big U—a frolicking green dragon that lived by the sea and sailed on a boat. As I began to focus on the dragon, I started to play and frolic. Everything else had a little less significance. Unpredictably, I found myself giving the chair a little kick, and then—almost without trying—found myself lifting it into the air, swinging with it, even dancing with it!

This was definitely the path of least action.

Try singing and focusing on your deepest self when you are working at something, or just walking, skiing, etc. Least action helps even when there is a lot to do. It is the easiest way in the sense of having the most fun and the best body feeling.

Snow White's seven dwarfs knew this principle as well, as Larry Money's lyrics to this popular song demonstrate:

> *Just whistle while you work <whistle>*
> *And cheerfully together we can tidy up the place*
> *So hum a merry tune <hum>*
> *It won't take long when there's a song to help you set the pace*
> *And as you sweep the room*
> *Imagine that the broom is someone that you love*
> *And soon you'll find you're dancing to the tune. . . .*
> *When hearts are high the time will fly*
> *So whistle while you work*

Again, here you relate not to the work but to the music, to love, and "when hearts are high, time will fly." Focus on your big U, and your work gets easier.

Least action in Taoism

In the *Tao Te Ching* least action may be symbolized by the attitude, "It furthers one to do nothing." The Taoists didn't really mean that you should not do *anything*, but that you should follow your most sentient awareness, your dreaming. According to the Arthur Waley translation of the *Tao Te Ching*, "The Sage arrives without going, sees all without looking, does nothing, yet achieves everything" (Chapter 47).

But *how*? In Chapter 5 of the *Tao Te Ching* (Stephen Mitchell translation) it is stated:

> *The Tao doesn't take sides;*
> *it gives birth to both good and evil.*
> *The master doesn't take sides;*
> *[she] welcomes both saints and sinners.*

From the view of the zigzagging mind—from the big U or larger picture it creates—what appears as a problem to the everyday mind is just another path, even a necessary path, even if this path seems weird at first. A path is just a path. Follow process, follow your teacher, the big U, the dreammaker, and then what is happening will no longer be good or bad; instead, your commitment to your inner experience, your tune, will be the point.

▷ Things to Consider

- Least action underlies quantum physics, relativity, Taoism, aikido, and psychology as well.

- Whistle while you work.

CHAPTER 12

Journey Principles

The Sage arrives without going,
sees all without looking,
does nothing,
yet achieves everything.
—Lao Tse[1]

In the previous chapter I quoted these words from the *Tao Te Ching* to stress the concept of least action; namely, that the sage does nothing and achieves everything. The psychological analogy of the least-action principle, the big U, is a metaphor for the physicist's pilot wave. Various spiritual traditions and religions have different names for this encompassing quality. I am thinking of the many names for *God, the sage, Allah, Yahweh, Christ, the Buddha mind, emptiness, dreammaker.* These names all speak about a kind of intelligence or force that moves us, without our even trying. However, in this chapter I want to discuss the journey nature of "arriving" and "going." Least action is not only about "not-doing" or "not achieving"; it is also about the nature of the overall journey and the way it organizes our moment-to-moment paths. The big U can be experienced as an earth-based force or an intelligence trying to manifest through each life event and perhaps also through our entire existence.

I indicated in the last chapter that least action is connected to a kind of "knowingness," a sentient awareness that is very different from a causal explanation of life. Least action is a "journey principle" because it describes a natural pattern that organizes events as we move through distance and time. Journey principles are less dependent upon the circumstances of any given moment than they are on the action of the entire path. They are teleological, and imply that what is happening must fulfill some principle, some goal. Each event at any given moment in your life is an example of, and organized by, a larger principle, the principle of least action linked to the whole of your life. This principle manifests as the big U, and is different for each individual.

Feynman showed that the least-action principle is true for each point and for the whole journey as well.[2] If the curved line in Figure 12.1 represents your lifetime, then any given point on this path represents a given moment or day. Most frequently, you might think that what is happening today is caused by a given incident in childhood. "Aha, I am feeling bad today because of what happened yesterday, or because my parents did not like me" or because I am physically ill. We all know how important history is and how it seems to determine a great deal of what happens. Causal explanations fit the little u especially well—those parts of us that identify with today's consensus reality, which in turn is based upon a perceived material existence and linear structure of time and space.

The journey principle is different. It says that whatever happens at this moment is not simply determined by the past. The present moment is part of a larger journey showing your myth with the least action relative to the given circumstances. Since least action holds not only for each moment but also for the whole journey, momentary processes are determined in part by a mythic and cosmic totality toward which life is striving. In other words, what you have done until now, and what you will do, must all add up to your mythic direction: the least action, the easiest way, for you to move through life. From the least-action viewpoint, there is no cause of why things happen; events are purposeful in the sense of adding up in the final calculation to your overarching principle, your personal myth. Every moment something catches your attention, each dream, as well as the great decisions of your life, was arranged in part by this principle.

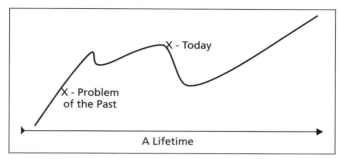

FIGURE 12.1 **A lifetime journey.** *Causal principles* state that what is happening is due to the past. *Journey principles* state that your entire life seeks to realize least action through history.

Perhaps this sounds too all-encompassing to the little u in us. Feynman, too, was in conflict over least action's break with causality. In speaking about photons, he said that light particles "know" how to follow the path of least action—even if we rebel at the thought. "All your instincts on cause and effect go haywire when you say that the particle decides to take the path that is going to give the minimum action," Feynman writes. "Does it 'smell' the neighboring paths to find out whether or not they have more action? . . . *It isn't that a particle takes the path of least action but that it smells all the paths in the neighborhood and chooses the one that has the least action.*"[3] (Italics mine.)

Instead of dropping causality, Feynman and others have shown us that causality—that is, Newtonian mechanics—can be derived from the principle of least action applied to quantum phenomena. In other words, causality is not just correct and useful for explaining everyday events in terms of time and space. The causality of classical mechanics can be seen as part of least action. Causal thinking by itself can be limiting, even depressing. It may explain some things, but it does not always explain our feelings, intuitions, and dreams. We need the principle of least action to explain why it is that at a given moment, we notice this and that, dream one thing and then another. Something in us is constantly seeking a greater, overarching (big U) perspective.

Something is helping us see that all the events of our lives—including the causal ones—are part of a larger story or myth trying to unfold.

Jung called this greater story, your personal myth. He wondered how synchronicities, meaningful connections between outer events and inner experiences, fit into this myth. Now from the big U perspective we find a possible suggestion. Peak experiences, amazing occurrences, synchronicities occur to us in part to show us the way, the path our myth is trying to take in the moment, the path of least action.

Peak experiences

Just as the quantum wave or pilot wave is the governing path for particles, the big U path is the least-action path for people and communities. When we have lost our passion, excitement and ease about life, or when we need to find our path, it can often manifest in what we feel is a peak experience. Just as the pilot wave is a complex number, a mixture of real and imaginary numbers, the big U and its appearance in peak experiences seem partly real and partly dreamlike. Whereas our little u is mainly identified with space and time (and forgets that it, too, is a parallel dream world!), the big U experience, our personal myth, is a mixture of the real and the imaginary.

To verify this idea, just remember back in your lifetime to a moment when you had a peak experience. You can define this type of experience in any way you like. Perhaps you just felt loved by someone or some people, or you had a grand realization. Some people may have had something like a god experience; others speak of realizing the interconnectedness of all things.

Peak experiences are usually moments when a central part of your personal myth breaks through into everyday reality with an exclamation—! It is a moment of remembering who you really are and what your life is about. Such experiences may remind you that you are actually on an immense journey. You are not just living for today and tomorrow. If you can, recall one such experience now; if you have had several, focus on one. Make a note about this powerful time right now. What happened? Where were you? What did you discover or realize?

How was that peak experience needed to remind you of the larger path you are on? When you have pondered that experience, perhaps you can ask yourself how that experience and path may be linked to your big U, and may have been organizing large sections of your life.

Individuation, self-actualization

Recalling this peak experience or its connection to your personal myth may give you a sense of how it operates as if it were a kind of intelligence in the background of all that you are doing. The myth is a journey principle trying to realize itself, so to speak. In a way, it uses your everyday self—everything and everyone around you—to realize itself. It probably organizes your history of relationships, what you have learned and studied, who or what were your teachers, and even where you are living. If you know your myth and are close to your big U, you feel congruent with life. If you are not close to your myth, you can feel lost and dissociated. We will look into the mystery of peak experiences again in a later chapter; here I merely hoped to give you a sense of the power of your process, how life feels easiest and most motivated when you are close to that myth.

Forerunners of the big U, or concepts related to it, can be found in most modern psychologies; think about Maslow's theories of self-actualization. He said we must fulfill basic needs such as hunger and thirst, then find security, and eventually become who we have always been. He said a musician must make music, an artist must paint, and so on, in order to be ultimately at peace. He sensed that there are causal aspects of life that must be fulfilled, and a kind of big U aspect. If he were alive today, I would say to him that the big U actually helps organize the more basic needs.

The big U also makes me think about Jung's individuation process: By trying to reconcile opposite tendencies within ourselves, by bringing together our ordinary self with the deepest realms of dreaming, Jung said a sense of wholeness would reveal itself as something unique to each individual. If Jung were alive just now he would be pleased, I imagine, to understand more about the geometry of individuation, the process of realizing the big U as a vector, and how it is related to least action and the rest of physics.

Purpose and teleology in physics and religion

One of the greatest physicists of the last century, Max Planck, said that there may be a larger purpose to life. After he won the Nobel prize for the discovery of energy quanta, he pondered least action and concluded that it had "an explicitly teleological character."[4] Other physicists hotly debate the teleological or purposeful implications of the least-action principle. The notion of purposefulness reminds some of the old conflict between science and religion, the battle waged since at least the fourteenth century in Western Europe and whole world. The conflict between animism and objective science during Leibniz's time seems to have transformed today. Today, the tension felt by many scientists between spiritual beliefs and the natural sciences, subjective experience and rational thinking is giving rise to new movements connecting the hard sciences with experiences and beliefs about consciousness. Every physicist such as Feynman who anthropomorphizes, that is, treats apparently nonhuman things as human, is unwittingly taking part in these new movements bringing science, psychology, and spiritual traditions together.

Fermat's principle and light

Feynman pointed out that nature is driven by a future state. As we saw in the earlier quote from him on page 125, he felt that nature sniffs all paths and chooses the ones that will finally add up to least action. He undoubtedly realized that he himself, like most of us, sniffs various paths before choosing one. Before making a decision about a future project, before we decide to actually do it or how to do it, we go through the various possibilities in our mind. We think, "Oh, I could do it this way or that way." In our minds, we take each way, each path, exploring and sniffing the one that feels best, which has least action.

Feynman explained Fermat's principle in terms of sniffing. Fermat said that a ray of light traveling between two points takes the path of least time.[5] This principle is a specific example of least action that, for light, becomes the principle of least time. Feynman said Fermat's ideas gave us an intuitive sense of least action. In his *QED*, Feynman imagined a lifeguard on a beach (Figure 12.2). He said that the lifeguard was like a light beam.

When someone screams for help in the water, the lifeguard (or light photon) quickly imagines or explores various paths to take in order to rescue the person. This is an emergency! Which path takes least time? Feynman explained that light went through different media much as our imaginary lifeguard must go through sand and water. The final path chosen was the path of least time.

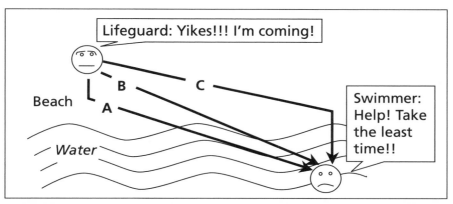

FIGURE 12.2 **Fermat's principle.** To save the person the lifeguard takes C, the path of least time, least action.

Let's go through this in detail. Say John is drowning, and you are the lifeguard on the beach. John needs help, right now. Which path would you take to get to him as quickly as possible? You could take the path of line A (Figure 12.2)—that is, run directly to the water, then swim a straight line from that point to the victim. Yet this path takes a lot of time because once in the water, you have to swim a long way, and you move more slowly (and may exert more energy) in water than on land.

Perhaps you should not run straight to the water, but rather take the straight line from the lifeguard tower to the victim—line B. That seems to make sense at first, for this path is the shortest distance. A sensible choice—until you imagine experiencing that path; then you realize you'll still have to swim quite a ways, and that takes time.

It turns out that running along the shore, parallel to the water, and then straight out to John—path C—is the best. Why? It is fastest! You can run quickly on the beach, and as a result of the short distance in the water, you will get to John in least time. Path C uses least time and least action, so preserving John's and your "force of life."

Feynman intimates that photons or particles of light are like people. The principle of least action makes them seek the fastest and best way to do things. Light particles sniff out various paths and choose the route with least action. How do they know and sniff? How do we know how to dream and find our way? Even before Feynman, Planck, pointing to psychology, observed that "the photons which constitute a ray of light behave like intelligent human beings: Out of all the possible curves they always select the one which will take them most quickly to their goal."[6]

We shall never be able to prove, as far as I can imagine, that photons actually think. We would have to prove that the universe itself thinks. That is why I suggest that some primal form of sentient awareness belongs to everything in the universe. Our sentient awareness, the viewpoint of the big U, often seems to take over in emergencies to carry us through things in the best possible manner, the easiest, perhaps the one that has most meaning for us. The big U is a kind of bodyguard. While the little u usually trusts only known or causally explainable paths and exhausts itself trying to *do* things, the big U uses less effort and not-doing. To get a sense of the subtle intelligence of the big U and its journey principles, let's focus on somatic experience.

The sleepwalking exercise

The following inner work is based on following subtle inner signals. You may have already noticed that following the outer visible signals of people is the easiest way to understand and get along with others. Now I encourage you to follow your *own* subtle signals. These appear most

readily when you are in a reduced or altered state of consciousness—
when you sleep or sleepwalk.

Sensing

1. To begin with, ask yourself if you can let go into dreaming. Ask yourself if you have used your everyday mind enough. If the answer is no, first try respecting that everyday mind more. Is there something you first need to do or to plan?

2. Once you have gained permission to enter through the gate into dreaming and dreamtime, you need to become used to your sentient awareness to lucidly follow subtle sensations and flirts as they try to catch your attention, showing you where to move and where to focus your attention. Experiment with trusting your sniffing ability in exploring the various earth-based paths and directions around you. Relax and follow your awareness. To begin with, write down your goals. What would you like to gain? Do you want to know something about your self or about your work or relationships? Note these down.

3. What are you trying to do these days and how do you usually do it? Make a hand gesture and sound demonstrating your "doing," and note this gesture and its meaning on paper. You will need to come back to this sketch later on.

Walking

4. Now look around the room you are in and feel and then mark a spot (on paper or on the floor) where that "doing" of every day life is located. Explore least action and its zigzagging wisdom: Relax and ask your mind if it will allow you to experience dreaming while awake. When you get this permission, try "dreaming"—that is, try using the altered state of "sleeping" that reminds you of dreaming. Become lucid and notice what is trying to happen around you.

   In particular, imagine and experience your body asleep while awake and sleepwalking. Actually stand (or if you have trouble standing, move your arms and upper body in a sitting position) and use your lucid movement awareness while dream-walking. Wait for something to catch your attention or to tell you in which earth-based direction to move. Something in the space around you may flirt with your attention. When something catches your attention, catch it! Move sentiently toward it or toward that direction. Slowly sniff out the path and the thing that caught your attention. Explore each thing, and then wait until something else catches your attention and move there.

5. Let your inner quantum compass turn you. Use awareness and let the earth move you as you explore various directions and objects. Move along one direction until you know what it means or until the object that caught your attention has explained itself to you. Then relax again and continue to explore the directions around you until your awareness tells you that you found the right thing and direction. Take your time and remember to continue moving in a zigzag fashion until you find the right place and direction.

Pondering

6. When you are done, discover the meaning of your final direction and experience or object. Where did you end up and what meaning does this place have for you? Does the meaning of this spot help you with the question you posed at the beginning of this earth-based meditation?

The final path is probably one of your big U paths. Can you sense how it and all the other paths were organized by the same least-action drive? From the viewpoint of the final path, what is the significance, if any, of the various locations you visited while you were dreaming while awake?

The mystery of the bathroom

One of my clients who did this exercise (Figure 12.3) wanted to know what to do with his life. He was a student and hoped to discover what to do after his studies. At first, he began literally sniffing the various books in my practice. He liked one or two, but then said that they were not what he was looking for. He meditated for a moment and then turned, saying that the window caught his attention. And so he sniffed out that direction. He went to the window and looked out. He said he was looking for something, and he thought it might be

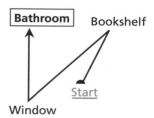

FIGURE 12.3 **Dreamer's zigzag path in my office, organized by least action**

outdoors, but it wasn't. So he backed up, turned, and said his body wanted him to go to the door in my office. I suggested that he follow his dreaming body, even though I had originally told him to stay in my office. Out he went into the corridor and into the bathroom and closed the door!

I walked after him and waited outside the bathroom. I suggested from the outside that he should maintain his sentient awareness with whatever happened in there. A minute later he came out again, and he was smiling from ear to ear. He said that he had found the path! The thing he was looking for was something he had forgotten about: his own body. He almost cried as he spoke.

To make the story short, he reminded me that he had wanted to know how to move forward in his life. I recalled the energy sketch he had made of his everyday life: a repetitive / / / / / . His ordinary way of doing things was to do things step by step, with severe regularity.

My client's final direction into the bathroom told him that the answer to his question was to follow the subtle impulses of his own body. He was shocked and thrilled with his dream-walking. He struggled with himself for a moment, and then said that he wanted to change the direction of his educational program and study physiology. Today, looking backward in time, I notice that this client did not immediately change his program of study, but waited till his studies were completed, and then began a professional sports career. That is how his dream-walking experience of following his body emerged in everyday life.

The mystery of path awareness

At any given moment there are always many path options available to you. These paths are determined in part by the times, by where you are, and of course, by who you are. Your dreaming process sniffs all paths and follows the big U, the least-action path. Looking back you may even notice that all along you were following the quickest and relatively easiest way to realize your full being. From today's viewpoint, perhaps a journey principle, your myth or least action has been guiding you.

▷ **Things to Consider**

- Causality says that present events are due to past ones.

- Least action is a journey principle. Present events are part of an overarching story line trying to manifest.

- Lifeguards work best when they sniff all paths and choose the one with least action.

- Remember the quote from the *Tao Te Ching* mentioned in the beginning of this chapter: "The Sage arrives without going . . . "

Part II

The Universe's View of Body Symptoms

CHAPTER 13

The Essence of Body Symptoms

If I have even just a little sense,
I will walk on the main road and
my only fear will be of straying from it.
Keeping to the main road is easy,
but people love to be sidetracked.
—Lao Tse[1]

According to the above quote, the big U is the one that makes most sense; it is the main road. But then, people love to be sidetracked. In other words, when you are in an ordinary state of mind, you identify with or choose a sidetrack vector! This split within us is consistent with the origin of everything, and the reason why therapists will always have work to do. With path awareness we live on track as we basically are, but then, we stray, we get sidetracked. That's when symptoms, relationship problems, and world difficulties arise. And that is why I have devoted Part II of this book to finding our track in the midst of—and with the help of—body problems. Parts III and IV will explore using path awareness in the midst of relationship issues and world problems.

The meaning of dis-ease

If keeping to the main road is easy, then disease—*dis-ease*—refers to the lack of ease, even to "dissing" or denying this ease. Dis-ease is the

137

opposite, in a way, of least action. The experience of disease, the experience of symptoms as "not me," is typical for the everyday little u. Everyone tends to deny the existence of their big U at one point or another, regardless of how developed they consider themselves. In this sense, identifying as an everyday person only, and simply doing whatever it is that you need to do and think ought to be carried out during the day is necessary. Without identifying with the little u, there is no relativity, no other framework with which the big U can get to know itself. Dis-ease is a way of getting to know *ease*.

The everyday little u usually follows the clock and rarely uses sentient awareness. Without awareness of other *parts* of yourself, you begin to experience life as filled with *parts* that appear as symptoms and people or events that seem angry. You fear that these ("dissed") parts will attack you or at least get in your way. Death itself may seem to be lurking behind every tree as you move far from your path. However, the point of all these perceived threats, symptoms, and events may not be to kill you but only threaten—shake up, loosen up—your little u. The threat of death mainly serves to loosen the primary identity's hold on life. If you relax this identity and center on the big U, you feel better. This and the next two chapters should give you hints about how to transform symptoms into meaningful paths.

Dreambody

Transforming medicine into a rainbow medicine is the goal of my book *Quantum Mind and Healing*, which deals with real body problems and their connection to relationship and social issues as well as the body's dreamlike behavior. Now I want to extend the material in that prior book with new principles and methods of path awareness.

The idea that your dreams can be seen at the surface of the real body was a breakthrough idea for me that I formulated in my first book, *Dreambody*. Today, much of process-oriented psychology is based, in part, upon reading dreams from body signals. Dreams and other subtle impulses and information move the body; they in-form, or change, our physics and physiology. Thus, our little u may intend one form of behavior, but the dreaming process in the background can move us in another behavior. This conflict in behaviors is the origin of second or double signals. Ongoing double signals are a sign that we are "dissing" the big U and its various parallel worlds.

Just as we can imagine pilot waves "in-forming" material objects, so we can feel how dreams "in-form" the body. That is why it is so important to work with the subjective, imaginary, and dreamlike experiences of the body. We can pick up early feelings, signals, and flirts and use them constructively in everyday life. Our whole self, the big U and its somatic experience in the form of the dreambody, is the real body with which we identify in time and space and also the dreamlike behavior of signals and dreamland experiences we often marginalize.

Neglected and persistent double signals and flirts cause us to become tense, and un-easy. When disease bothers us, the first approach of most people today is to assume that they are suffering from real bugs, bacteria, or other pathogens. Medicine is obviously very important and can be a matter of life and death. However, many, perhaps most, symptoms escape understanding and causal explanations. As a result, today's allopathic approaches in medicine may not always be sufficient to resolve dis-ease–creating processes.

The doctor is always in

One of the central messages of the first chapters of this book is that if you follow your awareness, your process becomes your greatest teacher. Translated into biophysical terms, this derived principle suggests that if you follow your sentient awareness, your healer is always in. The one who heals splits and creates health and wholeness is sentient awareness.

Experiment with the idea that the healer is *always in*. Sit quietly and don't move much for a moment. Just follow your breathing. Then notice what motions your body tends to make, and where it wants to move. Don't move there for the moment; just notice the direction and the associated experiences, feelings, and fantasies. Now move slowly and with awareness. Follow those movements and the direction your body is trying to take. What is the meaning of the direction your body is trying to take? What is the effect on your overall body feeling if you move in that direction?

Perhaps you noticed that your healer is always in. The doctor's office is open for you 24/7. You are never alone—your own personal healer is right there, and you don't even have to knock on the door and make an appointment—or pay a fee. It is the most amazing and inexpensive medicine in the world. Sentient awareness is least action. If you neglect your awareness and self-reflection, you must begin speaking in terms of dis-ease or symptoms.

Caduceus healing

Your dreaming shows itself in your body at one moment or another in terms of flirts, double signals, fantasies, aches, pains, and their directions or parallel worlds. In a way, in any given body area—especially where there are symptoms—each flirt or fantasy is a fragment from a story or dream. The dreambody as a whole is the superposition, or sum, of all those parallel worlds. Whereas your real body can be seen on a photograph, your dreambody can be guessed from double signals or felt and seen in dreams. Beneath these dreams are sensations and experiences of things that cannot easily be said in words. I describe this area as the essence area, the pilot wave, the big U. In the dreaming body is the pilot wave, quantum theory, least action, and the knowingness or intelligence of a quantum mind, the big U. The multiplicity of terms for this essence region occurs because of the impossibility of explaining and verbalizing experience that is otherwise ineffable and can only be felt. If you know the big U, your body feels together, and you know how to go about healing your internal rifts. One day soon I am sure this healing sense will be measurable. In any case, access to the big U accords healing power.

An important symbol of healing is the caduceus, the staff often associated with Aesculapius, the ancient Roman and Greek god of healing (Figure 13.1). Often identified in mythology as Hermes' staff, the caduceus is a staff around which one or two brown nonvenomous snakes are entwined. Often at the top there is a pair of wings.

I am caught by the similarity between those two snakes and self-reflecting waves. That healing staff reminds me of a quantum wave or pilot wave reflecting itself. Among other things, the caduceus symbolizes the experience of healing, of self-reflection, of knowing your deepest self, of the big U reflecting on itself and making itself conscious in everyday reality. This corresponds to the subtle and ineffable experience of the big U. You feel well regardless of the mess you are in.

FIGURE 13.1
The caduceus, the healing staff

There are many approaches to experiencing this theory in practice. In what follows, we will explore the parallel worlds of a body or symptom area in terms of vectors. Then, beginning with the most difficult parallel world, we will seek the big U with one essence method or another.[2] (Readers interested in the mathematics of how essence methods work and are related to the big U can read Appendix 10, "The U and Essence Experiences.")

Shamanistic approach to parallel worlds and symptoms

The essence method is best understood with body experience. When you are ready, ask your everyday mind to relax and take it easy. Let's shift from thinking about things to exploring the body experience of one of your symptoms. (Be gentle with yourself, with any frailty or body limitations.)

1. When you are ready, *describe your most troublesome or worst body symptom* and the area of the body involved. What was this body area like before there were any symptoms there? In other words, what in your own experience, is the basic nature of that area?

   (For example, in one of our seminars we worked with a woman who had a spastic bladder. Linda pointed below her lower stomach area and described that area as "very unknown." She said that the spastic bladder felt like a "very restricted area." Before that symptom, the bladder area was simply "unknown and carefree"!)

2. Using your sentient awareness of little things, and as lucidly as possible, *slowly move your hand toward that troubled area* (or the whole body, as the case may be. If your whole body does not feel well, place one of your hands at a distance from your body and imagine that hand as able to sense your whole body). As you move your hand slowly and with awareness, describe the first two flickering sensations or experiences that flirt or catch your attention in connection with that area. As you move your hand slowly toward the troubled body area, stop when you become aware of some small experience trying to reach your awareness, even if it's irrational. After you notice this experience, make a note about the feeling-image or story. Then move your hand closer to the body area, again noticing if one or more parallel worlds appear, and describe them briefly as well.

   (As Linda moved her hand toward her spastic bladder area, she said, "Oh! That is weird. I felt a piece of iron or a barrier in there!" We made a note about that and encouraged her to continue moving her hand slowly toward her bladder. Next she said, "Strangely enough, I experienced fresh air and wind blowing" as she moved her hand closer to her bladder.)

3. From the various parallel worlds of flirts that just popped up, *choose the weirdest or most troublesome or amazing parallel world*, whichever that is for you, and act it out. That is, using controlled abandon, become a shaman—and for a few minutes go as deeply as you feel comfortable into experiencing and shape-shifting into the images and story involved. Use your most sentient awareness, feel into the most troublesome part or figures in that story. Become it, act it out using movement, feeling, and images to create a story about it.   (Use care for your physical body while you do this.) Let nature teach you and guide you, as you explore this parallel-world experience until you know what it is expressing, until you know its secret.

   (In our seminar, Linda enjoyed "getting into" and playing the steel barrier. She stood ramrod straight and said as firmly as she could, "I am a cold and impenetrable world! I am imper-turbable"! She laughed, saying that normally she was so very flexible, warm, and outgoing that she enjoyed the contrasting "power of steel.")

4. Now ask yourself, *What is the essence of your experience of that weird parallel world?* What is the seed, that *almost nothing* out of which this experience arose? What was the essence or original impulse prior to the troublesome nature of this parallel world experience? To do this, you may have to act out the experience again; move it, feel it, and then, while feeling the same inten-sity, slow the movement down more and more, slower and slower, until you feel its initial seed or essence, the almost nothing before it became so big. Trust your imagination and experience; this can be very irrational. Be lucid and feel what that essence is. Once you have found that essence, name it.

   (Linda stood for some minutes acting like the steel barrier. Then she said that the root of this experience was to be very inhuman, in fact, to feel very remote, like the universe! The essence experience of that piece of steel was not so much coldness as *detachment* from the social world and connection instead to the universe. As she stood in front of us feeling this essence, it seemed as if time had stopped. Linda entered into a kind of meditation, almost a blissful state, and said after a few minutes, "This detachment is something I have been longing for.")

5. *Feel the essence carefully and become it in your body.* Let it move you and make sounds that go with it, if you can. Take time with being this essence and living in its world. Make a quick sketch of this experience and give it a name. How is this essence an important part of your overall psychology? How has this essence already been trying to grow in you? Now take your time feeling the essence again, and *let it tell its story through poetry, music, dance*—whichever is easiest for you and whichever naturally flows out of this experience.

(Linda sketched what she was experiencing as the essence of steel [Figure 13.2] and called it "infinity." She began to "dance" this picture, or rather

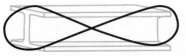

FIGURE 13.2 **Infinity, an essence experience of steel**

she let it move her. With her feet placed firmly on the floor, Linda swayed back and forth, explaining that this movement was her experience of freedom and infinity.)

6. Still feeling the essence in your whole body, *ask how this essence experience makes sense of, relates to, or helps your overall life situation.* How does this experience relate to the other parallel worlds that arose when you moved your hand closer to the symptom in the beginning of this exercise? How does the essence make sense out of that most difficult parallel world, its story, its figures? Are these figures in some way related to your personal or cultural history?

(Linda said simply that the big U, the essence of the steel, the swaying experience, felt like her experience of the other parallel world, the "wind." After her work, she said that she was surprised to find detachment "hiding" in her bladder! She also said that the big U tied together many worlds, and that now she now wanted to go back into Buddhism, which is where she first experienced the detachment that came out of her body symptom.)

Healing

Healing in the sense of medicine means reducing the pain or removing the cause of symptoms. That is an important definition, but it can marginalize other parts of us, including especially the big U. Reflecting upon the essence of one of the parallel worlds of a symptom can be healing in the sense of realigning you with your basic self, the U that ties your various experiences together.

Getting in touch with the deepest U may have immediate effects on the body or the way in which you use this troubled area. In the largest sense, the big U is the medicine; it is the essence or the Way. It is a kind of background map of the overall situation. It is the ease behind dis-ease. Perhaps this is what Lao-Tse meant in the quote at the beginning of this chapter:

> *If I have even just a little sense,*
> *I will walk on the main road and*
> *my only fear will be of straying from it.*

In the next chapter, we will consider why we stray.

▷ Things to Consider

- The caduceus is a staff entwined by two snakes.

- The caduceus symbolizes healing, the self-reflecting U or pilot wave.

- The U appears as the sum of vectors or the essence of the worst.

- Use that essence as a medicine.

CHAPTER 14

Parallel Worlds in Medicine

Keeping to the main road is easy,
but people love to be sidetracked.
—Lao Tse[1]

In the last chapter I used a quote from the *Tao Te Ching* to introduce the idea that we need to find our main road, the Way, the healing or essence of dis-ease, the big U. In repeating the second part of this quote here, I want to stress this idea, and also explore a second idea: namely, that people love being sidetracked. Why do we love being sidetracked? In a way, why do we make ourselves uneasy? To answer this I want to explore the geometry of symptoms.

Imagine if you can that instead of being a person, you were the entire universe. What would awareness mean for you then? How would you self-reflect? You would have to have some implicit form of duality for sentient awareness to arise. Something about yourself would have to catch your attention; something would have to bug you. To really catch your attention something would have to seem very wrong, or pester you. Sentient awareness arises and before you know it, the bug itches. Then you feel forced to scratch and reflect on that itch, like it or not. Suddenly, you are not just a quiet, harmonious, stationary universe but one that is evolving into bugs, itches, and hands to scratch with.

As I pointed out in Chapter 3 about path awareness, bugs are crucial to directional consciousness. That may be why we need to occasionally (or quite often) be sidetracked, to use Lao Tse's word. Bugs and itches lead to scratching and eventually to consciousness of who we really are or can be. In that moment, itching subsides. My guess is that most of us would only briefly think, "Who needs bugs?" before getting bored. And then the whole thing would start all over again. Consciousness is a process that requires bugs.

Sometimes the bug is only a dream, sometimes a symptom, a person, or a world event. At least during physical life, the point is that tickles are creative. Perhaps that is why the astrophysicist Stephen Hawking said that from the vacuum of zero-point energy field, the universe tickles itself into existence.[2]

The bug is immortal—thank "God"

Emptiness or harmony may not be the final goal, as it is in some spiritual traditions. In fact, because of the uncertainty principle, there is no absolute emptiness without a tickle. That idea fits what I know about people. Emptiness is a momentary state, but bugs are always there. The individual, the group, will always have to be bugged by someone or something. Your relationships will constantly turn up with new stuff to think about, perhaps because these relationships seek to know themselves, because the big U is trying to reach awareness. Detachment and enlightenment are, in principle, *momentary* states of knowing your big U. In principle, they cannot last long.

Symptoms disappear, but something else pops up again. Healing is a momentary thing. We are each a curious cosmos trying to know ourselves. A true facilitator—that is, someone who loves following nature—follows her own body, relationship, and group and world bugs. They bug her, and then she shape-shifts into their essence or the big U, and the bugs become her teachers. The bug seems to be immortal. So having symptoms is not due only to outer causes or an inner lack of awareness. They occur because you are a universe in the process of consciousness. In other words, sidetracking happens; we need and love sidetracks. In a way, something deep within us wants to be bugged and sidetracked in order to know itself.

Animating symptoms

In the last chapter, I suggested that symptoms are related to troublesome parallel worlds, and that the essence of these worlds may lead to wellness experiences, sometimes to momentary healing. Now I want to explore sidetracks and approach that big U by animating parallel worlds and adding them. That means I am going to ask you to imagine each of these worlds, including the world of the most fabulous imaginable healing medicine—even if you have not yet found it in reality. I am going to ask you to draw that medicine and to animate it, to give it the *vis viva*, the living force.

The animistic and artistic power of myth and modern medicine

Are you ready?

1. *What is your everyday self like?* Write down the answer to this question, and call it #1. (For example, just now my everyday life is very busy.) What is your most unusual self like? Note this in writing, too, and call it #2. (In my case, I typically have a lot of energy—which makes my present tiredness a little unusual.)

2. *Name a symptom that you'd like to explore*, whether one you feel now or a symptom in your past. Unless you absolutely want to focus on the same symptom, select a different symptom than you chose for an earlier exercise. (For example, in my own case, finding a symptom is easy: A few hours ago I drank some bottled water, and now I feel sick. A touch of stomach poisoning? I looked at the date on the bottle, and it should have been thrown out seven months ago. I wish I had looked at that date before I drank that water.)

3. *Feel or remember feeling the symptom at its worst*—or imagined worst—and describe the symptom's most disturbing energy or

imagined disturbing energy. Make a note, and call this #3. (In my case, the most disturbing energy is the rumbling feeling of a coming explosion of diarrhea or food poisoning. There are already some windy explosions down there!)

4. *Move your hands in a way to express the symptom's energy*, and then imagine a puppet that could represent this symptom energy (your #3). Feel the symptom, and let the energy make a line drawing. (In my case, it was easy to sketch what my digestive system feels like [Figure 14.1].)

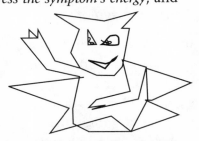

FIGURE 14.1 **Diarrhea demon!**

5. *What real or imagined medication (or method) helps to relieve that symptom?* If you are not taking any, what might help the most? Describe it. For example, you might imagine breathing, yoga, anti-anxiety meds, muscle relaxant, cooling medicine, homeo-pathic pills, energy pills, etc. Note this down, and call it medi-cine #4. Feel its nature and move your hands in a way to express the medicine's energy. Then imagine a puppet or picture that could represent this medication. (The simple remedy for my symptom is simple: a huge rush of cool, soothing water. My picture? A tsunami—with a head—that flushes the diarrhea demon out of my system [Figure 14.2].)

FIGURE 14.2 A tsunami flushes everything out.

6. *Now create and let your puppets dialogue[3] with one another* about your symptom (your #3) and the medicine (your #4). (Figure 14.3) With crayons and paper plates, create puppets by feeling their energies and letting those energies create the puppets.

If you don't actually make puppets, at least sketch them on paper. Hold up one paper plate and, using it like a puppet, express its energy. Then do the same with the other paper plate. Let these two plates dialogue with one another for a few minutes. They do not need to resolve things, just get to know one another.

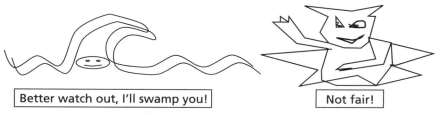

Better watch out, I'll swamp you!   Not fair!

FIGURE 14.3 **The tsunami and the demon**

(In my case, the tsunami "medicine" said "Watch out! Your time is almost up. I am going to swamp you!" In self-defense, my diarrhea demon said, "Not fair. All I want is total freedom to break out!" The tsunami began to think, "Hmmm, we really have a lot in common— flow and freedom . . .")

7. *Now with a sense of these energies, add movement to this experience.* Put your picture or puppets aside, and use your earth-sensing quantum compass to find the directions of your four parallel worlds—your usual, unusual, symptom, and medicine selves. Recall the experiences of #1 through #4, and find a starting point *.

   Once there, feel #1, your everyday self—feel it in your body, turn and find the direction it is pulled toward or headed toward, and walk a few steps in that direction.

   From that point, feel #2, your most unusual self in your body. Let it turn you, find its direction, and walk a few steps there. Do the same with #3, your symptom energy; and #4, the medication or healing method. Mark your ending point **. (If you cannot walk easily, you can perform this step this by moving your upper body slightly in various directions, then tracing the paths on paper.)

8. *Find the superposition of all your paths—find your big U.* Go back to the beginning point * and from there directly to the end point **, in a straight line. Walk slowly and feel the meaning of this big U (in Figure 14.4,

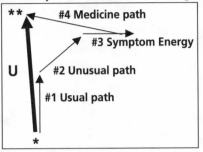

FIGURE 14.4 **Paths and parallel worlds of my diarrhea**

the dark, thick line) and its direction. Trust your experience and intuitions, the slight flickers that occur as you walk, even if they seem irrational. Walk it again and use your awareness and your wonder to explore the rhythm of this U. Let it move you. Now walk that path again and hum or sing its rhythm. Let the path of your big U move you in a sort of dance, and let a story arise about it. While singing, feeling, and moving this big U, feel its mythic pilot power—even make a quick puppet-like sketch of it.

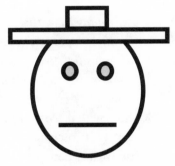

FIGURE 14.5 **Ommm, the Big U**

(Figure 14.5 illustrates my big U sketch.)

9. *Explore how all four paths may be important*, especially from the viewpoint of the big U. How does your big U include your everyday self, your most unusual self, your symptom energy, and the medication? (After all, your final figure is a product of superposing various vectors and feelings and, in principle, includes all of them.) In particular, how is the symptom necessary? Explore if and how the big U's viewpoint includes, understands, and appreciates the symptom energy and its medicine. Explore how this big U wants to influence your everyday life, your friendships, your work, and other aspects of your experience. (My own big U vector, Figure 14.4, is headed

toward midnight at the top of the world, the North Pole. The sketch of my big U experience, Figure 14.5, includes a sense of that pole, a kind of meditative figure with an overview of life. The figure is humming *Ommmm* to itself. I noticed that this big U figure includes the sharp-eye quality of the symptom, the diarrhea demon—which appears in the linear mouth and hat —and also the roundness or fluidity of the tsunami, my so-called "medicine.")

10. *Feel your big U in the symptom area, if possible.* That big U energy may be healing in the allopathic sense. (Mine was. I made one quick trip to the bathroom, and that was that.) Perhaps your symptom is reminding you of an energy with which you are often at odds, but really need to utilize with more awareness. That backlight energy, that sidetrack (to use the words of Lao Tse from the beginning of this chapter) is possibly not only in your body, but also projected or found in the people you like the least. It is a nonlocal energy, shared by all. The essence of one part of you is, in principle, the essence of everything because of nonlocality.

11. *Finally, take your medicine!* If it is a real medicine that you are taking, then paint the figures on the medicine package or bottles. (Do the same with all your health supplements.) On one side put the medicine spirit, and on the other side paint the demon that the supplement is working against. On the bottle cap paint your big U. (See Figure 14.6.) Taking your medicine is now a meditation and a great way to remember yourself, all your various directions! And if you are part of a pharmaceutical company, take note. Leave space for people to sketch their figures!

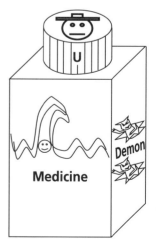

FIGURE 14.6 **The New Medicine container.**

Symptoms may be the fastest way to consciousness. That means least effort, though not necessarily least itchy.

▷ **Things to Consider**

- In a way, something in us loves or somehow needs sidetracks.

- The body problems bugging you can be the origins of your medicine.

- Paint all vitamin and medicine bottles.

CHAPTER 15

Stress Fields, Math, and Myth

It is best to erase all personal history, because that would make
us free from the encumbering thoughts of other people.

—don Juan[1]

Body problems are connected to what the medical world calls stress, the therapist calls complexes, and the physicist defines as fields. In Chapter 9, I discussed the various ways in which electrons in quantum electro-dynamics (QED) move through fields. These various methods may avoid the experience of annihilation and the creation cycle typical of both psychological and physical fields. The shaman, I said, had a choice. She can remain in her fixed identity and be annihilated (so to speak) by her antimatter opposite, or she can detach from her normal identity and time, use sentient awareness, and move free of time through, and out of, stress fields.

In the last chapter we saw that vector work creates another possibility. When faced with symptoms, you can relax your ordinary identity, use your path awareness, and find your big U to deal with troublesome energies. Whether you follow your sentient awareness and step out of time by following the essence of a troublesome energy, or use path awareness and vectors to find the big U, the world of body problems and stress becomes

155

the world of dreamlike opportunities. You can choose to move with the big U forward, backward, or out of time without insult or injury. Now I want to go further into the nature of fields and show how they are connected to what psychologists call *complexes*. By following her deepest directions, the shaman can accept, instead of condemn, problematic fields and flow with them. Studying complexes and their connections to fields will lead to altogether new as well as ancient methods of gaining freedom from stress.

Chemistry and complexes

Before the emergence of quantum theory, before Feynman's explanation of least action and quantum fields, psychologists called the most intense psychological fields *complexes*. They may have taken the word *complex* from the Latin word *complecti*, which means *to braid* or *to weave* (Figure 15.1). But it is more likely that the early psychologists of the last century followed the chemists of the eighteenth and nineteenth centuries who used the term *complex* to refer to bunches of ions that are weakly bonded together.

FIGURE 15.1
Complecti

An ion is an atom or group of atoms that acquires an electric charge by losing or gaining one or more electrons. Remember atoms? With the addition of more or fewer electrons, atoms become electrically charged and are attracted or repelled by other atoms. In this way salt (sodium chloride), for example, is formed from sodium and chlorine ions (Figure 15.2). Again, a complex in chemistry is a bunch of ions bonded together via electrical charges.

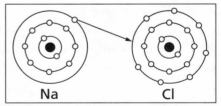

FIGURE 15.2 **Salt.** In an ionic bond, electrons are shared between atoms having too many or too few electrons.

Psychological complexes

At the end of the nineteenth century, Freud, Jung, Adler, and others developed the idea of the complex and used it as a metaphor in psychology.

Jung used *complex* to mean *exaggerated feelings* and *feeling-toned associa-tion*. He found he could measure complexes with a stopwatch (the pre-cursor to the lie detector test).[2] Words such as *mother* or *father* could be detected as delayed associations. Jung later explained that complexes were organized by archetypes, which appear in basic images or forms. Much like the chemist's complexes bound by electric fields, Jung's com-plex was a group of memories, feelings, and interpretations bound up with an archetype (a father complex, for example).

Complexes are field sensitivities

It seems likely that Jung and Freud, both of whom studied medicine, associated the word *complex* with chemistry, with electric charges or fields. In a way psychological *complexes* are sensitivities to polarizations, to electric-like fields. I think of fields as having both real and nonlocal natures, as physical and psychological. Just as there is an electrical field around chemical complexes or ionic groups, fields surround people as well. Fields are associated with structural patterns such as braiding, the image from which the complex is derived (Figure 15.1).

Many therapists deal with complexes as local field effects, assum-ing that they originated from powerful past events. The idea of a moth-er or father complex (Electra or Oedipus complex) refers mainly to per-sonal experiences. Such terms hide their mathematical, structural, physical, and universal nature. Working on complexes surely means understanding them, but something of their intensity and polarizing nature frequently seems to remain around the person.

In any case, both physical and psychological fields are both local and nonlocal. They are personal and located at a given spot, and at the same time have connections to distant locations. Instead of speaking of "having a complex," I prefer to speak in terms of being "sensitive to particle fields." This means noticing fields in oneself, in others, in the air. Fields are real; that is, they can be measured in terms of forces. But fields are also imaginary; that is, they can be dreamed as particles and powerful figures. Field sensitivities are problems from one viewpoint and gifts from a more compassionate (or big U) view. Some people seem to be born to be sensitive to specific fields. At one time we were all sensitive to the earth's field, which is a combination of gravitational, electromagnetic, and spiritual elements. We needed such sensitivities to avoid dangers and find food.

Jung's complexes

It's important to work on fields—that is, to take back projections—and also to learn to dance with fields. Jung himself was such a dancer. One of my Zurich analysts, Barbara Hannah, told me a story: When Jung was 78, he gave one of his last talks at a church in Basel about the psychology of religion. An interest of Jung's was explaining theology to church people, for his father was a minister. Jung had what he called a "negative father complex," so he was always working on his father (like all of us with fathers and mothers or absent parents).

Barbara Hannah went with Jung to Basel to learn from him and care for him, for he had had a heart attack a few years earlier. After the lecture, tired, on the steps of the Basel church, Jung explained the connection between God and the self to a minister who didn't agree with him—instead of caring for his own health and going home. The minister eventually left, and Hannah upbraided Jung then and there for jeopardizing his health in this way. "C. G., what *are* you doing?" she remonstrated. "After all these years, why are you spending so much time speaking to your father? You ought to know better."

Jung turned around on the stairs, Hannah told me. "I am only 78," he replied. "You don't work these things out. They become something more in time." Jung's father problem was not just a problem, but a field process.

Complexes, fields, and weather systems

Fields create polarizations and forces that affect physical objects—in fact, that can even devastate the body. Let's explore them.

What are the worst field situations that you avoid and which are you attracted to? What is the most difficult situation for you? What kind of situation or body stresses do you feel when you are in those fields? What exactly do you feel in your body? In a way, you may be something like an electron, pushed and pulled about by nature's electric or electro-magnetic fields.

What typically happens to you when you meet that situation? How do you behave? Some people feel overloaded; others get stressed, feel under intense pressure, get dizzy, or freeze. One client told me that when she felt unwanted, she wanted to die. Others say they get sick if they feel people don't like them.

In some places or around some people, fields are so strong that we can feel them move us about. We can sense fields as protective or repellent barriers. Fields are often associated with moods. Individuals, couples, and whole countries can be in pessimistic or optimistic moods or fields. Furthermore, fields and moods are often projected onto weather systems. Cloudy days are heavy fields and make many feel low. Sunny skies make most feel lighter. The oceanfront in Oregon and Northern California is often foggy; the Native Americans of these particular areas speak of gods emerging from these foggy fields. The Yuki people of the West Coast spoke of a creator called *solitude walker*—or in their Wintu language, *Taiko-Mol*.[3] He was a world creator, and his story shows how fields can create the world.

According to the story (there are various versions), in the beginning there was only water, and over it was a fog.[4] On the water was foam. Nothingness moved round and round and from it, in the water, came a voice. (Awareness was present at the beginning in a kind of vacuum.) Something came up quickly in the water, and it was called Taiko-Mol, pathwalker. He floated on the water and sang. In some versions of this story, he stood in the foam and dissolved the foam. Taiko-Mol was constantly talking to himself. He said, "Let's do it this way! . . . No, let's do it that way!" The pathwalker established the earth and its directions. That is how the world came about, out of a field of water and fog according to the Yukis.

Storm fields in China are still personified by dragons. The Chinese, Japanese, and Koreans all spoke of the weather as the Great Dragon, who is behind thunder and whose spirit lives in the rivers from which it arises. The Chinese emperors have been called Sons of the

Dragon or "dragon faced." Small wonder that we are afraid of thunder and stormy fields (Figure 15.3).[5] And small wonder we avoid people who look angry.

FIGURE 15.3 **Chinese dragon power:** stormy weather

Weather gods exist the world over.[6] Thunder is represented by one of the powerful Scandinavian gods, Thor. Like physical fields in QED, Thor is both the creator and the destroyer. Sometimes pictured with a crown, Thor has a special hammer

FIGURE 15.4
Thor's hammer

(Figure 15.4) that boomerangs when thrown, going forward and then backward in time. Ancient Hinduism talks about the "Maya field," a burning area surrounding the whole world. Spinning at the very center of the world field of fire is Nataraja, a dancing Shiva (Figure 15.5). Sometimes male, sometimes female, Nataraja spins blissfully, creating and destroying the universe.

FIGURE 15.5 **The dancing Shiva Nataraja, creator and destroyer**

This figure is associated with the sacred word *aum* or *om*, the central mantra of creation, the first manifestation of the Hindu divine ground of all being (Figure 15.6).[7]

Earlier in the book I pointed out that in any field there is creation, annihilation, and, with sentient awareness, the potential for liberation and freedom from time. That idea was modeled after Feynman's QED (quantum electrodynamics) theory, today the standard in quantum field theory. If we recall that the very idea of fields (or complexes and the moods they generate) comes

FIGURE 15.6 **Divine ground, OM (or AUM)**

from ionic or electric fields, we could say that Nataraja is an early configuration of Feynman's timeless electron moving backward and forward in time, free of ordinary reality. Long before QED, people knew that in every field there is the potential for annihilation—but also for freedom, by virtue of being at the center or essence of it all.

The field's U

This essence or U of the earth's field (of a person, world, or universe) is personified by Nataraja, or her/his symbol of OM. We can understand this idea best by imagining that if we are the victim of forces, we suffer. But if we are at the center of forces, and even feel that we need or create those forces, then we are no longer on the burning periphery being destroyed by Nataraja—no longer part of the periodic experiences of annihilation and creation. We are instead creating the world, we are the big U at the center, we dance the world into life.

Your big U is not only the center of oppositional vectors or the essence of difficult parts and fields; it is a creator of energies. At the end of the chapter you will have the chance to experience the prototypical shaman in yourself, who goes into the center of fields, finds her big U, and in a slightly altered state, uses it to carry you on creative stress-free journeys of path awareness beyond time.

Complexes and fields of stress are problems for our state-oriented thinking and little u. But for the big U, complexes can be timeless streams that carry us. Complexes for the shaman are earth powers that move her.

The lessons of Don Juan

What the physicist calls fields and particles in opposition, the psychologist may refer to as complexes and conflicting dream figures. Castaneda's shaman don Juan would have called these fields the *Nagual*, by which he meant the unknown, a totemic spirit, a master shaman who can move through the unknown.[8] Don Juan's use of *Nagual* is typical of essence and dreamlike terms whose exact meaning depends upon the way it is used in a particular context. When I think of fields, for instance, I imagine the Nagual in the sense that don Juan used the term: that is, it can be experienced, but not easily explained.

To follow fluid paths through the Nagual, don Juan said, you have to disrupt your personal routines. Our fixed identities and routines are like houses: They can be blown away by wind storms. You are a woman, born into this race, into that clan. You are a man with these health issues, with those beliefs. You have this religion, that education, culture, intelligence, gifts. These are all fixed identities. But with awareness you may have much more that helps you with otherwise difficult fields.

The shaman's U through the Nagual

How would you describe yourself today, and what direction does your ordinary self go in? Take a moment and feel your ordinary self, and let the earth tell you which direction that ordinary self is headed in. Make a note about it; you may need it later.

What is the greatest tension/force field pulling at you these days? Take a moment and try to choose one that comes up now and describe it as best you can. Then imagine this field as a weather system. Try to see that system with a human face; try to sketch it.

Explore feeling this weather-field system and imagine some image or being behind it. Sketch it. Feel, walk, and note its direction (Figure 15.7). While walking this direction, feel its rhythm and let the direction dance you in one way or another. What or who does the image behind this dance tend to annihilate and what sorts of things does it create? Make notes about its direction and dance.

FIGURE 15.7
**Field face +
direction**

Now let go of your personal history, of your momentary identity, whatever that may be. Explore being a shaman in the sense of letting yourself sense the deepest part of yourself and ask your body to find its direction. Where is this big U path headed? Walk there, and while walking, feel and let yourself dream and be dreamed along this path. Shift from being a dreamer to being the dreamed; let the U dream you, carry you, so to speak. Relax your personal routines, feel this deepest U's rhythm and the way it dances/moves/sings you. Let your momentary identity relax a few minutes and dance the U's dance. Stay lucid and notice your dreaming dance.

Finally, while still experiencing this U, explore the direction of your ordinary self and the most difficult field or complex. If possible, try to experience the possibility that you have dreamed up or created your ordinary self and the tense field and direction that were pushing you about. As the big U, explore the directions of the troublesome field and your ordinary self until you have some compassion and body understanding of their dances.

Then continue on dreaming, lucidly noticing what happens and what you are learning. Note what meaning, if any, that troublesome field had. How do you feel physically in the moment, and who are you?

Stress may not be due to complexes but to our fixed identities that are afraid of, upset with, or resist powerful force fields. The shaman's potential path is one of nature's timeless streams. Or more simply, as don Juan says in the quote at the beginning of this chapter, "It is best to erase all personal history." Then our journey, the big U, can operate with least action not just over the course of a lifetime, but moment to moment through the strangest stormy weather.

▷ Things to Consider

- The chemist's notion of complexes, of shared electrons and electric fields probably preceded the psychologist's notion of complexes and fields.

- Nataraja's dance creates the world field and is also free of it.

- With less personal history and more U, the demons of stress fields turn to rivers.

CHAPTER 16

The Second Training in Dizzy States

Spinning with your ally will change your idea of the world.
That idea is everything; and when that changes, the world itself changes.
—don Juan[1]

The big U appears in every moment as the background direction leading you to notice tiny flirts, and in your lifetime as the overall direction of the journey moving through problems, body symptoms, peak experiences, shamanistic trance states, and big dreams. In this chapter I explore how the big U appears in our relationship to the universe through dizzy states of consciousness. We'll work with altered states of consciousness, with spinning and circle dancing. Circular movements, like those found in the martial arts or dervish rituals, remove personal history long enough for you to feel a new kind of center that can create helpful insights into difficult situations. One of our greatest allies is spinning.

Mysticism reviewed

The pioneering American psychologist William James wrote that mystical experiences are *ineffable* and difficult to verbalize. Mystical experience is *transient*, he said, in that you can't hold onto it. It is *noetic*, in that you know things but can't quite say them. To these insights of James, I suggested earlier in the book two additional factors: that the big U is also *nonlocal* and *superpositional*, by which I mean that it is compassionate. It contains and embraces all our parts. The big U is a great earth-based teacher, an ally of shamans. Being compassionate, the big U is naturally encompassing and encircling. It is not surprising, then, that spinning and circle dancing have been used worldwide by many peoples to relate to nature, to the universe.

Spinning in mythology and spiritual traditions

In *Hidden Dance* Amy Mindell explained that in order to resolve their greatest problems, to align themselves with nature, to know when to hunt and plant—in general, to relate to the universe—earlier peoples ritualized circle dances.[2] These circular or spiral dances mirror the seasons and the universe, and by participating in them, our ancestors attempted to create a good relationship to fields, to the weather, to create better lives and community. Here are some of those ritualized circle dances.

- **Santo Daime.** We experienced the power of circle dancing as a means of healing individuals and communities in the Amazon with the native people living in the forests near Manaus. As practitioners of the Santo Daime religion, these Brazilian natives believed strongly in the spiritual benefits of their sacramental tea, Ayahuasca, which they incorporated with elements of shamanism, Christianity, and Yoruba practices.

    Practitioners dance all night in revolving circles with everyone in their community—the elderly, toddlers—everyone together in a collective community making a healing ceremony. I had experiences there that are still helpful to me today.

- **The dervish.** Perhaps the best known circle dancers are the mystical Islamic group, the Sufi dervishes, followers of Rumi (1207–1273). Neither Sunni nor Shia, they consider Sufism to be the essence of all religions. For them Islam and Allah are forms of the natural order. The Sufi practiced spinning to know God and the universe. They speak about Mount Meru as the centering backbone of the spinning universe. In their philosophy, the Indian Ocean itself circles around this mountain.[3] That symbol implies that the devotee becomes a mountain, allowing life (as the ocean) to flow around her or him.

My personal experience with the power of dervish rituals indicated to me that spinning interrupts your normal identity and opens you up to amazing experiences, to what I experienced as the universe itself. As you spin, your body finds a way to re-center, as if it were a mountain around which events move.

- **Dancing Shiva.** Remember Nataraja (from the previous chapter)? That dancing Shiva spun in the middle of the circle of fire, symbolizing freedom from the world of Maya. Shiva was quiet, almost blissful. These pictures and ideas also represent the possibility of stillness in movement, of centeredness in the midst of creation and annihilation.
- **Quantum spins.** According to quantum physics, every particle in the universe is characterized by a spin.[4] In a similar manner, individual people also have a spin or way of being. In an exercise later in this chapter, some readers will spin only clockwise, and others only counterclockwise. And the rates of each differ. People, like particles, have very different spin characteristics.

When you spin, your process or body wisdom becomes the teacher. Each of us has a particular spin associated with our particular body and our relationship to the universe. It is that relationship we shall be seeking later in this chapter's exercise.

Spinning in the Chinese martial arts

It is this relationship between us and the universe that is central to the Chinese martial art Ba Kua Chang. In general, becoming adept in the martial arts is possible only for the most dedicated students, for these arts are not about fighting or winning but about what I am calling the big U and its use in relationships involving contact and conflict. I have been most interested recently in the roots of Ba Kua Chang, which reaches back in time before the Tai Chi form of martial art.[5] It is a Taoist art based upon a walking meditation that consists of moving around a circle of trigrams.

To understand the general meaning of circling in conflict, try to imagine fighting with somebody who is spinning! Without preparation, you might get confused or dizzy! Imagine the use of spinning or circling metaphorically in conflict. Say someone accuses you of something: You're spinning if at one moment you say, "Well, yes, you're right" and at the next moment, say, "No, you're wrong"—that is, you yield, attack, yield, etc. You are not identified with only your ordinary self, but are constantly shifting directions and revolving. In a way, the Ba Kua master is in Tao with what is happening—she or he is like the universe, moving with the changes that are present. He uses his big U to move through stress fields.

The Ba Kua method uses the eight trigrams from the *I Ching* (*Book of Changes*), which describes an ancient system of cosmology and philosophy and is the oldest of the Chinese classical texts. According to Bruce Frantzis, a student and teacher of the internal martial arts, there are two basic approaches to learning the Ba Kua martial art—a pre-birth and post-birth method—and both involve the trigrams.[6]

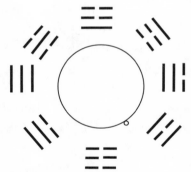

FIGURE 16.1 The Bakua Chang practitioner walks around a circle surrounded by the trigrams.

- *The pre-birth method* (*hsien tien*) is a meditative or internal method that involves circle walking exclusively. The purpose of this method is to recharge your original energy, or the first battery (so to speak) that you had while in the womb. This energy is imagined to come from the cosmos and can be felt while walking meditatively around the eight trigrams. (See Appendix 8 for more about Taoism and the eight trigrams.)

While moving around, the practitioner experiences the various directions and energies of the earth and universe, and visualizes or feels the universe twirling her about. According to this method, circle walking optimizes the original powers we received from the universe. (See Figure 16.1)

- *The post-birth method* (*hou tien*), according to Mantak Chia, stresses "fighting applications, not its meditation aspects. The post-birth method is done in straight lines rather than by walking a circle."[7] In this method one practices the various fighting postures associated with the specific trigrams. Whereas the pre-birth method connects the body to the original energy coming from the heavens, the post-birth method maintains that energy by various physical means, such as exercising, practicing fighting postures, resting, and eating properly.

First and second training

I think of the various methods in terms of a *first* and *second training*—an idea I got from a conversation with Zen master Keido Fukushima of Kyoto.[8] For me, the post-birth is a first training relating to methods and structures. In contrast, pre-birth training is a kind of second training emphasizing inner work and a spiritual attitude. The second training is about our original relationship to the universe, whereas the first training involves cognitive learning, facts, and methods. The second training is really needed before, during, and after one's education is formerly completed.

In the second training you learn to perceive and connect with the powers of life that move you while alone, in relationships, out in the world; while sitting quietly, flying through the air, or landing on the ground. Normally, you probably identify with the little u; your attention is toward what you are doing, what your obligations are in time and space. You feel you must *do* things. At night, however, we give ourselves up to the universe and spin.

In an earlier chapter we discussed getting to this sense of liberation through sniffing and sleepwalking. In the immediately preceding chapter, we used our sense of the direction and the deepest part of ourselves in the body. Now we will use spinning. If you have trouble standing and spinning, you can sit (or lie) and move your head or even just your eyes in a circular fashion. The point of the exercise is not to get dizzy but to spin carefully and approach the point of dizziness with lucidity. While at that point between the worlds, where you feel you might lose your balance, use your sentient awareness to catch and track the fantasies and experiences trying to emerge.

Be careful when doing this exercise. Some people have to spin only a very little to become dizzy, whereas others have to turn rapidly and many times. Your body will direct you. Try to spin until you feel some connection with the universe. Then, just before getting dizzy, remain as sober as possible and while moving, lucidly catch the kinds of experiences that pop up. You will be dreaming while awake, so to speak. The fantasies that emerge at this point may be very important.

Spinning with the universe

A good beginning method is to write down how you experience your ordinary self today. Sense the direction of that ordinary self. Who are you today?

Then ask yourself a central question that has been on your mind. Perhaps you want to know what you should do next. Feel the earth around you and let it tell you the direction of this central question.

Put this information to the side for now, and if possible stand up and prepare to circle around a point:

1. Place your left foot in one place, and move around it by pivoting with your right foot.
2. Keep your eyes partially open, and spin slowly at first, moving only as fast as needed to almost get dizzy. At that point, just before you get too dizzy, stay alert.
3. Remain lucid while you are moving and sense the universe, noticing any and all experiences trying to emerge. Perhaps you

will feel yourself being moved by some force. Feel how your body dialogues with the forces of the universe. While moving, feel and imagine these forces, and follow your body and your fantasy, trusting your sentient body awareness to care for the overall situation. Move at the rhythm and motion that makes you feel best. Trust your body and the flirt-like experiences, the fantasies and feelings that arise.

4. Note these experiences and describe them in a sentence. Still spinning, allow a short story to emerge; tell it to yourself in a few sentences. While in the dance of that story, explore the parallel worlds of your ordinary self and your problem. Note any experiences and insights that arise.

5. Finally, use your awareness dance to benefit your everyday life. While still spinning, look at the question you posed in the beginning of this exercise and let your dance answer that question. Then go on with your dance, letting it go where it wants. Name the dance and ask it about your future tasks. Your body will tell you when to stop dancing. Remember the nature of that final dance, its timing, rhythm, space, feeling, and story.

A middle-aged client asked me what the next step in life was and how to deal with her business problems. She began spinning—and at the moment of getting dizzy, she felt an invisible force moving her about. She was initially angry at this force for pushing her around: *Submit*, the force told her. So she gave in to it—and to her surprise began to enjoy the experience of being slightly altered. Suddenly she caught a fantasy: she saw the force leading her into a cave, where people would visit her because she had become a kind of diviner that could give them answers.

After her process she explained to me that she was thrilled with this experience because she had wanted to retreat from her business, but had not admitted that to herself yet. Being more inward was her next step. Listening to the cave was her calling!

The secret to dreaming

Feel the powers of the earth and universe. They are as surprising as they are new for many people. Remember your little u and the story you just learned about. Remember the feeling of being connected to what moves you on earth. How has this story been trying to arise before? In what way is it characteristic of something very basic about you, perhaps an aspect of your personal myth? Apparently when our momentary identity is relaxed, when we are dizzy or dreaming, we can better feel the big U as the force of the universe moving us in our individual lives.

Make a note about how the experience of spinning wants to change the world of your everyday self. Build your everyday self into the story of the big U, and don't stop dreaming that story until it includes both the big and the little u. In the case of my client who finally submitted to the force, the wisdom from the cave was calling to the everyday person to be more inward in all that she was doing.

The point of these body experiences is not only to explore the body's creativity, but also your relationship to the universe—and then to use this relationship on earth. The big U changes your sense of the world and of everyday life. Don Juan said it best:

Spinning with your ally will change your idea of the world. That idea is everything; and when that changes, the world itself changes.

▷ **Things to Consider**

- Circular movements remove personal history long enough to feel a new kind of center that can create helpful insights into difficult situations.

- The big U is a story, a dance, and an earth-based or cosmic experience appearing at the point of dizziness.

- The second training is learning to sense the universe dreaming our big U and story into life.

Part III

Where Relationships Come From

CHAPTER 17

The Geometry of Love

To meet an ally without being prepared is like
attacking a lion with your farts.
—don Juan[1]

The analogy to don Juan's comment is, in my mind, dealing with the Nagual of relationships *without* your big U. You need to be prepared. Use your path awareness. In principle it is part of the new paradigm of deep democracy. Democracy is an important older paradigm normally understood to mean the free and equal right of all people to be represented. *Deep* democracy extends democracy to include the free and equal right of all *dreams* and *essence experiences* to be represented.[2] By itself, democracy is insufficient to reduce war and conflict in relationships of all sorts, whether in closest friendships or the connection between nations. Without recognition of the dreaming background to relationships, power instead of awareness, rules instead of consciousness, dominate. Deep democracy requires sentient awareness of changes, flirts, dreams, as well as everyday reality.

Trying to work on relationships or world issues is one of the greatest challenges. Such work is like meeting your "ally," the spirit which at first threatens to annihilate your consciousness. However, with sentient awareness, the shaman can turn those issues into an opportunity. To deal with relationship issues, you need to respect the consensus-reality issues, the dreamland map, and the essence-level or big U experience of the overall relationship direction. The U lends us the necessary elder-ship to appreciate all the roles, feelings, vectors, and people character-istics involved in relationships. The goal of this chapter is to find the U, the geometry and the sacred space we share.

Relationship problems

Relationship issues are the microcosm of world issues. Everyone, every-where seems to suffer from similar relationship problems in pairs, teams, and groups. At one time or another, most feel unappreciated. Many people are bothered by competition and jealousy, revenge and aggression. And although people are aware of feeling victimized by another or a group, few are aware of being an oppressor. In a way, the human world is characterized by victimhood; virtually everyone denies being an oppressor.

Relationship problems are legion; they take up much of our per-sonal lives and historical past and present. Why is it somehow easier to figure out how to walk on the moon than it is to walk on the earth and resolve an issue with an old friend or relative? There are, of course, as many answers to this question as there are people. But one answer seems outstanding. In working on the moon project, we experience ourselves as outside the moon or on a spaceship. On the other hand, while working on relationships, we experience ourselves as inside and miss the potential for detachment from our perspective. The alterna-tive? We need to recognize our feelings of love, hate, rejection, aban-donment, revenge, hurt, and anger—*and* find a third viewpoint that allows us enough detachment to respect the feelings and stories of oth-ers. I thoroughly recommend the path awareness exercise at the end of this chapter to everyone who is interested in discovering this third viewpoint. It is the viewpoint that can change the world, each person at a time.

Relationship methods

There are many different schools and methods for dealing with relationships. At one point or another, all methods can be important. Some people look at their dreams to work on relationships, others talk to God; many see their spiritual or religious helpers. Some go to therapists or shamans. Some rely on gossip, a main staple of help-seeking people from all walks of life. When we were in Kenya, we went to witch doctors who told us that they would listen to partners describe their problems, and then send them home while they worked on it for the partners. Their method of work is probably the oldest, though least recognized currently, of all relationship methods: a nonlocal focus on the space between the two people involved.

There are many individually centered approaches, psychodynamic and analytical approaches, and various systems approaches. Some focus on the influence of multigenerational processes on relationships; some focus on the self-esteem of the individual; others on power and hierarchy issues. Feminism helped to awaken us to the whole area of relationship work that involves gender differences. And multiculturalism brought in the influences of different cultures, races, and stressors on relationships as well. All these methods are more or less important, depending upon the people, issues, processes, and timing involved in any particular conflict situation.

The three-tiered approach of deep democracy is based upon sentient awareness and, in principle, contains the other methods. To resolve issues—

- Listen to the individuals.
- Find their dreaming in the moment.
- Go to the essence of experiences.

The basic idea is that relationships are not just between two or more people but also include their *shared parallel worlds*.

At the least, process-oriented awareness work includes noticing the reality context of the people involved, what the issues are, and how individuals identify themselves. Are the participants talking about money or about not being heard? Do they identify themselves as heterosexual, bisexual, transsexual, gay, or lesbian? What differences exist in terms of race, religion, health, age, gender? What feelings can you see in signals that have not been yet verbalized? Who has the most and the least rank in a given situation? When people speak of their deepest feelings, remember that those feelings are nonlocal and may belong to everyone, including you. Work with the field around the individuals, not just the individuals as isolated, contained entities. To find the essence level, have the individuals experience, guess, or feel the almost entirely impersonal, ineffable, hard-to-formulate background to their strongest experience.

In my book *Dreambody in Relationships*, I focused on how signal exchanges between people can be seen in dreams and how the first dreams or the first big experiences in relationships organize overall long-term patterns for those relationships. I also focused on what we called high dreams and low dreams, rank, roles, and ghost roles in relationships. All of these methods (and more) belong to what I called the first training in the last chapter of that book. That training requires skills and understanding, learning how the visible level in relationships is connected with the world of dreams.

However, without a second training—without direct access to and identification with the big U—you are either the observer or the observed at any given moment and not a sentient third. Without that U, we are either on one side of a tense situation or on the other, and we easily forget the friendship and meaning of the relationship.

The map: a sacred space between us

To get to the sense of nonlocality, we need to focus with sentient awareness on the subtleness of the earth-based directions. To find subtle shared experiences and eldership—the vectors or sacred space between us—we must use not only our everyday awareness but our most sentient abilities. If you allow yourself to notice the background space to a situation, there are few problems that cannot be helped. That space is filled with a blueprint.

Let's look at a relationship map (Figure 17.1). In the space of real everyday life, we are two (or more) people. In the dreamland space we share, however, there are also the figures of our dreams. At the border of the essence world, which cannot really be formulated, there is a quantum compass, a sentient earth structured by earth-based directions (consistent with, or projected onto, the area around us or onto north, south, east, west). The essence world manifests itself as the big U— as its diverse directions, dreams, and finally as you and me.

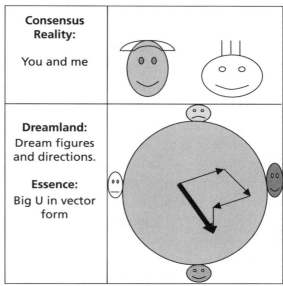

Consensus Reality: You and me	
Dreamland: Dream figures and directions. **Essence:** Big U in vector form	

FIGURE 17.1 **Relationship map**

The essence and dream worlds are nonlocal and not easy to formulate in words. Perhaps they are mathematical, patterned, sacred spaces. The best I can do (the future will formulate these spaces in a more differentiated fashion) is call the big U the wave/particle, or vibratory/directional intelligence of the essence world, the common ground we share. Like the pilot-wave or quantum-wave function in physics, the big U is the (usually) hidden pattern or intelligence appearing in spontaneous sounds, songs, directions, dream images, and behind the everyday actions of everyone involved in the relationship being considered. As we have seen in individual life and will now see for relationships, the big U has the characteristic of a nonlocal, *knowing* intelligence. In principle, it embraces and uses everyone and everything in the relationship. It needs the diversity of worlds and figures that creates the sense of relativity and the possibility of awareness and consciousness.

The background U goes by many names. Some call it God or love or the "one with a million names," depending upon the peoples, cultures, and times. Remember John Wheeler's universe in Chapter 2 (Figure 2.2). His universe is shaped like a whale trying to look at its tail; a whale reflecting on itself. In a universe with just two people, the U manifests as an intelligence that uses one to look at the other, and vice versa. This mirroring function is the essence of relationships, the awareness potential. A relationship can feel like an entire world, and if it is very troubled, many feel the world is going to pieces. On the other hand, with a sense of the U, even parting can be a warmly agreed-upon relationship experience.

Everything changes. Remember the early Taoists who imagined the beginning of the universe as yin and yang emerging as a person and a bug (Chapter 3)? Physicists see even the emptiness of a vacuum as a potential bug ready to create reality. So even the most blissful state in a relationship cannot last forever; something is always about to bug us about the other person. The whale's tail itches or flirts with its eye. The big U is itching to know itself. That is perhaps one of the grand reasons for all experience, whether alone or with others: for awareness to know itself—and perhaps, helping the universe to know itself. In any case, the possible genesis story of relationship work is, "In the beginning there was the bug. . . ."

Sand painting

The beginning of the universe is portrayed by Navajos as a sand painting (Figure 17.2). Here we notice again the vector-like directional figures and structures, as well as the overarching U-like figure spanning from one end of the painting to the other.

Not just the Navajo, but Africans and Tibetans and others use sand paintings to heal and understand the blueprint of the cosmos. In our Kenyan healing, our shamans spent hours first drawing their sense of the dreaming universe on the ground. Then we had to sit on the intricate diagram they had drawn. We had to be *in* that dreaming. And after the healing, they washed it all away.

The word for sand painting in the Navajo language means *where the gods come and go*. Any one picture of the essence and dreamworld, any one map of vectors, is transient; don't hold on to it. The artist's feeling of being moved by the earth is what counts. People the world over who do sand paintings say, "Erase and re-create the sand painting every day." The blueprint changes, though the big U, the universal power behind them, may be steady. Parallel worlds change and shift to meet different situations, but the basic patterns, pilot waves, remain. Likewise, the graphics behind who we are as individuals, couples, and groups are not frozen for all of time. Vector diagrams need re-creation every day. Sit in the midst of the sand painting.[3] Create the map, sit on it, and the earth structure may give you a sense of identity with the larger picture, the big U.

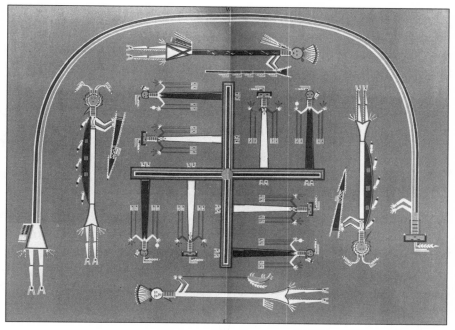

FIGURE 17.2 **Navajo sand painting**[4]

The observer and observed are parallel worlds

Each relationship is the sum of many worlds. In Chapter 4 we focused on how the observer and the observed are parallel worlds. What catches your attention depends upon which part of you is looking. There are many ways to work with relationships. In what follows I will suggest the observer/observed method because it is relatively simple. What catches your attention about another person depends upon that person and also upon your own state of mind at a given moment. The observer and observed are two of the parallel worlds in the relationship, which just about everyone can readily experience. (In the next chapter I will suggest a more complex method with more parallel worlds.)

For example, the thing that might catch your attention about a coworker might be her or his loving nature, coldness, or rankful behavior. But then who in you is looking? Upon meditation you might find that the observer of coldness is one who needs love; the observer of rank-conscious behavior might be someone who feels abused. Coldness and love, or ranking and abuse are possible parallel worlds of given relationships. The relationship is not one or the other of these experiences, but the sum of all.

The big U

Like everything else in the universe, planets and trees, individuals and groups, every relationship is the sum of its parallel worlds. Remember: Worlds are parallel in the sense that they are usually disconnected from one another. They may live on the opposite sides of town, so to speak. Thus at any one moment, one person is seen as cold, the other as loving, one is powerful, the other hurt, and so on. When you are in one world, then the other person seems polarized in a world of her or his own. But the bottom line is that these worlds are shared and nonlocal. This is why roles suddenly flip, as you become the other, while the other picks up your old role.

While doing earlier parallel-world exercises (that is, in moving your hand toward an object or toward your own body), you may have noticed all sorts of parallel worlds popping up. All you did was move your hand slowly and with awareness. I assume—and you probably noticed—that some form of awareness is just there and able to notice things. In other words, something in you is aware of the details of your relationships to objects, relationships, and even your own self. Some will say that awareness belongs to the dreammaker, the one who notices all the fragments. The little u notices things and gets fixed on one viewpoint, but the big U sees all the sides and is noetic—that is, *knowing*. Graphically speaking, the U is the sum of the parts and levels.

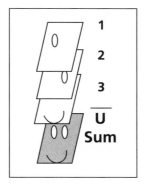

FIGURE 17.3
Relationships are the sum of parallel worlds.

There are three parallel worlds of the face picture in Figure 17.3: a left eye, a right eye, and the mouth. The sum is the face, or in this analogy, the big U (the grey area).

Who is looking at that relationship?

The map or relationship blueprint is composed of the directions associated with each of these worlds. Your normal or little u viewpoint is usually identified with only one of the worlds, one part of the relationship's map. We usually look at things as one parallel world looking at another. Without realizing what we are doing in relationships, we become but one dream figure looking at another. That's the beauty and difficulty in relationships. There is a constant process of role switching. First you play one and I the other; a week later, we switch.[5]

Allow me to demonstrate this role-switching exercise with my wife Amy. I begin by meditating on Amy as she sits across from me. In the moment we are dealing with a difficult outer project. I am serious, and she seems very reasonable, very linear. Now I will relax my everyday mind. As I do, I relax my gaze, and see her with half-closed eyes. I notice something about her flirting or trying to catch my attention. What is that? One of her earrings, sparkling at me (Figure 17.4). It reminds me of something about

FIGURE 17.4
Amy's earring

her, something I feel as her sparkling nature. Now without saying more about that, I want to sense the earth-based direction of that earring. I associate or feel the earth-based direction of that earring as heading south. Somehow the earring belongs with the sun, with Mexico.

I ask myself, *Who (in me) is the observer of that flirt?* The answer is a noncognitive one: As I study Amy's earring, I sense a part of me that loves that earring; it is a linear part of me that needs its warmth. I look at her earring; which is to say, the linear part of me is fascinated by the earring. Aha!—so *I* am the reasonable and linear one. In any case, the linear part of me is associated with the northeast. Why? That is where my body moves when I feel my experience of lin-earity. Perhaps that is the northeast United States, where I did my earliest college studies. If I began at the point * and walked the direction of the observed earring to the south, then I can walk the path of the observer—that is, the linear part of myself, which goes northeast (Figure 17.5).

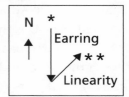

FIGURE 17.5 **Observer and observed**

Now I want to find the big U in our relationship. I go back to the beginning point and walk that U line to the end point ** (Figure 17.6). The experiences of this U are very characteristic of my relationship with Amy. For me that U vector heads toward Kenya, the world of commu-nity warmth, and the cool clarity of shamanistic insights. The shamans were magical, but were successful because they were also very warm and very reasonable! I had to walk the U line several times to feel and real-ize these associations. When you do this exercise, you may also need to walk that U line several times to recognize its meaning.

In any case, that U deepened my contact with Amy—for at the moment of the flirt, I was thinking that *she* was in a linear, reasonable mood. I thought we needed another kind of mood to deal with the outer reality situation we were involved in. The shamanistic nature of our big U helped me understand how *I* was in that linear reasonable mood. Moreover, I suddenly realized how important that mood was in dealing with that real-world situation we were both trying to solve. I laughed and told her about my insights. Without knowing directly about the big U I had experienced, Amy said, "Remember those shamans from Kenya? In some situations, their reasonable behavior was just what was needed!" Warmth and reasonableness were nonlocal, and both were needed in our project.

In any case, shape-shifting, at least temporarily, into the mood and meaning of that big U is the goal; the experience will help you deal with whatever you do together with the other person. When you find the big U, your mood and the world changes; you may find yourself in a very different and improved spot to work on relationship projects or issues. The big U is the grand facilitator, the pilot or guide with compassion for the various parts.

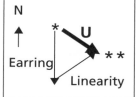

FIGURE 17.6 **The Big U**

The relationship exercise and parallel worlds

To approximate the big U in relationship work (and to do it quickly before, during, or after you are in contact with someone), we shall use only two parallel worlds, even though in principle, there are an infinite number. But the approximation of the big U can be very helpful and rapidly done.

1. When you are ready, *imagine or actually find someone with whom to work*. After imagining or talking to her or him, be silent for a few minutes and use your sentient awareness, give yourself space to relax. You can talk to the person again in a few minutes. (Perhaps in learning to do this with another person, you might even ask her or him to try the same practice.) In any case, with half-open eyes, gaze at the person in reality (or in your imagination) and notice something that flirts with you. Gaze or blink and notice something that catches your attention very quickly. You may notice a few different things; let your inner mind choose what to focus and call that the observed. What did you see? What did you observe? What does it mean to you? Make a note and/or make a quick sketch of that flirt. Now feel that observed flirt, get in touch with it, and let your body turn in many directions to find the direction that seems right for

that observed experience. (My earring line in Figure 17.6 was the observed flirt.)

2. When you are ready to add vectors and find the dreamland blueprint, take something to mark your starting point *. Then feel the direction of the observed and take a couple of steps in that direction; maybe you will even understand something more about that direction. (If you are not able to walk, you can just move your upper body in that direction from a sitting position.) Can you feel how that direction is nonlocal? How is it shared by you and the person you are working with in some way?

   Note to the observer: What part of you needed to see that flirt, that "observed?" Can you sense or feel the observer part of you that needed to see that observed? When you feel and know who that observer is, feel the observer's direction, take a couple of steps and mark the ending point, **.

3. Return to the beginning point * and walk the direction to the end point ** (Figure 17.7). Walk and feel what happens to you as you walk the U line. Walk until fantasies and feelings arise that indicate the meaning of

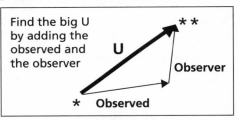

Find the big U by adding the observed and the observer

U

Observer

* **Observed**

** **

FIGURE 17.7 **Adding relationship vectors**

that path. Trust your body and your experiences. Is there a feeling or story about that path in your mind? Let your experiences create a short story.

4. How could this story and feeling be a possible guide? How might you use that feeling in relationship with the person you are with or thinking about? From the viewpoint of the big U, you may sense how all of these different paths are all nonlocal, needed, and belong to both of you. The big U is, in principle, the essence of your map, your sand painting. It is a kind of intelligence that needed those two viewpoints of the observer and the observed to know itself. In any case, that U is an

intelligence that can work with the situation. If you are working with a living friend who is sitting next to you in the moment, ask your friend to create her or his sand painting version of the relationship and share it with you. Compare your various experiences of the relationship's U.

Please remember, this work is a sand painting. The winds of time blow it away. This picture is meant for today: Sit on its ground. It is the sacred space between you. Renew that space tomorrow. That U will probably always be the easiest way, the least action, least effort, and the greatest sense of friendship or love. The first training in relationships is learning to find the blueprint. The second training in relationships is relating as a whole person, shape-shifting into U.

▷ Things to Consider

- Relationships at one level are sand paintings; they are geometry.

- The observer and observed are nonlocal parallel worlds.

- The big U or essence of a relationship is the sum of worlds.

- To deal with relationships without the big U is like attacking a lion with your farts.

CHAPTER 18

Compassion as Love in Action

You have been given an abstract gift: the possibility of flying on the wings of intent.

—don Juan[1]

The story of the observer and the observed is more awesome than any of us usually realizes. Without awareness of the big U, I think of myself as being the force behind what I look at and what I do. But with sentient awareness, I notice that nonlocality was present before there was a little me, or little u. In the consensus reality of psychology, we speak of our projections on others—but the truth is, no one really knows where projections come from. Similarly, experiences of the observer, observed flirts, vectors, the big U—all these arise between us, just as much as we arise because of the underlying blueprint of relationships. The story of the big U in the background helps us get beyond the problematical aspects of projection. As I will show in this chapter, this helps us deal compassionately with even the most radical relationship scenes.

Second training in relationships

Most of the time, our relationships are built on secrets, things we do and feel that we think we'd better not say. But one of the biggest secrets

189

should not really be kept: the big U and each person's sense of the dreaming mind. After the first important meeting with someone, agreeing to go on only with mundane everyday life keeps the U a secret. Keeping that secret eventually becomes irritating and boring, if not worse. Share the big U with others! Get to know the overall big U direction of a relationship and tell your friend about it; you will feel more certain of yourself and the other. Do some form of the first training; learn about signals and roles, vectors and flirts. Work on some form of the second training; shape-shift and become the relationship's intelligence that needs the two of you to express itself.

One of my colleagues, Waynelle Wilder, injured her brain in a serious automobile accident, yet recuperated to write about it some months after the accident. Here she describes her connection to the man who accidentally drove his car into hers.

> *Shh, shh, shh, I am whispering, patting his head. It is not really his head; it is a hat on his head, although I am sure I feel his hair under the hat. He is crying and cooing "Oh no, oh no, oh no." And with call-and-response mantra, I echo back "Shh, shh, shh." We are caught in a strange embrace; he is squatting outside my car window as I pat his head-hat. I am still trapped inside the car. I realize I have never felt such compelling compassion until now. Each tear he sheds catches my eye and feels like my own. I know he is crying and moaning in pain, but I am the one bleeding. Somehow the incongruity doesn't register. Our connection seems natural.*
>
> *I don't feel physical pain, only anguish about the pain. I am seeing and hearing from the man on my left side, squatted outside what used to me my driver's side window. His skin glistens like black diamonds. I am curious why he is upset, but I know I need to comfort him, "Shh, shh, shh." His tears are mine, a strange ecstasy. "It will be all right, I know it will." He argues back, "Oh no, oh no, oh no, it will never be."[2]*

Waynelle's altered state, compassion, and poetry speak to me about her sense of oneness with the situation, an awesome embrace of all that is happening. That is a big U experience—compassion, a gift. The big U is like the pattern or intent behind a situation. Don Juan says it best: "You have been given an abstract gift: the possibility of flying on the wings of intent."

Relating to bears

The big U is a gift, but at the same time it can be developed. Let me describe another situation: developing a relationship with a black bear. Compassion helped me with this uninvited guest. Amy and I were recently troubled by that bear on the Oregon coast. He visited us frequently at night, overturning garbage cans and ripping up parts of our house. I promptly borrowed a rifle from a friend—but happily never used it, choosing other methods instead.

Since we live 300 feet from a national forest, there will always be a valid debate about whether our property belongs to us. For the little u, the human viewpoint, our house definitely belongs to us. But from the bear's viewpoint, it is his. Nonlocally speaking, we all live together and nothing belongs to anyone—but most of us rarely have access to this view. The awesomeness of the earth cannot be owned by anyone—something our Native American ancestors knew well.

In any case, the most radical encounter with that bear occurred about midnight one night as Amy and I were talking in the kitchen. I

FIGURE 18.1 **Black bear**[3]

said to her that I thought she had a lot of power. At that moment, we heard a roar. We looked at the door where that sound came from and saw through our glass door what seemed at first sight to be a monster making a huge racket. A few feet from where we were standing inside the house, a black bear (Figure 18.1) was shoving boxes around on the front stairs. Only a glass door separated us from one another. Face to face with the bear who was ripping up various parts of our property before going into winter hibernation, we quickly decided to use parallel worlds (a method involving various flirts I will lead you through at the end of this chapter).

I remembered that exercise because we had just been working on it that evening, perhaps one hour earlier. In any case, I looked at the scene and had no trouble whatsoever noticing what was trying to catch my attention in this situation. Bear teeth! Looking at the bear tearing up some boxes a few feet away, all I could see at first were his teeth. I was not certain if he was going to charge; my basic instincts told me to be careful and watch those teeth! As I stared, I also encouraged myself to notice other experiences of the bear. I noticed that his black fur caught my attention. This fur seemed strangely cozy to me, even though at the same time I was terrified. Under the circumstances, the flirt made little sense to me but I remembered it. While standing there, staring at each other, finally a third flirt popped up in my attention. The black bear suddenly stood stone still. He was so quiet as he stared at us, eye to eye, as we stood inside the house looking at him through the glass door.

With Amy's help I quickly felt and "walked" the various flirts and parallel worlds that had just caught my attention (Figure 18.2). Those teeth were hot! They went to Florida. After taking miniscule steps, I walked in the direction of Miami. Then I felt the cozy fur, which went toward Latin America. The stillness—hmmm, that took me a moment, and away I went toward a Zen experience I'd had in Kyoto, Japan.

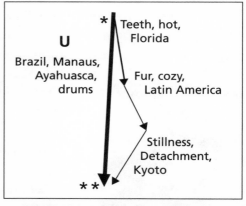

FIGURE 18.2 **Relationship with the bear**

I walked these three vectors very gently, using the slightest meditative movements of my head. The resultant big U vector went straight to Manaus, on the central Brazilian Amazon, where we had taken part in that Ayahuasca ceremony some years early. While still standing near the bear, in a split second I caught an association to that ceremony: drumming. It had been loud and powerful. Without thinking another moment, I promptly went into our living room, grabbed our Haida drum from the wall, and began drumming as loudly as possible.[4] The arrow next to the drum is the direction of my big U (Figure 18.3).

FIGURE 18.3 **U and Haida drum**

I began to drum in front of the bear, which was only a few feet away. At first the bear just stood there; perhaps he was staring at us in amazement. He listened, then suddenly turned and ran off into the distance. What a relief! We cried for happiness.

But deep down in my heart, I felt more than a relief. I felt deeply in contact with the earth. I can't quite verbalize it. I felt the fierceness of the teeth, the heat of the south. I experienced the fur, the warmth of Latin America. And I knew the bear's stillness as something connected to the power of nature, the feeling of the earth, the sense of something in the sky and the waters. Finally, all this combined to give me the overall feelings of what I call the big U, which in this moment meant aboriginal life, the amazing communities near Manaus on the Amazon and on Haida Gwai. The Haida animal dances I experienced reminded me of the oneness of all beings.

The drum or the big U feeling behind it sent messages I cannot communicate with words. It speaks of my love for people and nature, of my respect for life, terror and fierceness, and in a way, of my sense of oneness with the world of the bear. From a purely consensus-reality viewpoint, the sound may have scared the bear away. But from a more sentient viewpoint, from the feeling of the big U, the bear awakened or reminded me of a kind of peak oneness experience. I recalled some time later, with Amy's help, that after all, bears played a central role in the first dream I can remember in life.[5] In a way, I was meeting my own life. Amy felt the same about herself, but that is another story I'll tell at another time.

In any case, the drum expressed a kind of compassion for terror, fierceness, and stillness. Perhaps the bear came to remind us of our link and indebtedness to all aboriginal peoples and to ourselves. My point is that the big U is a relationship creator and an elder—even in situations that seem impossible. The power of the U usually works without hurting anyone. The sum of the parts is a guiding force. As long as we are only identified with just one character, one parallel world, or one part of the relationship, we panic, become uncertain, feel attracted or repelled, and marginalize other parts of the situation.

The relationship's guide

In principle, every moment, every relationship, and every relationship situation comes with a guide. Remember, from Chapters 7 and 8, David Bohm's overarching idea about a quantum wave pattern that describes a given material object? Every material object in the universe—every particle, every person, every chair, every planet, even the universe itself—has a quantum wave or a guiding pilot wave associated with it. In relationships, this guide is often deep in the background (unless, like Waynelle, you are developed enough to suddenly have access to it in a traumatic situation). The U is a guide, a wave, a vector, and a dream or relationship myth. Do you recall from Chapter 7 (Figure 7.4) the various vectors of the flashlight? How some of its possibility waves went backward? Those backward-moving waves are needed because all the possibilities together add up to the most likely characteristic. The big U helps you, allows you, and nudges you over the lifetime of a relationship to zigzag along each and every one of these directions at one time or another, to adjust to life's variations.

Compassion in relationships

In this exercise we'll thoroughly explore the background and various parallel worlds of a relationship.

1. To begin, choose a relationship—an intimate relationship with someone in the present or past, a troubled and difficult

relationship, or anyone appearing to you in the moment. Then we shall find the big U and how to use it in that relationship.

2. Remember the first dream, experience, or impression in that relationship. Write that down; you will need it later. Then note any problems or projects in your relationship with that person.

3. Now find two or three parallel worlds of the relationship: Using one hand as an awareness instrument, move it slowly toward the relationship which you can imagine in your other hand.

Catch the flickering experiences that arise. Call these experiences parallel worlds 1, 2, and 3 (and however more or less that you experience). Make notes and give them names (e.g., teeth, heat). Ask yourself if these parallel worlds have already been apparent or recurring features of that relationship? Which flirt is potentially connected to your sense of relationship or friendship? If the person is an intimate partner, which world is linked to your sense of sensuality or sexuality?

Explore backlight: Which parallel world is most likely to be the backlight, that is, the most troublesome or awesome? Unfold this backlight, act it out and sketch it. What is its belief/value system? (For example, in my relationship to the bear, the most troublesome world was clearly the "teeth," the fierceness.) How is this backlight world connected potentially to your toughest (or imagined toughest) relationship problem with that person, and your sense of uncertainty in that relationship? How is this backlight energy nonlocal: that is, how is this energy in both of you, in the rest of the world around you, possibly in your body problems, and in your relationship troubles with others?

Now find the U's compassion: Put something on the floor to mark your starting point, and add parallel worlds. To do this, feel world 1, find its direction, and move there. From that spot, do the same with worlds 2 and 3 and put something on the floor to mark your ending point. Now add the worlds by feeling and walking from the beginning point to the end point. Feel the U's rhythm, song, and meaning and name that experience. Make notes about this relationship U.

Consider Sam, who was scared of Jake—although actually, it was Jake who was jealous of Sam. This jealousy provoked Jake into always making negative critical comments that scared Sam. So Sam put his image of his relationship with Jake in his hand and looked at the two imaginary figures. Then he slowly moved his other hand toward the one with the figures. As he did so, with sentient awareness, he was shocked to notice a knife popping out of his imagination. The knife was the first parallel world in which stabbing was happening. Continuing to move his hand slowing toward the imaginary figures, Sam said that the second parallel world was depressing; he said that Jake was really depressed. And the third world was simply wind. Sam felt the earth-based directions associated with each of these parallel worlds: the knife (world 1), depression (world 2), and the wind that blew from east to the west (world 3) (Figure 18.4). When Sam found the big U, it felt like liberation or detachment, "something going north, to the arctic!" Sam was shocked and more than pleased.

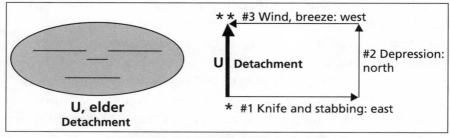

FIGURE 18.4 **Relationship with a jealous friend**

Complete your own inner work: you should walk the various vectors (Figure 18.4), then feel and imagine the U direction again. If possible, sketch the experience of the U as a humanlike being. Sketch the U, using the feeling and energy of the experience. (Perhaps the facial figure in Figure 18.4 will suggest how to use your own creativity.) Finally, shape-shift and become this figure; stand and move as it might stand and move. Trust your body experience and second training. Shape-shift; make the U's possible motions and sounds or speak its words; let it "breathe" you, so to speak.

Perhaps you might be able to experience how you, as the big U, created the people in this relationship. Perhaps you created them to know parts of who U are? As the U, how do you see the most trouble-some parallel world? Do you have the sense of inclusiveness for it and the other parallel worlds? How is this backlight needed in one form or another? Recall your first impression or feeling or dream after meeting the person you have been working on. How was your big U experience already present in what happened at that time?

When you enter your second training, your big U will know what to do next in this relationship. It will deal surprisingly with your and the other's contact and distance, signals, double signals, and rank differences.

Here is what happened to Sam. He completed his work on the relationship with Jake. Sam's detached U experience saw Jake's stab-bing, critical comments as merely speaking out. In fact, from the U's perspective, "Jake's speaking out was needed," Sam said. "Bluntness belongs to the total picture."

A few days later, Sam actually met Jake and told him about his experiences. He told Jake how his direct style is really needed, and that with detachment Sam would be blunter as well. Jake was shocked and cried. No one else liked his direct style of confronting things. Then Sam warned, "But watch out! Don't speak out too often, or else I'll return your stabs!" Of all things, both men laughed until they both had tears in their eyes. Apparently both loved being met in their spontaneity and freedom.

The big U deals surprisingly with relationship situations. Waynelle comforted the man who crashed his car into her. I drummed for the bear. Sam got tough with Jake. The big U is compassionate in the broadest sense. While the little u may not know or like certain directions and remain upset and uncertain in relationship, the big U needs all the directions.

That U is everyone's birthright. It is an incredible gift; but to find it we need to relax our everyday little u for a few minutes and focus on shifting into the second training. As don Juan said in the quote from the beginning of this chapter:

You have been given an abstract gift: the possibility of flying on the wings of intent.

▷ Things to Consider

- You don't know yourself until you know the U's compassion in relationships.

CHAPTER 19

The Shaman's Relationship Spin

If the Beloved is Everywhere,
The lover is a veil.
But when living itself becomes the friend,
Lovers disappear.
—Rumi[1]

Sensing the big U enables you to flow with least action in relationships. During such times, neither you nor your partner is the main point. The big U provides connection not only to the real situation, but to the sense of independence from what others call reality. Relationships require training to work best. Do some form of first and second training to help yourself and the other.

In Chapter 17 we explored the big U's guidance in relation to the observer and the observed. In the last chapter, we used the U's path awareness to develop awareness and compassion. In this chapter, I want to explore the alchemy of relationships and describe a dervish type of spin dance for friends to find their big U.

Where we are so far

Because it is normally marginalized by most people, I have been emphasizing the big U. However, from the viewpoint of deep democracy, the big U is but one of many relationship qualities. Awareness of consensus reality, or CR issues, rank, history, locality, age, nationality, race, sexual orientation, religion, health conditions, etc., is important. Remember the significance and diversity of dream images and the non-local, shared nature of roles in dreamland. Our myths and stories are not just personal; they are nonlocally present throughout the whole universe. Many fear death or the loss of an important relationship in part because the reality of nonlocal experience is not sufficiently conscious. The signals, double signals, and body symptoms arising at the surface of relationship issues have roots in that dreamworld we all share. If one person is not well, everyone is not well in some way.[2]

I have called the nonlocality of dreamland a sacred space to emphasize the necessary focus and awareness needed to reveal the geometrical structures. Sentient earth-based awareness notices evanescent flirts and vectors, the common ground of relationships. With the second training, then, you can shape-shift into the big U, transient as this may be. Having access to the big U, in turn, makes it easier to notice signals, rank differences, double signals, and personal details.

The exercises I have suggested throughout the chapters are meant to stimulate awareness and are not necessarily a fixed program unto themselves. They are a form of body awareness and earth-based training to find the various vectors and the U. Every relationship situation is a chance to learn more about one's relationship to the universe.

Your teacher's path through moods and fields

Take a minute to check in with yourself; close your eyes, if you feel comfortable doing that. Once you are aware of yourself, feel your deepest self and find where it is located in your body. Then stand and feel your deepest self inside of you and when you are ready, let the earth tell your body with which direction that deepest self is associated. Let the earth turn you to the direction associated with your deepest self and move there. As you do that, notice any feelings or irrational ideas associated with that direction, and the rhythm and movement of that path. To feel that rhythm, you must walk in that direction; only the earth can teach you about itself. Feel the rhythm of this deepest part of yourself, your big U and its implications. Make a note about this experience. Consider that direction and those earth-based feelings to be your teacher.

As we've done earlier in the book, we will explore how to use that teacher in order to work on moods and fields—this time in relationships. Everyone knows about relationship moods; just visit your family or go into a friend's apartment. Sense moods and fields around shops and educational classes. There are depressed and manic fields—fiery, heavy, dull, tense, yet also very ecstatic and elated fields. We know from earlier chapters that moods are fields structured by background figures as well as by annihilation, creation, and zigzag detachment processes. Now I want to emphasize the earth-based and dreamlike nature of these fields.

In the problem is the solution

Because of the timeless motions of the big U that are possible in every field, problem fields contain their own solutions. Alchemy, the earlier form of chemistry in which matter was still imagined to be animated, pictured the beginning or *prima materia* stage of all material processes as containing potential transformation. The solution was in the process, so to speak. At the center of these processes was the spirit Mercury, who facilitated turning base materials into gold and the panacea that would heal all things. There is no evidence that alchemy succeeded in these particular goals; but thanks to Jung and his students, we realize that alchemy was a symbol for not only what physics was to produce (e.g., the transformation of one material into another), but also of human transformation leading to greater wholeness.[3]

Sometimes Mercury was called the living water or the magical trickster; sometimes he would be seen in dreams as the old wise woman or man, as the Self, the magician, some very magical spirit, or the fool (Figure 19.1). Jung called Mercury the god of the unconscious. In any case, take note of Mercury's staff

FIGURE 19.1 **Spirit Mercurius**

with its snakes—the caduceus that I understood as a symbol for self-reflecting waves that make the pilot wave or big U conscious.

Like the early alchemists, I too can see Mercury as an image of the spirit in nature that creates the panacea, a big U experience that flows and zigzags through the field processes that turn our everyday mind into frozen, static, and unmoving states.

In his study of relationships and of trans-ference, Jung showed how the alchemists imagined themselves as "transforming"—beginning as separate individuals, "dying" in the sense of losing their original conventional postures and identities, then evolving into a hermaphrodite (Figure 19.2).[4] And in that fig-ure again, we see a symbol of the big U, a unity containing all figures and even parallel worlds.

FIGURE 19.2
Hermaphrodite. Symbol of the big U

Look forward to monsters and fields

Remember that moods and fields are often seen as atmospheres or weather systems. Usually we become aware of them when they bug us.

FIGURE 19.3
Gloomy weather

Without awareness, we usually identify some per-son as the problem, instead of sensing the nonlo-cal nature of the atmosphere. However, the mood is in the air, so to speak (Figure 19.3).

If you are not careful, then you too will be infected by a field—which means that you cannot move freely in it; you are like the proverbial elec-tron that swings between creation and annihila-tion. To facilitate transformation in such fields while being in the midst of them requires the second training. Most of us are more familiar with being the victim of fields and relationship issues. We are rarely aware of sustaining difficulties by our insistence on remaining in our ordinary u, which negates the importance of roles, rank, ghosts, and other possibil-ities.

To get in touch with that U, use vector walking or simply feel the deepest part of yourself in your body and find its direction, as you have done throughout this book. However, perhaps the most powerful way of working with a field is to relate to its *universal direction*—that is, its orientation to the universe. Spinning is a powerful body-oriented method of getting to the big U, especially when the little u is fixed, static, and frozen into a stationary state.

Circle dances renew relationships

More than any other body method in my experience; spinning is the most rapid means of relaxing the grip of the little u. Spinning dissociates you from personal history. I mentioned earlier how many cultures created round dances to mirror the universe and to feel contact with the circling stars and the motions of the universe. The dervish dances of which I spoke were—and are still—performed in part to release the dancer from the bonds of this world. The effect of the spinning is to remove personal history; the tall cylindrical hats the dervish wears symbolize the tombstone of the ordinary self (Figure 19.4).

FIGURE 19.4 **Dervish**

Spinning can be an ecstatic state, as every child knows. Adults who spin frequently experience themselves as being part of the entire world and in direct communication with God. As a teacher, my best experience of using spinning to help people occurs by strongly encouraging the development of lucidity in the resulting altered states of consciousness. Turning is very different from standing still in relationships. Standing still and talking is related to what we normally do; we remain fixed in one position. We ask questions from stationary states. To find answers, we ask *others* to go into a trance or possibly flip coins. Then we notice the answer; one side or another. But the process of *creating* answers can occur through spinning: the spin is a twirling process that occurs when the coin is freed from your hand and can follow the process of least action as it spins through the air.

Instead of getting one answer at one time or another, spinning enables us to get in touch with the big U from which answers come. Spinning helps us get in touch with the sentient awareness of change that occurs in relationship to gravity. When we spin, we free ourselves from particular answers and get to know ourselves as a process of change; we then understand the relative importance (or unimportance) of all possibilities. We know that any answer, any state, is just temporary. Because spinning tends to create dizziness, it puts us in the hands of gravity and opens up the world of dreaming, of freedom from our normal position on the earth.[5] Because the little u is no longer in control, the experience of spinning is like dreaming, a form of "least action." That is, what you experience may seem as if it is coming from the universe.

Let me explain. While spinning, the experience of dizziness interrupts the control of the little u, as I've noted. In this sense the body's kinetic energy comes closer to the potential energy given by virtue of gravity, as if one were freely falling. Because of this least-action (kinetic is close to potential energy) free-fall phenomenon, we sense gravity more clearly than normal. Your dream world, your metaphorical potential energy, is due to the fields you live in—call them your relationship to the earth and world. My potential energy comes, in part, from you and your psychology, and from the times. It comes from the world situation, and the sea, the earth, and the universe. In brief, your potential is linked to the whole universe, and through interaction with its field, you get to know your own personal myth, your position in the universe. Least action in psychology implies that whatever I do kinetically with my life, whatever motion I create, my body seeks to live as close as possible to my potential energy, the universe, or the fields in which I live.

Whirling together

When you spin during this exercise, be careful. Follow your body. Go only as quickly as you feel comfortable. Begin very slowly and notice all the various experiences. You can put your left foot in one spot and kind of pivot around it with your right. As you spin, move only to the point *just before* dizziness occurs. At that moment of slight disorientation, your body will teach you about its ability to deal with your relationship situation by its movements and the fantasies that occur. Many speak of how the earth or the universe moves them. This exercise may reveal your connection to the universe, that is, your big U.

You can do this exercise on relationships alone, in twos, threes, or as a community (further in the book I will discuss how to do this exercise in teams and with large communities). Circle dancing with others has always been a way of creating community. The method I am suggesting is tailored for relationships. As noted, you can do this alone, but it is best if you do this with a friend or partner(s).

Are you ready?

First, note any areas of interest, projects, problems, or difficulties in a relationship with someone you want to know better, meet, or renew your connection with. The person need not be present for the first part of this work, but at some point, it is important to spin together, as I will shortly describe.

If you are with someone else: each of you moves off to one side, each to her or his own inner space, to find the parallel worlds of the relationship. Take one hand and move it toward (your imagination of) the other person in relationship. As you move your hand slowly toward that relationship, notice two or three parallel worlds that arise. Make notes about them and find their directions. Feel each and just note their directions. You don't need to walk the directions at this point.

Now spin and dance and find your big U by putting your left foot in the center and keeping it there as you let your right foot pivot around it like a compass. As you move, try to feel the universe turning you in such a way and at a rate that you feel well. Use lucid attention until you are almost dizzy—then note any altered experiences that arise, continuing to move until you feel you have found the right rhythm and experience and story. Let a story unfold from these experiences. As you did before, sketch the energy of this story and name it.

Before interacting with your partner, use the big U movement and story to explore the various parallel worlds of the relationship. While staying in the experience of spinning and moving and storytelling, feel and explore the various directions of the relationship. I can't tell you how to do this exactly. If you allow yourself to move and stay within the feeling of the story, when you ponder the directions of the relationships, your body will explain things to you in a way that suits you. Please make notes about your insights immediately afterwards.

When you and your partner(s) are both ready, don't just talk and share your experiences together; let the universe move you as individuals. Spin and dance together! Share your stories briefly while still moving. Continue on with your movements at the same time—follow her or his spin dance experience. Follow your own body and notice how your movements approach and retreat from the other. Follow your own big U as it teaches you how it interacts, merges, or moves independently of the other. This process cannot be described exactly because it is a combination of your body feeling and the sense of the other. Simply know that you are dancing with your big U—with life itself—and with the other(s) as well (Figure 19.5).

The relationship of you and your big U to the universe will inform you about how to find your final dance together. Stay sober and lucid while moving. Your body will know when a final pattern seems to emerge. At that point, still while dancing this pattern, allow a story to emerge between the two of you. This time you will be storytelling with the other person. You are both moving and talking together. One of you might say, for example, "Once upon

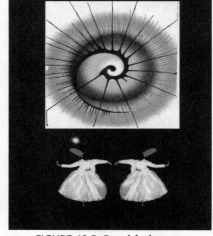

FIGURE 19.5 **Dervish dancers**

a time . . ." and the other adds, ". . . there was a forest." And so on. Your joint story may put both of your big U stories or myths together. This relationship story may be the core of your friendship.

At another point in time, or now, if you are both interested, you might discuss how that relationship dance pattern and the story that emerged want to go on. What task does that story suggest for your relationship together? What does it imply about the relationship gifts and problems? If yours is a long-term relationship, ask if what happened in the dance appeared in your first experiences and dreams in the relationship.

Relationship is a dance. Everyone's dance is different; no one form will ever be enough to describe relationships. Some dances are wild, some are gentle, some loving, some feisty. Some of the relationship dances I have seen were so slow, the people barely moved; others were fast and wild. Some dances used independent movement processes, whereas others totally merged into one form, one movement.

FIGURE 19.6
Flying bird

When I danced with Amy, she told me that the mythic description arising from her spinning was that of a bird, flying freely (Figure 19.6). When I spun, my story focused on the movements of the sea. Together, we danced our individual patterns, until they flowed together and ended forming what we felt was a boat. Facing each other, we leaned backward while supporting each other with our outstretched arms (Figure 19.7). The story that emerged was that of a boat on the sea, rocking back and forth. In between our outstretched arms, other people could board our boat.

The final patterns are superpositions of two movement processes: That boat was a superposition of her wings and my experience of the sea. Together we became a boat on the sea. However, no description of such processes can suffice. You must try it to understand.

FIGURE 19.7 **Leaning back and holding hands**

Like all the patterns and insights that emerge, these dances are sand paintings. See them, recognize the patterns emerging, and use them to solve problems between individuals and in the world, if you are so drawn. Then let the patterns go. Remember, the many sand painters from around the world agree that the sand panting is "where the gods come and come," to borrow a Navajo description. Sit in the sand painting of the dance, experience the earth, and re-create the experience again the next day. Experiencing the process, not just a static state, is the point.

Do your second training and learn to shape-shift to relate to the infinite. When you have questions, let the shamans spin. The dance is a big U, an altered state of consciousness, a vector, a myth, a teacher, and an advisor about the future. Perhaps it created us to do its work? This is how I understand Rumi's poem, quoted in the beginning of this chapter:

When living itself becomes the friend,
Lovers disappear!

▷ Things to Consider

- To find your relationship myth, dance together.

- The second training in relationships is learning to spin.

- Relationship dances are sand paintings.

- Use the patterns that emerge, then let them go and find them again.

Part IV

Eldership and World Paths

CHAPTER 20

The Group's Wisdom

To him who holds in his hands the Great Image (of the invisible
Tao), the whole world repairs. Men resort to him, and receive no
hurt, but (find) rest, peace, and the feeling of ease.
Music and dainties will make the passing guest stop (for a time).
But though the Tao as it comes from the mouth, seems insipid and has
no flavour, though it seems not worth being looked at or listened to,
the use of it is inexhaustible.
—Lao Tse[1]

The *Tao Te Ching* is right. Merely talking about the Tao—or about aspects
of it, like the big U—seems insipid relative to experiencing it. Yet in any
community she who gains access to her big U creates something more
exciting than peace. As the Tao Te Ching says, under these special circumstances, things roll along with music. Others join the path.

However, judging from my experience with organizations of all
sorts, with families, teams, cities, and nations, the little u directs and
constantly clashes and bugs others. To be deeply democratic, we had
better find a way to affirm the little u—all of them! The laws of physics
imply the need for diversity; we have different atomic elements, different vectors behind the particles composing our atoms. Psychology is
the same. We need to affirm diversity. But deep democracy implies that

to affirm diversity, you have to have a metaposition. That metaposition is the big U; it can turn any organization into a community.[2]

The world needs elders who seek the big U and do not forget the importance of the little u's. The lessons of this book can be condensed into one injunction: Find and follow the organizational sand painting, the blueprint that includes everything. When we don't, nature predicts that anything an individual or business marginalizes will react and undo whatever the organization wishes to do. Nature insists upon all histories, all paths, and peoples.

World problems

Most of our little u's oppose diversity; that is why all our groups, teams, organizations, and nations prefer popularity to negative feedback, wealth to poverty, and ambition over laziness. From the viewpoint of the big U, these little u consensus-reality directions are all important because they relativize one another and make discovery of the big U so interesting. Furthermore, without the little u's, we might not have any sense of the backward and forward directions in space and time. Whether we profess democracy or not, all of us—our nations, businesses, and organizations—agree on one point: Hold on to identity and avoid or marginalize diversity in ourselves, teams, and whole groups. Yet, despite this aversion to diversity, all of us dream of that world or of a spiritual leader who will care for all.

Our world has at least several easily identifiable problems:

- *Bitter conflict.* Our one-sidedness leaves us surprised when another side pops up to disturb us. This side may appear as the "others," or as the earth and fate herself in the form of a flood, earthquake, or other natural disaster.
- *Inadequate global theory.* Our one-sidedness also leaves us without a global theory that joins people with each other and with the cosmos.
- *Unequipped elders.* Even if we had a global theory, we would need elders to lead us in practicing it. This book has been an attempt to create such a theory and a suggested eldership training.

We need a global theory that is based in first-level training methods to learn the needed skills, and a second-level training to use those skills. Regardless of the methods and theories we apply, without the second training, our efforts to change the world will amount to nothing more than compassionless marginalization and oppression.

Death of the organization, life of the community

Every organizational problem is individual as far as *content* is concerned. But the *process* related to problems seems generic. Any problem indicates the need for the big U because from its viewpoint, what the little u calls a problem is really a marginalized path, a backlight.[3] Thus, organizations fearing financial problems or conflicts challenge all of us to remember the U of ourselves and organizations. Uncertainty due to change, whether outside or inside the organization, is natural and normal, and can be relieved by some form of fluidity training focused on discovering, exploring, and walking even the troublesome vectors. A group that seeks and finds its main path, its U, will function as a community team that is carried by friendship and inspiration. U is the deepest reason for being; it is the group's real mission. From the U's viewpoint, the fear of, or apparent demise of, a group becomes an opportunity for rebirth. But this ideal itself is but a point in a moving river. Like individuals, groups must fear their fate in relation to others and fight for life before dropping those little u views to explore viewpoints that put them in touch with the overarching elder of the inter-organizational process, the big U.

Whatever we do as individuals, everyone who is now living will be dead in about 120 years. Organizations may live for shorter or longer periods of time, but until now, none is immortal. However, the vectors that move us exist in other time dimensions. The U behind the vision promoting communities and organizations may be perennial, though their people and outer forms change.

Defining organizations

Let's define an organization as a group of people identified by a common purpose or shared interest—like a business. Each organization is characterized by consensus-reality structures such as its history, identified purpose, networking method, rules, rankings, and management policies.

Organizations usually do not identify with their dreamland or essence structure, yet all organizations have them. In contrast to the specific consensus-reality nature of organizations, the dreamlike structures and associated social feelings and processes not only create but also disturb the community. The organization's social or feeling atmosphere is a field created, in part, by the relationship between roles and ghost roles (that is, roles spoken about but not identified with, "the others"). Just as individuals dream about themselves and others, the roles of a group consist of the parts with which it identifies and the "others."

I have devoted other books to a discussion of community processes, so I will be brief here. I have sketched various dreamland roles (Figure 20.1)—a dominant figure, usually the boss, mayor, or CEO. Then there are "the others," unsavory figures that most of us avoid—a criminal or thief, for example. These are the main and backlight vectors into which all individuals slip, but which are essentially nonlocal, shared experiences that can be found in every community.

FIGURE 20.1 **Community.** The big U can't be seen directly in essence. It is a kind of hidden vision, center, sum, and background "pilot wave" behind the overt roles (the "boss") and ghost roles (the "thief") into which we get pulled.

All groups speak of the (roles of) good and bad people or events, the future and the past, the oppressor and the oppressed. These roles and ghosts are like masks floating in the air, waiting to be acted out. At one time or another, we all identify ourselves and others as one of these masks, usually forgetting that roles are both real *and* imaginary. Native

Americans and aboriginal people everywhere were wiser about the ghosts and roles; they put on masks and shape-shifted, dancing to express the different animals and earth spirits moving their communities. Although today most roles and ghosts are marginalized, they still require our attention. Whenever we give parties, roles should always have a place to dance, whether literally or figuratively. People come and go, but roles are time-spirits: they change slowly over long periods of time.

The essence of any organization has as many names as there are cultures. Earlier people may have referred to this essence or big U as the *genie*, the spirit of a given place or clan. The *I Ching* speaks of the *well*, saying, "The town can be changed, but not the well," not the source of life. In precolonial times, communities danced their ghosts and may have been closer to the well, to their deep sources. My idea that businesses are organized by the big U, or by Bohm's concept of the pilot wave, uses other metaphors for these wells or genies that nourish and guide us. My main experience of organizational essences today is the U as a path—as the Way.

I have sketched the essence of organizations as a wave-like and vector form underneath the various faces (Figure 20.1). Though the big U can be thought of as a group's vision or purpose, the deepest U processes are ineffable and cannot be easily formulated. Even the stated purpose or vision of an organization is rarely its real U. This discrepancy may be why supposed visions can be as irritating as inspiring. For example, merely saying you are interested in democracy does not ensure that you are democratic. (Not, at least, in the sense of deep democracy.)

The U as a healer

To support sustainable businesses, organizational theory must include all of its consensus-reality structures *as well as* dreamland and big U experiences. This is easier said than done in public situations because the U is far more than a cognitive idea. To comprehend it to any degree—to realize the meaning of the sum of all the organization's consensus-reality and dreamland experiences—requires lucidity and some kind of second training. That sum, like the superposition of dreamland roles or ghosts, is an earth-based directional path; it is a U feeling. We need the U to help us heal in the sense of resolving our splits and rifts. Difficult as it is to describe the U, it is nevertheless an immense power—the kind of thing that attracts us to some communities and makes us hope that our highest dreams will be fulfilled. Though we usually expect others to model that U, everyone's effort and awareness are needed to actualize it. For most purposes, however, it would be a help if even one person in a hundred could actualize the U. Because of the U's power, that one person, even without much social rank, can be helpful. Think, for example, of Joan of Arc. That young maid of Orleans listened to the voice of St. Michael and led France to survive impossible situations.

You can get to the U through quantum theory, dreams, spiritual beliefs, contemplation, spinning, or using the walking meditations I have introduced in this book. In times of great trouble, the big U emerges spontaneously as a peak and healing vision, such as the visions of Black Elk.[4] (I will explore those visions more in the next chapter.) At the end of this chapter, I suggest how doing an Observer/The Observed exercise can help you find the organizational blueprint.

In rare cases, the name of the organization gives us a hint about its big U. This reminds me of Naropa, a large American Buddhist University in the United States for whom Amy and I worked some time ago. We studied Naropa's organization and discovered that the university's founder, Chögyam Trungpa Rinpoche, had named the school after a legendary figure who decided to spend his life seeking his teacher, Tilopa. Wherever Naropa turned to find his teacher, he ran into trouble—robbed one time, beaten another. Finally, in the last moments of his life, as Naropa prepared to commit suicide, Tilopa his teacher appeared as a blue spirit and enlightened his pupil by telling him that he, Tilopa, had been behind all the apparent problems Naropa had met along the way. In this way Tilopa saved Naropa's life and enlightened him.

For Amy and me, the essence of this story is this: what seems like a difficulty is actually a teacher in disguise. The essence or big U of this legend might be useful for many individuals and organizations. On the path of life, we can only meet our teacher. In any case, we used that big U story; it was a helpful and powerful ally. Simple as such ideas may seem, they are powerful enough to create whole institutions, organize them, and in times of need, resolve tensions. The U of organizations does not really *do* things, but rather carries them by inspiring those involved.

The facilitator's preparation

Finding the big U of Naropa University was relatively simple. You can find and use the vectors of any organization by determining its essence, its U and dreamlike direction. The U is the essence and the sum of all the dreamland figures, all the real people, animals, and material aspects associated with the community.

Facilitating your own community, your own culture, town, or world while being part of it is paradoxical. After all, how can you be both a part and the whole at the same time? My answer is that we are both part and all-parts or whole. We are all capable of a kind of aikido, Ba Kua Chang, and dervish dancing. The purpose of the combined first and second trainings is to allow and encourage you to appreciate your everyday self and the little u of others. In the first training, we learn about ghosts and roles, edges and hotspots, and discover the group's blueprint and center.[5] The second training focuses on using the big U awareness as a metaskill to facilitate tensions by flowing with and between parts, supporting each as if they were part of the organization's zigzag process wisdom. Of course, all such work must be adapted to the particular situation and culture.

In this exercise I will use a second-level training exercise based upon the observer/observed polarity discussed earlier in the book. This exercise is relatively easy and can be done rapidly, both before and during organizational interactions.

1. *Think about a group you would like to help.* Remember, you are a member of the world community, the universe of all beings, national communities, city, cultural, and family groups. You may be part of a business or sports group. Choose one of these groups or organizations and we shall focus on trying to facilitate their scene. After you have chosen one you want to know

more about, just think about the group's members. Who are they, where are they, what do they do? Where are they?

2. Relax, and while thinking about those group members, let your eyes close and pretend that, as they open, you can see the group again. What catches your attention about that community in the moment? Is it something or someone? Is it known or something you don't really want to know too much about? If there are several things, let your deepest mind choose on which to focus. Whatever it is, write it down. Call that the *observed*.

3. Now ask yourself, *Who is the observer of that community?* What part of you needed to see that particular flirt? Don't be self-critical; just notice this part of yourself and make a record of the name of it. Call this part the *observer*. Now add together the "observed flirt" and the observer. When you are ready, mark a starting point * (Figure 20.2). Stand and let your body

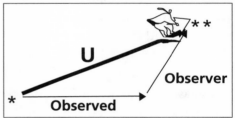

FIGURE 20.2 The big U path comes from the sum of the observer and the observed.

and the earth tell you in which direction that observed flirt goes. From the end of that line or arrow, remember the observer in you and let the earth and your body move you a few steps in the direction associated with that observed. Mark the spot on which you are standing, **.

4. Finally, with your most sentient mind return to the beginning * and walk to the end point **. Walk that U line until you know the meaning of its direction and path. Develop your path awareness and walk that U line until you begin to feel its earth-based spirit, the path of that group, carrying you. Walk until you know that U line as something moving you, at the same time, as the group's path. Imagine using this path, or rather feeling it as you facilitate the group and help it realize its potential as a community.

Working with violence

I used this exercise with a large group of which I am part. That group's conflict situation is very common, and so I will discuss it without giving many personal details about the organization.

Some time ago, the CEO of a large organization asked me for help with a potentially violent situation. At first I was uncertain I could help, because I am a member of the group myself. The CEO brushed aside my hesitations, however, and launched forward to describe the situation: A section of the organization was angry and threatening to be violent. They were the "attackers." They felt that the CEO and the rest of the management were neglectful and unaware of their rank and privileges.

The Observed. Before the meeting they had invited me to facilitate, I used the observer/observed method to prepare myself. Alone, I meditated on the organization. The part that flirted with me in the moment of my meditation was the CEO—it upset me to realize that he repelled me. And although John F. Kennedy's philosophy makes sense to me, it irritated me when the CEO insisted that "people should not ask what they can get, but should say what they can give the group." Unless it is wielded with great sensitivity, this philosophy can marginalize many people.

The Observer. When I pondered who in me was observing that CEO, the answer was immediate. The observer was the everyday person in *me* who feels marginalized! In a split second I realized, "Oh, oh! I have the same problem as the group itself!" On one side is my human everyday self with its ordinary needs, and on the other hand, I am the CEO marginalizing some of my needs for the benefit of others. I got nervous, realizing that the CEO and attacker are all mine—rather, they are nonlocal ghosts in me and in that organization. My own childhood abuse stories were coming back!

The Sum. I went on and added the vectors that addressed the concerns of the CEO and the Observer. The CEO went toward Washington, D.C.—that is, southeast from Portland, Oregon (Figure 20.3). The observer went to the East Coast of the United States, where I grew up. That direction is associated with the Statue of Liberty for me. (For my family, that statue has always been associated with a sense of freedom.)

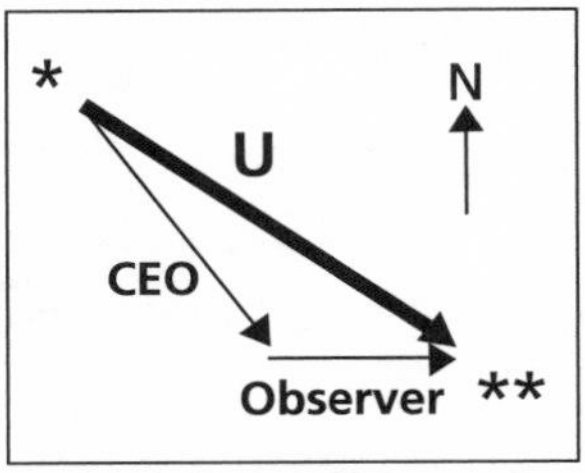

The overall or U path went to Kenya. As I walked there, I felt moved by the memory of my experiences in Kenya with Amy. I felt a kind of shamanistic trance in which I was contained by a heartful community experience.

FIGURE 20.3 **Group U as Kenya**

I felt so well walking that U path that I could hardly wait to meet with members of that organization. I felt empathetic not only with the marginalized people, but also with the CEO and his Kennedyesque goals! When I actually met with that organization during their conference, however, I was nervous at first. So I recalled my U, the warm-hearted deep community experiences in Kenya. As we began the large group process together, I closed my eyes for a moment and felt something drawing me towards the shamans in Kenya. I imagined and briefly spoke out loud about how I myself was both the CEO and the attackers—they were all me. I could or would not have normally done this; perhaps my own and the group field allowed it.

In any case, this act seemed to shorten and ease that large group process. A very tense atmosphere had characterized the beginning of the process. After I spoke, people were sympathetic to me. Even those who had been arguing stopped for a moment. "You poor man," they said. "It must be hard to have all those terrible inner conflicts." They did not realize at first that I was talking about *them*! Instead, they became interested in giving me hints about how to resolve *my* inner conflicts. After hearing their recommendations, I told them I was experiencing my self as the group, and the group as me. To my surprise everyone became quiet. Then they broke the stillness with laughter. To make the story brief, the tension in the atmosphere quickly dissipated and was replaced by a warm feeling of community. It was almost magical. Without a cognitive discussion about what had occurred, at that point everyone simply agreed that there had been enough anger. There was no sense in arguing any more, and everyone sat down to work things out.

Your work

If you got to the U of the community in this exercise, you too probably know that both the observer and the observed are you as well as the group. Your inner work is preparation for your outer work. In many ways, you are the world because of the nonlocality of parallel worlds: the observer and the observed, the dreamer and the dreamed. Finding the U will help you step out of the hold of the little u, out of everyday time and space in order to grasp the whole—within yourself—and then take that larger view back to the group. The U is a kind of energy that does the rest.

Perhaps the *Tao Te Ching* quoted in the beginning of this chapter says it best: "To him who holds in his hands the Great Image (of the invisible Tao), *the whole world repairs.*"

▷ Things to Consider

- The world is missing a global theory and elders to actualize it.

- To help an organization, find its blueprint and the big U.

- If you use that U, organizations become communities.

CHAPTER 21

The Way of Black Elk

Ultimately, you must forget about technique.
The further you progress,
the fewer teachings there are.
The Great Path is really No Path.
—Morihei Ueshiba[1]

The most useful idea I know for dealing with political and organizational problems is to find the group's design, the shared direction I have been calling the U path. When you have found it, it is sometimes easier to embody than speak about. As the great Japanese martial artist Ueshiba says, it is at once The Great Path and no path at all. Training uses methods, but the point is the experience. Community paths are mysterious, ineffable, difficult to express. When we find the path, it is noetic—knowing and wise. Yet because it is transient, we easily lose track of it. It is ours and everyone's—it is nonlocal, appearing anywhere at any time. Within the context of a given organizational situation, the community U is a peak experience. We feel carried by it. It is the stuff of myths and fairy tales, sand paintings and meditations, visions and vectors.

Community as a totem pole

Perhaps children know the U best. They seem freer to dream it. The following Haida tale of the first totem pole reveals this dream aspect of the community's core.[2]

Once upon a time the young boy Sta-th and his father paddled their canoe out to sea to fish. Suddenly the boy saw an amazing image in the water. The parent and child both looked into the sea and saw a picture of their community. This picture was just the same as their everyday community, but with one additional element: a tall pole created from a tree, into which was carved many figures—a great bear at the bottom, and salmon, fox, and eagles at the top of the pole. They returned to their island and shared their vision with their people. Eventually the Haida built their first totem pole (Figure 21.1).[3]

FIGURE 21.1 **The first totem pole**[4]

There are several important elements in this story.

The child. It was a child who first saw the vision. The Haida were happy to hear of the vision; they sang and danced all night until the sun came up in the morning.

The times. In real life, however, the consensus-reality times (not described in this tale) are more complex. Like all First Nation peoples, over the past several hundred years the Haida have suffered greatly from oppressive colonial policies enforcing the domination of mainstream European religion and culture. From what I have heard, the totem pole tradition is several hundred years old. Such symbols of the big U occur at a time when communities are threatened, at a time when the Haida are trying to relocate their culture and their roots. Just as individuals may receive healing dreams when life is threatened, communities receive great visions on the brink of death.

Superposition. In the story the people and their community existed, but not the pole. The totem pole is a literal sum of many dreamland figures superposed upon one another: the great bear at bottom, then the salmon, fox, and eagles on top. Some of the Haida told me that the tops of poles—the lookouts—were once imagined to watch over and care for their families, clans, and communities. Rising high above the people, the wooden pole watches over the people fishing at sea and the folks on land. Though there are many figures on the pole, it is made of one tree. As such, the pole is a symbol of the big U's caring, superposition, and watchful awareness over all beings.[5]

Black Elk's vision

At the age of nine Black Elk received his famous visions for a healing community of the Oglala Sioux. The Sioux lived throughout the Great Plains of North America until they were exiled to the Pine Ridge reservation in South Dakota.[6] In *Black Elk Speaks* the Sioux elder begins with a description of the powers behind everything: the "four corners of the universe"—north, south, east and west—which Black Elk claims are really one spirit. These directions, furthermore, are "grandfathers" whom Black Elk needed because, as he said, "nothing can be done by a man alone."[7]

These "powers of the world" gave the nine-year-old Black Elk the gift of a special vision: the "grandfathers," the nation's hoop. They said to Black Elk, "Behold a nation; it is yours." And a voice said, "Behold, they have given you the center of the nation's hoop to make it live." And herein, said the visionary, lies the "holy man's duty":

> To restore the nation,
> to nourish the nation,
> to make the nation live,
> to make it leaf, blossom, and flourish,
> to make the nation walk in a sacred manner,

to make the nation walk "in a manner pleasing to the Powers,"
to help the nation "go back into the sacred hoop
and find the good red road, the shielding tree."[8]

Black Elk reminds us of the meaning of eldership. He says that to bring the people and culture back to life, we must walk and find the "red path"—a symbol for the ancient spiritual tradition of sensing and following earth-based directions, the four corners of the universe, the grandfathers. The sentient earth's awareness was his personal teacher and community guide showing him what to do. Take "the center of the nation's hoop" and help the nation "walk" its path, that is, "walk in a sacred manner . . . in a manner pleasing to the Powers."

The mythic Haida child's water vision and Black Elk's dream remind us of earth-based awareness, of geometry, of wisdom from our aboriginal sisters and brothers, of the aboriginal nature in those of us who are not aboriginal. When I recently reread Black Elk, I realized that in a small way I was hoping to understand and renew my own and everyone's relationship to the earth's powers as the center of our nations. Once you know and feel the big U of a community, you know the earth, the common ground shared by all. In principle, the big U will teach you what you need to know to work with organizations, with the world.

The second training in organizational work

Vector work in combination with group process skills (described in *Deep Democracy of Open Forums*) has been helpful to us in working with aboriginal communities, the military, businesses, religious groups, high schools and universities, government groups, athletic teams, and high-tech laboratories.[9] I described new first-training skills in the last chapter. To these I would add all the inner work and relationship methods of this book. Remember to walk the main group experiences and the various earth-based directions associated with people and communities.

But these various methods are applied best with the big U. There is no one way to do the second training or learn how to find the big U. Perhaps it is something one grows into, at least for brief periods of time.

Just as there are many paths to the top of a mountain, any second training method that enables one to be partially detached from the tensions of a group and follow a path that can be shared is important. Meditation, inner work, walking vectors, spinning to know your own big U, compassion for all directions—these are all helpful. The second training is as important as first-training skills because these are difficult to use in the midst of extreme inner and organizational tensions. When you feel afraid and timid, insecure or uncertain, a greater power is needed than the consensus-reality powers of people and institutions you must deal with. That is why the bottom line of community work is, to use Black Elk's phrase, following the four corners of the universe.

Earlier I discussed the big U's compassion as more than just a conscious attitude, but as a second-level training experience. For compassion means much more than merely being nice. Compassion involves openness to the earth as a directional guide—which in turn allows you to zigzag, to go deeply into one direction and then sentiently and deeply explore another. Using the U's sentient awareness makes group processes feel safer as viewpoints become possibilities in the larger scheme of things. Compassion lets you zigzag and sniff out all paths, in Feynman's words. Remember the teachings of the shaman don Juan. Temporarily relax your personal history, and be dreamed.

Far from being a task, community work can also be a peak experience. In a way every big U experience is a peak experience, because it is a way of least action, the easiest way through difficult times. It is a path—which, as Ueshiba says, is really no path at all. It is rather an earth-guided, dreamlike vector through real and imaginary spaces and times. It is a wave and song experience. Find and sing it when you are alone, and in the midst of community.

> *Then a song of power came to me*
> *and I sang it there in the midst of that terrible place where I was . . .*
> *A good nation I will make live.*[10]

After reading Black Elk's words, I realized that by sharing his culture's sacred visions, he was creating a new tradition. By telling us about that power that brings nations to life, he not only hoped to preserve his visions so they might help his own people, but all peoples. "My story," he said, "is the story of all life."

▷ Things to Consider

- When the community is endangered, the big U appears to children who can look into the water.

- The big U is a totem pole, one tree with many spirits.

- The community's U is the voice of the four grandparents.

- The U is the story of life; it sings, dances, and renews community.

CHAPTER 22

Conclusion: The Universe's Mother

There was something nebulous existing
Born before heaven and earth.
Silent, empty,
Standing alone, altering not
Moving cyclically without becoming exhausted
Which may be called the mother of all under heaven.
—Lao Tse[1]

Today I know that whatever is possible, it is actually occurring in our lives, dreams, and on this magical earth. The whole of us, that U, is the sum of all these occurrences. Far from being a static experience, this U is the wisdom and guidance behind what seems to be the madness of life. That U is a zigzagging dancer who values each occurrence. In the quiet of the night, that U is indistinguishable from the earth's voice, showing us when to turn this way or that way. I'll never forget to listen to the grandparents, the East, South, West, and North.

Looking backward over the course of writing this book, I sense that something unknown led or pushed me through various zigzags, through various chapters. These are paths I have walked with you, sniffing each one to find the way. Now, at the end of the book, I just walked them as paths again, experiencing each of them, and finding the U (Figure 22.1).

To start, I meditated on and walked my original motivations: my interest in the future of psychology and its intimate relationship to physics and aboriginal wisdom, especially Native American rituals. Then, wondering how I could ever convey the idea of earth guidance to general readers, I found many inner

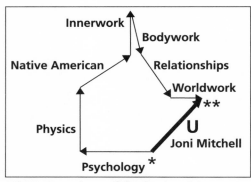

FIGURE 22.1 **The U of this book and its connection with Joni Mitchell's "The Circle Game"**

work exercises from my dreams to help. The feeling of inner work goes to the North Pole, the world of solitude and oneness with the universe. This felt too far from people, and thinking of this book's readers helped me turn toward the south, into the worlds of body work and relationships. You moved me to apply the fundamental sentient awareness principles to friendship. The resulting relationship chapters led me to the power of the shamans we met in Africa. Spinning alone is amazing, but together with another person brings the kind of hope you only find in dreams.

I then wondered, what is the meaning of inner work, health, or a good relationship if you must both die because of war? The earth moved me once again to re-explore worldwork, this time using vectors. I was shocked to realize that behind what might seem like hell is a peak experience trying to restructure the everyday world of organizations. I was thrilled to notice in my seminars around the world that even the most extroverted organizational executives and social activists were interested in spinning themselves into connection with gravity—experiences they could then use with groups. When I walked this book's worldwork vector, it pointed east toward New York. Now walking in that direction I can feel the optimism of the rising sun. Why? I wanted to integrate psychology and physics, worldwork and Native American spirituality, Black Elk's four grandparents and martial arts.

Now I am standing at the end of the worldwork arrow, **. I'll go back to my beginning point *, then travel straight as a bird flies to the end **. Experiencing the U line is very irrational. What will I find as the sum of all these chapters and ideas? The U moves out toward north-central Canada, the arctic North Pole. What I suddenly realize is that this vector was the same as my wife's (see Chapter 10). Amy's big U for the musical piece she was working on went with Joni Mitchell into Canada's deep north. I think of Joni and recall a lyric of hers: "And the seasons, they go round and round."

As I hum and then sing "The Circle Game" aloud, I begin to realize that the song expresses my interest in nature, in the periodic psychological forces of change, in the physics of spinning, time, and direction. The subtle, quiet northern remoteness of that song reminds me of Native American and aboriginal earth-based spirituality—the sense behind the quantum compass. Joni Mitchell's "Circle Game" is a U that gives me a feeling that everything is connected. Spirits, people, and particles are all exploring paths, moving according to an earth-based yet grand cosmic blueprint that is out of sight.

Answer to Einstein

Joni Mitchell reminds me of Einstein's cosmos. I hear Einstein wondering about its pattern: "I want to know God," he said. "The rest are details." And I hear myself answer, "Albert, God is the sum of all the details." God is far out there, in the unimaginable details of this and other universes, but at the same time, God appears as our lucid, sentient path awareness. God is not just something to understand, but something you can feel, the pull of a star in the nighttime sky, the inexplicable impulse to go this way or that.

What Einstein called God, Jung called the unconscious, Lao Tse named the Way, the "Tao that can't be said." Native peoples feel the sentient earth or Great Spirit. Buddhists speak of original nature or Buddha mind. David Bohm thought of it as the pilot wave. The names we use for this noetic intelligence and resulting mathematical expression depend upon our culture, the times, and the moods we are in.

Leibniz called it the *vis viva*, the force of life. In the middle of the night, my body feels it as sentient awareness. In meditation or dreamlike states, the body knows the big U as that long sought-after sense of being carried, as a ship on waves at sea. After I know the U, everything seems right; without it, the various zigzags of life seem crazy. I love the crazy wisdom of the Tibetan Buddhist master Trungpa: splash with the water, move with the wind, first this way and that. This U is not a symbol of static wholeness, but a dynamic balance that can be found only with awareness, naïveté, or courage. Sentient experience leads us back and forth with path awareness, moving here and there as in a circle game through the seasons of sunshine and rain—and it all adds up to who we are. When you are linked to that U experience, you don't really zigzag at all. That is the outer viewpoint. From inside the U, you don't really move much. Instead you arrive without going.

But this state never lasts long. This reminds me of the Taoist and her bug I discussed earlier. Unity gives birth to dualities and re-creates the universe and the time and space of everyday reality. Suddenly after the sense of completion, the bug reappears—just when you thought there was a moment of peace. That damn bug makes us begin the sand painting all over again. Without the bug there would be no relativity, no duality, and no awareness. Just when you found the Way, the bug always reverses it. And don't forget backlight, the doubter, consensus reality, and the little u.

The little u complains: "Hey! What do you mean, 'you don't move much and arrive without going'? Wait a minute, not so fast . . . you can't finish yet! That's not the end! . . ."

The seasons go round and round and suddenly you are back again. Endings, like beginnings, are treasured only by consensus reality. Remember the little u; she belongs in the big picture. She says, "What are you talking about? Will it earn me a living?" My answer to her or him is, "I apologize—you don't need to think about that big U. Just do exactly and precisely what you need and want to do right now."

We need that little u. The rest will happen by itself; it must, if it is natural law. Forget about doing anything but your daily work, struggle with yourself and others, curse the unconsciousness of national leaders, enjoy TV, and have a good meal. Without trying, with least action, you'll awaken one night and remember that this life is a stage on which the big U will manifest itself. Then you will know for a minute or two that your everyday self is the potential mother of the universe. That little u is the universe's chance to get born on earth. You sometimes think of yourself as the random child of a meaningless and unknown universe. But from another point of view, you are the universe's mother, giving its directional nature a chance to be realized in everyday life. You can bring the stars to earth. Do that, for yourself and for the rest of us.

Yes, the universe is our mother. And in a self-reflective manner, we can be hers.

APPENDIX 1

Waves and Particles: Quantum Mechanics in a Nutshell

> *It is often stated that of all the theories proposed in this century, the silliest*
> *is quantum theory. Some say that the only thing that quantum theory has*
> *going for it, in fact, is that it is unquestionably correct.*
> —Michio Kaku[1]

A very approximate account of quantum physics for nonscientists sees matter as an unknown something that can be spoken of in terms of little bits of something called *particles*. Every particle has both particle and wavelike behavior. Waves undulate. Where they are intense, you are most likely to locate the associated particle. Wavelengths are amazing: they help determine the velocity/momentum—or "push," so to speak— that a particle can give. The principle of uncertainty tells us that if you locate the particle precisely in space, you lose track of other information, such as its wavelength. On the other hand, if you know the wavelength, you lose track of where the particle is. Measurement of one aspect makes the other indeterminate. An everyday analogy would be the experience of focusing carefully on one subject, and temporarily losing track of any interest in other subjects.

Quantum objects (particles) exist in superposition, a pattern called the *quantum wave function*. This pattern is the sum of many possible states. A particle has many states—or "worlds," according to the "many worlds" theory of quantum mechanics. When you measure a particle or other quantum object, the states (or wave function) collapse and you find only one state. Measurement collapses the wave function of many states into one—the measured state, so to speak. Physicists call that one measured state "real" and try to think of the others as possibilities, some more probable than the others. For physicists, consensus about reality occurs only with measurement.

Where do the other states go upon measurement? Here is where quantum physics borders on psychology and philosophy. Your view (as long as it has measurable conclusions) determines the answer to these big questions. All we can say is that the background to reality is weird—or as Feynman says, absurd. We don't know where matter is exactly located. We don't know where all the states of a particle are located either. They are nonlocal. They are everywhere.

What is my view of quantum theory? I love it. It reminds me of dream theory. The thing that counts most, however, is what works with a given individual, what consensus the individual experiences in relation to the reality you suggest. But the other parts of dreamlike processes that you can't see are also real for many therapists. You may not see these parts today, but they could easily turn up tonight in a dream or tomorrow.

APPENDIX 2

Zero-Point Energy

The pendulum of a clock eventually comes to rest. In quantum physics such an oscillator would not come to *total* rest, but would rather continue to jiggle randomly about its resting point with a small amount of energy—the so-called *zero-point energy*. Although it may not be observable to the naked eye, this jiggling has important consequences in physics: One is the presence of a certain amount of "noise" in a microwave receiver that can never be gotten rid of, no matter how perfect the technology. Physical things like pendulums and fields—like radio waves and light—have this jiggling, a property of incessant fluctuation. You can never get rid of it, even if you have the best vacuum on earth.

Vacuums are no longer possible because they actually jiggle with unseen activity even at absolute zero, the temperature at which all molecular motion is supposed to cease. Exactly how much zero-point energy a vacuum has is unknown. Some cosmologists think that in the beginning, when conditions everywhere were like those inside a black hole, the vacuum energy was high. Supposedly it "tickled" the big bang into occurring. In principle, the vacuum energy should be lower today; however, many think there is plenty around to tap. Some psychologists call this vacuum energy "dreaming" while asleep.

Zero-point energy makes noise unavoidable in electronic instruments, and can also be seen in the Casimir effect, that is, in the forces and pressures of the vacuum. See Appendix 3 for more.

APPENDIX 3

The Casimir Effect: The Force of Nothing

In 1948 the Dutch physicist Hendrik Casimir suggested the presence of a material force based upon the jiggling Heisenberg bit of energy in a vacuum. On zero-point energy "empty space" actually consists of varying jiggling energy and electromagnetic fields. There is no absolute vacuum. In fact, the waves in a supposed vacuum can, in principle, have any frequencies. Physicists can even calculate an average non-zero vacuum wave fluctuation energy of about half of a photon. Casimir thought that if we place two very tiny plates into a vacuum very close together, they would have room between them for short waves to move, but no room for the longer waves. The waves that are kept out will "press" against the two plates, or two mirrors, creating a force, today called the Casimir force, or the force of nothing. This effect of the pressure from oscillating fields was detected experimentally in 1993.

This effect can be imagined as the effect of waves on two boats near each other in the sea. The boats are pushed together by the waves that are too long to fit in between the boats.

In Figure A3.1 you can see that the little wave (with a short length) fits in between the boats (or plates). If two boats are placed at the crest of that little wave, then the longer waves that cannot fit in between the boats, will push on them from the outside and crunch the boats together.

The same thing holds for a quantum vacuum. If you have two mirrors instead of a boat, then the quantum waves of the supposed vacuum that do not fit in between the plates "push" them together.

Recent developments on the Casimir theory by Bernard Haisch and others, described in *Physical Review*, indicate that this "force of

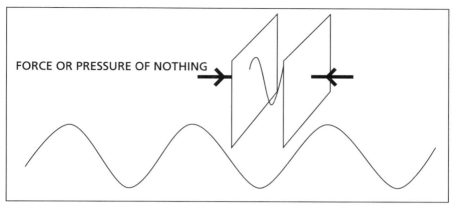

FIGURE A3.1 **Casimir's force of nothing**. Waves come from zero-state vacuum fluctuation. The big wave doesn't fit between plates or mirrors, and because it can't get "into" the little space, it creates a pressure between the mirror plates.

nothing" may be what is behind the force associated with the inertia of all material bodies.[1] If you give something a push, even a ball on the floor, the inertia of the ball resists the push. The inertia of a mass, its gravitational nature, and the general laws of physics have been an enigma until now. According to Haisch, the Casimir force of nothing may lie behind our sense of force. In other words, inertia arises because the invisible background of the universe resists sudden change. Mass and movement are coupled together, indivisible, in Haisch's theory.

Psychologically, the Casimir theory sounds like a specific instance of reflecting on something and marginalizing other things. Marginalizing one energy (or frequency) in favor of another gives us the sense of gravity, pressure, or force. If we are able to move with the various forces and vectors, we feel carried and don't experience a force, per se. Marginalizing creates pressure and force. Marginalization and pressure are interconnected. Because it's natural to marginalize, it's natural to have forces, and the sense of me and not me. The result—what we call consensus reality—is based upon separation, *here* and *there*, *present* and *past*, etc. The Casmir force is a metaphor for the tiny tugs and pulls, attractions and repulsions of which we become aware. Perhaps that force is an aspect of the awareness principle, of the dualistic, relativistic tendency of awareness. Our very nature, the nature of the universe, chooses between vibes or feelings and keeps others out. In a way, the Casmir force may be the subtle pressure we feel that pushes us around, and eventually towards consciousness.

APPENDIX 4

Feynman and Quantum Electrodynamics (QED)

The American physicist Richard Feynman (1918–1988) shared the 1965 Nobel Prize in physics for his development of the theory of quantum electrodynamics, the study of the interaction of light with atoms and their electrons. He contributed to the future of nanotechnology (the study of machines that are one-billionth of an inch big) and the theory of quarks (particles that make up elementary particles, such as protons and electrons), as well as superfluidity (a state of matter in which a substance flows with no resistance).

Feynman got his bachelor's degree from MIT and his doctorate in physics from Princeton under John Wheeler, who mentored many great students (among them Hugh Everett). Feynman's dissertation, "A Principle of Least Action in Quantum Mechanics," was characteristic of the manner in which he used basic principles to solve fundamental problems.

Feynman's work in quantum electrodynamics, which earned him the Nobel Prize, studied how electrons, positrons (particles with the same mass as electrons but opposite in charge), and photons (packets of light energy) interact with one another. Together with the work of others, QED still remains the most accurate physical theory known and is basic to standard thinking in quantum theory.

Feynman invented what are now called the *Feynman diagrams* to demonstrate how elementary particles interact with one another. Feynman diagrams give us an intuitive, space–time approach to particle paths. He suggested thinking of particle paths as moving from one point to another in space and time through regions too small to measure accurately. His method gave rules for calculating the tendencies and probabilities associated with each of a particle's possible paths. By adding all of these tendencies together—and squaring the result—we get the probability of the physical process most likely to happen and be measurable in everyday reality. The present book uses the added tendencies, or quantum wave function, as a metaphor for the big U, our basic and deepest personal and community pattern.

APPENDIX *5*

Gravity

In everyday life we know about gravity because we feel our weight on our feet or on our buttocks when we sit on a chair or the ground. We notice how the tides rise and fall, caused by the gravitational force of the earth and the moon. Gravity organizes the weather by pulling dense cold air down and letting lighter, warmer air stay higher up. Without gravity, all of us and everything else would spin off into space. Gravity is part of the sense we have of being living bodies on earth. Gravity is connected to whatever we call "home." Without gravity, the earth would fly to bits and we would live in outer space.

Gravitation is the force of attraction between all objects that pulls them toward one another. It is a universal force, affecting the largest and smallest objects, all forms of matter, and energy. Gravitation is a very weak force; but for huge bodies like planets, gravity's force can be large. In this way gravity governs the motion of astronomical bodies. Gravity keeps the moon spinning near earth, and it keeps the earth and the other planets in our solar system spinning around the sun. In fact, gravity governs the observable motion of all stars, slowing down expanding sections of the universe because stars and galaxies attract one another. Gravity makes black holes. When a star runs out of fuel needed to keep burning, gravity takes over and compresses the star into a tiny nothing, called a black hole.

Gravitation is the weakest of the four fundamental forces: It is weaker than electromagnetism, weaker than the weak and strong nuclear forces responsible for holding atomic particles together. Gravity is so weak that it has little effect on the composition of atoms. Unlike the other forces, gravity does not rapidly decrease over distance. As a result, unlike the other forces, it reaches great distances. Whereas electromagnetic forces or the forces between particles repel and attract and get weaker as the distance between objects increases, gravity only attracts—plus it maintains its effect over large distances.

Newton came up with a good theory of gravity, and Einstein refined it with his principle of general relativity as a characteristic of space. No one, however, including Einstein, knows what gravity actually is, or knows its relationship to the other forces. My guess is what I see and know for sure: Gravity is an example of deep democracy. All its levels are important. It is both real and dreamlike, something that helps us identify with being on earth, and at the same time, something that never leaves us, even when we are far from this planet. Furthermore, it is the only force that tends to hold all things together, all the time.

APPENDIX 6

William Gilbert's Soul of the Earth

William Gilbert (1544–1603) discovered the properties of the lodestone, the iron magnet. The word *lode* is related to the Old English word for *load*, which originally signified the course or way to go. Gilbert is credited with discovering magnetism. (Some also acknowledge him as an early colonizer, for he gave the European sailors the compass—and consequently the power to explore and conquer.)

Gilbert said in his work *De Magnete* (*On the Magnet*) that magnetism was the soul of the earth.[1] He said that the magnet was something that could teach us how to love the earth again. The lodestone had great powers, he said. "Iron is drawn by the lodestone," Gilbert wrote, "as the bride to the embraces of her spouse." According to Gilbert, behind our sense of direction is love for the earth.

Today biologists know that most animals have a magnetic sensor that allows them to find their way home. People used to think that it was the light of the sun that gave animals direction. Although the sun is one factor creating a sense of direction, animals can also find their way home at night because of their magnetic sensor. For example, if you put something on the bird's head that disturbs the magnetic field around it, the bird will get lost. Take off the disturber, and home the bird goes.

APPENDIX 7

Process Work at a Glance: Applications and Theory

Process work or process-oriented psychology is based upon awareness of change and has a wide spectrum of applications, some of which can be seen in Figure A7.1.

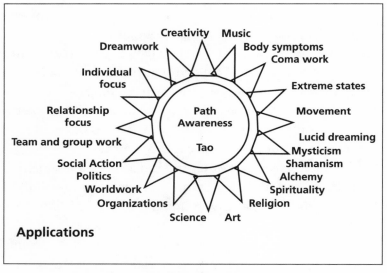

FIGURE A7.1 **Process work applications**

Some process ideas and metaskills updated in this book

Sentient awareness is a subtle, subjective, ineffable, noetic, passive, transient, and nonlocal process.

Awareness is—

Two-in-one, a unity with inherent duality.

Self-reflective, the tendency of two or more mutual observers to behave similarly.

Deeply democratic—it values real, dreamlike, and ineffable events.

A guide for the everyday mind; a multidimensional teacher of the way.

Nonlocal, evanescent, particle-like flirts, waves, and dreamlike pre-signals.

A quantum compass, an earth- or cosmos-based experience of being turned.

Uncertain—the everyday mind is always uncertain about dreamlike realities.

Superpositional—it adds up flirts, parallel worlds, and directions to create the big U.

A bug, sometimes a backlight or oppositional vector, experienced as a problem.

Moody, a force field in which creation, annihilation, and detachment occur.

A zigzag—process wisdom moving through all directions and balanced around myth.

Least action, as the big U, a teleological dreaming tendency that minimizes effort.

If you forget all this, don't worry. Happy birthday must be sung many times . . .

APPENDIX 8

Superposition and Vectors in the *I Ching*

Perhaps the oldest divination procedures known to us today are found in the *I Ching*, or *Book of Changes*. There the Tao of any given moment is represented as a sum of various states or possibilities that have an imaginary or dreamlike character. These states are derived in part by seeing the various results of throwing a coin into the air. In a way, the coin is influenced by the momentary field, or Tao. When the results of each throw are added on top of one another, they form trigrams and or hexagrams, in which digital symbols or numbers (like 0 and 1) are placed upon, or superposed upon, one another. Below you see trigrams or *pa-kua* that are said to be composed of not only "strong" or solid yang lines, but also weaker or dashed yin lines. (In their own way, perhaps the Taoists were the first to discover quantum computing—but that is another story.)

You can think of these diagrams as states of possibility, as basic directions, paths, or Taos (Figure A8.1). Notice that these various Taos are due to the superposition of basic states. Each state is composed of a solid line — or a broken line – –.

FIGURE A8.1 **The Tao as sum of "possibility states" in the *I Ching***

What guides the changes?

The principle of change is governed by the so-called Great Ultimate, or the Tai Chi, pictured as a swirling, spinning yin and yang lines moving about in a circle (Figure A8.2). Some Taoists consider this graphic representation to be the first manifestation of the Tao.

FIGURE A8.2 The empty circle is the Tao that first manifests as the Tai Chi, or the Great Ultimate—the connection between the worlds.

Directional thinking

In Figure A8.3, the "Great Ultimate"—the source of change and revolution in the universe—manifests as tri-grams and directions. Each trigram or state is associated with a particular direction on earth. (Figure A8.4) The Taoists, like most aboriginal peoples, believed that direc-tions had particular meanings.

FIGURE A8.3 **The Great Ultimate (Tai Chi) with trigrams**

The Tao manifested not only in terms of abstract feelings and concepts but feeling-based and earth-based directions as well.

According to the *I Ching,* to find and interpret the Tao for a given situation, not just any one of the trigrams or states is needed, but two trigrams placed upon one another. At left you can see the two trigrams

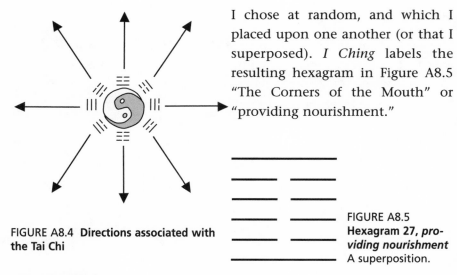

FIGURE A8.4 **Directions associated with the Tai Chi**

I chose at random, and which I placed upon one another (or that I superposed). *I Ching* labels the resulting hexagram in Figure A8.5 "The Corners of the Mouth" or "providing nourishment."

FIGURE A8.5
Hexagram 27, *pro-viding nourishment*
A superposition.

Vector addition

A given Tao of the moment is a sum of trigrams, so that the final Tao—that is, the final direction or path we must take in a given moment—is in principle the sum of directions. In Figure A8.6, I have added the two direction vectors that the ancient Chinese associated with the trigrams of Figure A8.5 to show an overall vector direction, the bold line.

Thus, the Tao—the most likely outcome, course, or way of a given situation—is like the quantum wave function, which is the sum of various vectors. The final bold line would correspond in quantum physics with the most likely possible outcome of a situation with two possibility states.

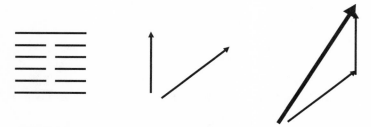

FIGURE A8.6 **(Left to right)** Hexagram of the *I Ching,* trigram directions, and vector addition

The Tao is therefore another name for the big U of a given situation. In some ways, therefore, *Earth-Based Psychology* updates the divinatory approach of ancient Taoism. The *I Ching* suggested thousands of years ago, that the total gestalt of a hexagram, the superpositional form of the hexagram could be used to understand the individual lines. Likewise, I am suggesting that the big U can be used to understand the meaning of individual subvectors. In a way, a hexagram is a type of pilot wave or big U vector that encompasses all its parallel worlds.

APPENDIX 9

Questions about Vector Addition

The original meaning of *vector* comes from the Latin word *vectus*, or *carrier*. Vectors correspond in psychology to the sense of being carried by a body-oriented, earth-based experience in a certain real or imaginary direction. Vector addition, or adding arrows together, as I describe in the text, is derived from something called vector algebra in mathematics.

In mathematics and physics the addition of vectors obeys a symmetry principle; it does not make any difference which vector you add first or last. The result is always the same in vector algebra. In particle physics and quantum electrodynamics, vectors representing the possible directions of particles (or "histories," as Feynman called them) are "bundled" or added in any order that you like.

The fact that it does not matter in what order you add the vectors in vector algebra corresponds to what I call deep democracy; each direction has equal value relative to the others. Feynman said it simply: An electron must "sniff" all the possible paths.

In *Earth-Based Psychology* I have developed a walking meditation based upon our sense of the earth. The calculation so familiar to many scientists and familiar to many aboriginal people may be new for many reading this book for the first time. The mathematical calculations are metaphors for personal subjective experiences we have all had, and which are presaged in Taoism, sandpainting, and many aboriginal traditions. The experience of following the earth—of turning and then adding directions, arrows, or vectors—is at first a body-oriented, noncognitive experience based upon our experience and feeling of the earth. It is natural for many questions to arise.

For example, occasionally the vectors may sometimes add up to zero—especially if the directions reverse themselves (Figure A9.1). This zero does not signify stasis, but a vibratory "almost nothing," even though

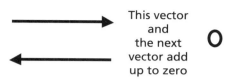

FIGURE A9.1 Sometimes two vectors add up to zero.

the outer situation may not appear to be moving. The point of the walking meditation is just simply standing on that point and letting nature inform you of the meaning of the resulting experience.

In a walking meditation remember that when you add vectors, it is good to try to experience them as horizontal directions on earth. They may be easier to add to begin with; once you are familiar with this procedure, you can use any direction you like, including of course up and down.

Also remember that when you feel pulled somewhere by the earth, you may feel pulled to what others call a real direction such as north, south, east, and west. Or you may be pulled toward something in the space you are presently in, or to a nearby place you imagine. Or you may simply feel something pulling you in one direction or another, without even knowing cognitively what it is. Go there to find out. Trust your body and the experience which arises.

Can you trust your own sense of vectors? Well, yes and no. Let me say first, Don't trust! Usually your rational mind can hardly believe at first that your body knows what it is doing—unless you are very body-oriented and have been practicing communication with nature. To your rational mind I would say this: Don't trust anything until it makes sense to you. Experiment—let your body show you something about the world you may not have known before. Then judge for yourself afterward. That is how to learn about and remember your *Earth-Based Psychology* and your path awareness.

APPENDIX 10

The Big U and Essence Experiences

There are many ways to sense the core or essence of a given experience. Some people can just guess it; others can meditate and feel the seed from which the experience emerged. Others need to express the experience in movement, and then explore that movement in slow motion until their body senses the essence of the experience. The big U is a more graphical method of getting to the essence of experiences.

Consider how the U relates to essence experiences. See the two body experiences or two vectors connected to directions such as hate (#1) and love (#2) (in Figure A10.1). They can be added, as in Part A, to reveal the direction and experience of the big U. In Part A you see the bold line, U, as the vector sum of the two thin arrows, #1 and #2. Part A represents experiences of the vectors #1 and #2 from the viewpoint of the big U.

In part B, the focus is on the subvectors—the little u and its time and space. To the right we identify with #1 (love, say) or #2 (e.g., hate). The big U, the sum vector, is here experienced or intuited indirectly as something that "ties together" the other vectors. However, this tie, the big U, is barely visible because we are focusing on, or identified with, a subvector such as #1. Thus the big U appears at best as a longed-for dream of a healing figure, goddess, or medicine that will cure all things.

In other words, there are at least two basic ways to find the big U, depending upon the focus or identification of a given person's starting point. If someone's identity is ready to explore the big U background, then this person can add vectors by walking their directions (as we have been doing in previous chapters) to finally experience and identify (temporarily, at least) with the inclusivity of the U. The second or

FIGURE A10.1 **Hate and love as vectors**. Left: **U** is experienced as inclusivity. Right: focus begins with #1 or #2 and seeks U as the essence or a common ground.

"essence method" is most useful when the person seems very attached to, or identified mainly with, the little u or another "subvector." In this case, we begin with the identification with that one subvector and seek its essence or common background. Here, focusing on the essence of any one subvector in principle will reveal the big U that ties all the worlds together.

Why does the essence of any subvector reveal a sense of the big U? Because the essence of any one parallel world or emotion of a given situation gives us a sense of the big U of that situation (at least as it appears from the perspective of #1). The essence perspective of #2 might be slightly different from that of #1; however, either perspective of the big U will still be sufficiently close to the U's nonlocal common ground or tie-in characteristics to produce important results. The theoretical principle in the background is that because of nonlocality, the essence of one thing in a system is the essence of everything. The essence of the total gestalt or big U can be found in any of its parts.

APPENDIX 11

Least Action, Kinetic and Potential Energy

In Chapters 11 and 12, we saw that Richard Feynman explained the quantum wave function as the quickest way for light to move through different mediums. Light, he said, was like a lifeguard saving someone in the water, choosing the path of least time or action.   Physicists use the term *action* in many ways.[1] In the law of least action, *action* refers to a mathematical quantity that depends upon the velocity, mass, and distance traveled by an object or particle. Action describes the way energy is carried and used.

For example, if you throw a ball in the air, at first the ball has a lot of movement or kinetic energy because your hand moves fast to throw the ball upward. The ball gains potential energy as it rises higher above the ground because increased height gives the ball increased ability to make a louder bang when it falls on the ground. Potential energy comes from the height (in the gravitational field), or from the increased distance from the center of the earth. At the top of its flight, the ball doesn't move much and therefore has little kinetic or movement energy. However, the ball has most *potential* energy at this top point. And then when it falls again, the ball begins to lose potential energy, which transforms into kinetic energy—or movement energy— just before you either catch it or it hits the ground.

Because energy cannot be created or destroyed, the total energy— that is, the kinetic plus the potential at any point—will always be the same. This constancy of the total energy is referred to as the *conservation of energy*.

Instead of dealing with the sum of energies, least action is concerned with the *difference* between the kinetic and the potential energies.

To calculate the action at each point along the path of the ball, you must subtract potential energy (PE) from the kinetic (or movement) energy (KE). To make the total calculation of action for the ball's path, you must make this subtraction at every point along its path, then add up this value for all points as the ball moves up into the air and back down again (and multiply each increment by time, as is required by the action equation). The answer is the total action.

$$\text{Action} = (\text{KE} - \text{PE}) \times \text{Time}$$

For the ball, a star, or even a little particle, action is essentially determined by KE - PE at every point on its path. The action principle says that paths that minimize action are favored by nature.

Given the amount of time it takes for the ball to reach the place you want it to go, you might think you could throw it higher or lower, faster, or slower. But nature denies your attempts: For a given amount of time available, the law of least action says that the ball will choose and "know" which of the various possibilities to take. The ball will find that single path with least action! Feynman and others speak of the ball—or its counterparts in the quantum world, such as an electron—as if it sniffs out all the paths and chooses the path that requires the least action.

Likewise, the Taoist sniffs out the Tao, to practice not-doing. You and I can now sniff various vectors, and use our earth-based psychology to follow our deepest dreams through time and live more fully on our planet.

ENDNOTES

Part I

1. Erwin Schrödinger, *Science and Humanism* (Cambridge, United Kingdom: Cambridge University Press, 1951), 51.

Chapter 1

1. Carlos Castaneda, *The Fire from Within* (New York: Washington Square Press, 1991), 205–214.
2. Arnold Mindell, *The Shaman's Body: A New Shamanism for Health, Relationships, and Community* (San Francisco: HarperCollins, 1993), 141. This work is an interpretation of don Juan's teachings.
3. See Appendix 4 for more details about Feynman, whose work has been wonderfully explained by MIT professor Edwin Taylor <http:/www.eftaylor.com/>.
4. Richard Feynman, *QED: The Strange Theory of Light and Matter* (Princeton University Press, Princeton, 1985), 10.
5. Arnold Mindell, *Inner Dreambodywork: Working on Yourself Alone* (New York & London: Penguin, 1990).
6. Arnold Mindell, *The Dreambody in Relationships* (New York & London: Penguin, 1987).
7. Arnold Mindell, *The Deep Democracy of Open Forums* (Charlottesville, Virginia: Hampton Roads Publishing, 2004).
8. Arnold Mindell, *Coma: Key to Awakening—Working with the Dreambody near Death* (London: Penguin-Arkana, 1994, 1995).
9. C. G. Jung, *Memories, Dreams, Reflections*, ed. Aniela Jaffe, trans. Clara Winstone and Richard Winston (New York: Vintage Books, 1989), chap. 11.

Chapter 2

1. Michael Shermer, "The Major Unsolved Problem in Biology: Three Books Try to Explain Consciousness" [book review], *Scientific American* (2004), n.p. <http://www.sciam.com/article.cfm?articleID=0009877A-D64E-101A-956483414B7F0000&chanID=sa006&colID=12>.
2. Carlos Castaneda, *The Fire from Within* (New York: Washington Square Press, 1991), 203.
3. Rebecca Solnit, *A Field Guide to Getting Lost* (New York: Viking, 2005), 17. According to Solnit, the Wintu people of California speak of western or eastern hands depending upon their directions. (Thanks to Susan Kocen for this information). Because of the almost universal earth-based intelligence of aboriginal people who worship the sentient earth, it seems likely that this identification of the body with directions is more widespread than presently documented in the literature.
4. Edwin Taylor and John Wheeler, *Exploring Black Holes: An Introduction to General Relativity* (New York: Addison Wesley Longman, 2000). John Wheeler's students included the well-known astrophysicist Kip Thorne, physicist Richard Feynman, and Hugh Everett, the originator of the "many worlds" interpretation of quantum theory.
5. Arnold Mindell, *Quantum Mind: The Edge Between Physics and Psychology* (Portland, Oregon: Lao Tse Press, 2000).
6. Amrit Goswami, with Richard Reed and Maggie Goswami, *The Self-Aware Universe: How Consciousness Creates the Material World* (New York: Tarcher, 1995). Physicist Goswami suggests a similar idea.
7. David Maclagan, *Creation Myths: Man's Introduction to the World* (London: Thames & Hudson, 1977), 56. My sketch comes from the sand painting found here.
8. There is more in the picture than I have represented here. For example, there is a bluebird of happiness and footprints along the rain-path, the three vertical lines that lead to higher worlds. The footprints approach from the east, and this path becomes the yellow pollen sacred path. Each corner of the sand painting represents a given direction.

Chapter 3

1. S. Hameroff, "Funda-mentality: Is the Conscious Mind Subtly Linked to a Basic Level of the Universe?" *Trends in Cognitive Science 2* (1998): 119–124.

2. Thanks to Jiro Isetani of Portland, Oregon, and Kanae Kuwahara of Tokyo for pointing out some of the basic Tao elements to me. Thanks to Ayako Fujisaki of Portland for using her dictionary (Koji-gen) that tells us that the origins of the Chinese character for *Tao* come from the *direction* or the *way* you are headed. (The middle part of the pictogram for Tao means *head* and the rest means *movement of legs*.)

3. Lao Tse, *Tao Te Ching: The Book of Meaning and Life,* trans. Richard Wilhelm (into German) and H. G. Ost-wald (into English) (London: Viking-Penguin-Arkana, 1985). Indeed, the interpretation in terms of awareness of directions and paths is made more likely by considering that the Tai Chi and Tao were originally expressed in terms of directions (discussed in greater detail in Chapter 5; see also Appendix 8). There are many possible translations of Tao, such as Richard Wilhelm's *meaning.* This translation makes sense to me, as the Tao that can be said. But *meaning* tends to divorce the Tao from the earth field and directions.

4. My book *The Deep Democracy of Open Forums* (Charlottesville, Virginia: Hampton Roads Publishing, 2004), offers more on the subject of awareness in organizations.

5. The reader interested in some basic quantum physics should explore Appendices 1–3.

6. Arnold Mindell, *Quantum Mind: The Edge Between Physics and Psychology* (Portland, Oregon: Lao Tse Press, 2000). Though it is true that particles may pop in and out of existence, the time over which they do so is inversely proportional to their energy (or their mass). Another way to state Heisenberg's uncertainty principle is the product of the uncertainty in energy and uncertainty in time must be no less than Planck's constant. So if you get virtual particles popping into existence, they do so for a short time.

7. See Appendix 2 for more about zero-point energy.

8. Stephen Hawking, *A Brief History of Time* (New York: Bantam Books, 1988, 1996).

9. This tiny force may eventually give rise to methods for exploring the hidden dimensions of string theory and clarify unified field theories. According to recent research, this force is connected to the experience of inertia—that is, the reason why a ball placed on a piece of paper remains where it is when the paper is suddenly pulled from under it. Harold Puthoff, along with Bernard Haisch of Lockheed Research and Alfonso Rueda of California State University, connect zero-point vacuum energy to this inertia: B. A. Haisch, A. Rueda, and H. E. Puthoff, "Inertia as a Zero-Point Field Lorentz Force." *Physical Review A* 49 (1994): 678. This research

implies that behind the famous formula defining force in terms of the inertia of mass connected to acceleration (F = ma) is this Casimir force, a force I think of as pressure or force of awareness. In other words, our everyday world appears to be mostly stable and resist sudden movements or acceleration because of that zero-point energy field. (See Appendices 1–3 for more information about the vacuum and the Casimir force.)

10. Michael J. Puett, *To Become a God: Cosmology, Sacrifice, and Self-Divinization in Early China*. Harvard-Yenching Institute Monograph Series, number 57 (Cambridge, Massachusetts: Harvard University Asia Center, 2002), 4.

11. Puett, *To Become a God*, 4. The exact text reads: "Long ago, in the time before there existed Heaven and Earth, there was only figure without form. Obscure, dark, vast, and deep—no one knows its gate. There were two spirits (shen) born together; they aligned Heaven, they oriented Earth. So vast—no one knows its end or limit! So overflowing—no one knows where it stopped! Thereupon, they divided and became yin and yang, separated and became the eight pillars. Hard and soft completed each other, and the myriad things were thereupon formed. The turbid qi became insects and the refined qi became humans."

12. My friend Ayako Fujisaki pointed out that the ancient Japanese people believed that there were bugs inside of our minds that create ideas and feelings. There are many bugs (*mushi*); expressions such as "He/she has the bug" for a bad mood. If you don't like somebody, without any particular reason, you say, "The bug doesn't like her." Feeling depressed or down is expressed as having a "bug of depression."

13. In earlier works, I have referred to bugs as flirts trying to catch our attentions.

Chapter 4

1. In an interview with Brian S. Cohen, "Being in Dreaming: An Introduction to Toltec Sorcery," *Magical Blend Magazine* (April 1992), 35.

2. Arnold Mindell, *Quantum Mind: The Edge Between Physics and Psychology* (Portland, Oregon: Lao Tse Press, 2000). Mathematically, the self-reflecting nature of awareness may be pictured as reflecting (or conjugated) complex numbers. The quantum wave is a complex number; it is partially real and partially imaginary.

3. Mindell, *Quantum Mind*, and Arnold Mindell, *The Quantum Mind and Healing: How to Listen and Respond to Your Body's Symptoms* (Charlottesville, Virginia: Hampton Roads Publishing, 2004). See discussion on John Cramer's transactional interpretation of quantum physics.

4. The mathematics of conjugation in physics reverses the time element in the echo wave.

5. Marie-Louise von Franz, *Number and Time* (Evanston, Illinois: Northwestern University Press, 1974).

6. <http://www.angelsandearthlythings.com/p-9.html>

7. In physics, *nonlocality* refers to what Einstein called "spooky action at a distance." *Nonlocality* is a property of the quantum world in which two states simultaneously collapse upon measurement of one of them. Looking at one state automatically gives you information about the nature of the other state. This phenomenon is the essence of what is called Bell's theorem. Bell took Einstein's philosophical objection to the spookiness of the quantum world and turned it into a testable proposition. Many experiments, such as the two-photon correlation studies performed by the French physicist Alain Aspect and his colleagues in 1982, demonstrated nonlocality. The strong correlations observed in these experiments suggest to most physicists today that we live in a nonlocal universe. In short, what happens right here and at this time could depend upon something next to me or something very far away in space, in time, or both space and time.

8. Physicist David Bohm: "The electron, in so far as it responds to a meaning in its environment, is observing the environment. It is doing exactly what human beings are doing." Rene Weber, *Dialogues with Scientists and Sages* (New York: Routledge & Kegan Paul, 1986), 69.

9. Why don't we focus on lucid experiences all the time? There may be good reasons to not necessarily be sentient about every experience. After all, if you were to notice every little ache and pain as you were crossing the street, you would be hit by a car. Marginalization is a really necessary thing when crossing a street, but it shouldn't be a lifestyle. Marginalizing parts of yourself can depress you. If you marginalize experience too much, it can bug you and become a symptom.

10. For more on how flirts connect with meditation methods, see Arnold Mindell, *Dreaming While Awake: Techniques for 24-Hour Lucid Dreaming* (Charlottesville, Virginia: Hampton Roads Publishing, 2000).

11. John Wheeler was the doctoral supervisor not only of Richard Feynman, but also of Hugh Everett, who assumed that there is a quantum state description of all matter that follows Schrödinger's wave equation. Everett then assumed that universal states were a superposition (a kind of addition) of several, possibly even an infinite number of, identical non-communicating parallel universes.

12. The wave function is a mathematical expression used to describe charac-
    teristics of a particle (such as its speed) as they change over time and
    location. The square of the wave function (i.e., multiplying it by itself)
    describes the probability of finding the particle at a certain point. See
    Appendix 1 for more on quantum theory.
13. Fred Allen Wolf, *Parallel Universes: The Search for Other Worlds* (New York:
    Simon & Schuster, 1989). The author describes parallel worlds in a clear
    and popular style.

Chapter 5

1. Carlos Castaneda, *The Fire from Within* (New York: Washington Square
   Press, 1991), 214.
2. Arnold Mindell, *The Dreammaker's Apprentice: Using Heightened States of
   Consciousness to Interpret Dreams* (Charlottesville, Virginia: Hampton Roads
   Publishing, 2001). This work contains a host of other ways of working
   with dreams. The approach in *Earth-Based Psychology*, however, is new.
3. The idea of adding up our parts or processes came to me while studying
   Richard Feynman's quantum electrodynamics. In later chapters I discuss
   how the central guiding pattern of objects (or their pilot wave, as David
   Bohm terms the quantum wave function) can be found by adding up all
   their various possibility waves or vectors—that is, all their possible tendencies or parts.
4. Likewise, in quantum physics, the quantum wave function and its substates are complex numbers; they are partially real and partially imaginary
   in the mathematical sense.
5. Since 1991 the Max Planck Institute of Psycholinguists of Nijmegen, The
   Netherlands, has employed psychologists, ethnologists, and linguists in
   order to research the manner in which people orient themselves
   (info@ngfg.com). The Aboriginal Gugu Yimithirr people of the northwest
   coast of Australia, for example, don't say, "This is my right-hand pocket
   in my pants or my left-hand pocket." Instead they say, "This is my western
   or eastern pocket." If they turn 180 degrees, the pocket designation
   changes accordingly. In other words, they do not orient themselves
   according to consensual direction relative to the body, left or right. (In
   fact, the terms *left* and *right* do not even exist in something like a third of
   all languages.) Thanks to Max Schupbach for introducing me to the
   Guugu Yimithirr.
6. Bruce Chatwin, *The Songlines* (New York: Penguin, 1987).

7. Ani Williams, "Riding the Celtic Songlines." < http://www.aniwilliams.com/ avalon_songlines.htm>.
8. Philip Rawson and Laszlo Legeza, *Tao: The Chinese Philosophy of Time and Change* (London: Thames & Hudson, 1973). For more on directions and the addition of direction in Taoism, see Appendix 8.
9. Discussed in Chapter 2.
10. For common questions and answers about walking directions, see Appendix 9.

Chapter 6

1. Carlos Castaneda, *The Active Side of Infinity* (New York: Harper Collins, 1998), 260.
2. Arnold Mindell, *Coma: Key to Awakening—Working with the Dreambody near Death* (London: Penguin-Arkana, 1994, 1995).
3. Download and read his account at <http://www.aamindell.net/download/ research/matthias.rtf>.
4. Amy Mindell, *Metaskills: The Spiritual Art of Therapy* (Portland, Oregon: Lao Tse Press, 1995).
5. There is a more thorough explanation of the math behind this quantum-theory rule in Chapters 8 and 9 of my book *Quantum Mind: The Edge Between Physics and Psychology* (Portland, Oregon: Lao Tse Press, 2000).
6. Mindell, *Quantum Mind*, 95.
7. Conjugating a complex number (that is, multiplying the number by its reflection) results in a real number. Here is how in numbers and words: $(a+ib)(a-ib) = a^2 - iab + iab + b^2 = a^2 + b^2$ That is, when multiplied, complex conjugates become real numbers, because by the definition of imaginary numbers, $i^2 = -1$ and because $+iab - iab = 0$.
8. Richard Feynman, *The Theory of Fundamental Processes: A Lecture Note Volume* (New York: Benjamin-Cummings, 1961), 1. Feynman states this rule as follows: "To every process there corresponds an amplitude, a complex number . . . the probability of the process is equal to the absolute square of this amplitude."
9. Mildred J. Hill, a Kentucky schoolteacher, composed the melody of this song. It was first published in 1893 as "Good Morning to All," with lyrics by her sister, Patty Smith Hill. *Time Magazine*, January 2, 1989, p. 88.
10. Hazrat Inayat Khan, *The Mysticism of Sound and Music* (Boston: Shambhala Publications, 1996), ix. In particular, see the chapter "The Value of Repetition and Reflection."

11. Arnold Mindell, *The Quantum Mind and Healing: How to Listen and Respond to Your Body's Symptoms* (Charlottesville, Virginia: Hampton Roads Publishing, 2004). In this book I write about a "quantum state crossover," suggesting that parallel-world dreams or body feelings are linked to the mechanical vibrations of sounds. In other words, sound may be healing because it reflects dream experiences, making them realizable through repetition. Repetition of dream figures in terms of sound is healing.

Chapter 7

1. Jean Paul Richter, ed., *The Notebooks of Leonardo da Vinci*, vol. 1 (Mineola, New York: Dover Publications, Inc., 1970).
2. A veteran of six space shuttle missions, Franklin Story Musgrave (1935–) was aboard the maiden flight of *Challenger*; with another crew member he performed the first space walk of the space shuttle program.
3. This meter is called a *photomultiplier*. It releases electrons when hit by a photon.
4. What I'm calling *backlight*, Jung would have called *shadow*—that undeveloped or unacknowledged part of oneself associated with people (of one's own gender) that are unliked. Still, I prefer the term *backlight*, for we are not talking about an absence of light, but of light raying out in opposite direction from our everyday minds.
5. Signals and communication theory are discussed in Arnold Mindell, *The Dreambody in Relationships* (New York: Penguin, 1987).
6. I consider compassion to be a mystical experience. In principle, the big U is encompassing; it embraces and contains rather than excludes parts. My idea of compassion is more than being nice; it is related to superposition, in which the whole embraces the dreamland directions. In other words, I am adding to the conventional meaning of the word *compassion*, "feeling with the suffering of the other or with the patient," the sense of feeling with all sides. The extended idea of compassion includes for me the Latin word *compassare*, which means awareness and measure. Compassion refers to "walking with the same step" and is an aspect of the Tao, the Way. In a process-oriented sense, compassion means being in step with what is happening, using awareness and being precise and feeling. This definition of compassion combines the clarity of scientific attitudes and the feeling capacity of the heart.
7. A popular version of Richard Feynman's theories appears in his *QED: The Strange Theory of Light and Matter* (Princeton, New Jersey: Princeton University Press, 1985).

8. Professor Edwin Taylor of MIT, as well as other physicists, uses the term *kernel function* or *propagator* to stress the mathematical and physical significance of quantum theory and Feynman's clock. For more on direction, see Taylor's excellent paper "Computers in Physics," *American Institute of Physics* (1998), 12(2), 190. Taylor elucidates Feynman's *QED: The Strange Theory of Light and Matter*. According to Feynman, the photon's "quantum stopwatch" hand rotates as the photon explores each path. Like other theories, quantum theory uses metaphors, talking in this case about paths and clocks. Are these clocks real? Do their hands actually rotate? Does the electron really follow all paths? What is important is that the direction of the arrow is determined by a little "stopwatch," whose hand is a rotating arrow, moving as the particle travels. But this is a very unusual stopwatch. It does not measure time. Feynman says, "The stopwatch hand turns around faster when it times a blue photon compared to a red photon" (p. 47). What is it that is "faster" about blue light than the red light? Not the velocity, not the rate of time itself (no relativistic effect here), just the frequency. The rate of the "stopwatch" is determined by the frequency of the photon. It is simply a mathematical device that gets us good results, and its very abstraction and dissociation obscure its correspondence to the natural characteristics and behavior of waves. In other words, the direction of the arrow at the end of the photon's path gives physicists the information needed to make calculations.

9. Most recently biologists and physicists have determined that the directional sense of humans as well as many other animals is a combination of an internal magnetic compass as well as the movements of the sun and planets. See in particular the Princeton University news release "Sixth Sense: Study Shows How Migrating Birds Navigate" (April 28, 2004) <http://www.princeton.edu/pr/news/04/q2/0428-wikelski.htm>. (The full study is published in the April 16, 2004, issue of *Science*.) Human subjects apparently know how to find their way "magnetically" but cannot explain how they do it.

10. As time becomes more digitalized, I imagine we will become more divorced from our body senses and less familiar with earth movements. The less we follow our bodies and the earth, the more we conflict with time. Already "time stress" seems to be one of the symptoms of following time instead of body experience.

11. Meditating or connecting with the big U line frequently results in a spontaneous flow of understanding that encompasses everyday problems, whether or not they have been consciously focused upon.

Chapter 8

1. Richard P. Feynman, *"Surely You're Joking, Mr. Feynman!"*: *Adventures of a Curious Character* (New York: W. W. Norton & Company, reprint ed. April 1997), 166.
2. The product of both uncertainties is never less than a certain constant, named after the German physicist Max Planck.
3. John Gribbon, *Q Is for Quantum: An Encyclopedia of Particle Physics* (New York: Simon & Schuster, 1998), 418.
4. Werner Heisenberg, *Physics and Philosophy: The Revolution in Modern Science* (New York: Pelican, 1958/1998), 194.
5. Arnold Mindell, *The Quantum Mind and Healing: How to Listen and Respond to Your Body's Symptoms* (Charlottesville, Virginia: Hampton Roads Publishing, 2004). Here I give examples of the reflection of childhood dreams in the rest of life, including chronic symptoms.
6. Arnold Mindell, *Coma: Key to Awakening—Working with the Dreambody near Death* (London: Penguin-Arkana, 1994, 1995).
7. Mindell, *The Quantum Mind and Healing*, 76.

Chapter 9

1. Quoted in Carlos Castaneda, *Tales of Power* (New York: Simon & Schuster, 1974), 292.
2. Arnold Mindell, *Quantum Mind: The Edge Between Physics and Psychology* (Portland, Oregon: Lao Tse Press, 2000). This work contains more on Feynman's quantum field views.
3. There are well-known physicists such as Stephen Hawking, Kip Thorn, Fred Alan Wolf, Amit Goswami, and many others who are pondering time travel.

Chapter 10

1. Lao Tse, *Tao Te Ching*, trans. Gia-fu Feng and Jane English (New York: Vintage Books, 1972), chap. 45. (Because each of the Tao Te Ching's verses is one page or less, I will note the verses as chapters.)
2. <http://blog.tmcnet.com/blog/wimax/wimax/brainstorming-origin.html>.
3. Alex F. Osborn, *Applied Imagination: Principles and Procedures of Creative Thinking* (New York: Charles Scribner's Sons, 1953).

4. Milestone Films, a boutique distribution company in New Jersey, restored and digitized the film *The Mystery of Picasso*, which has been dubbed a national treasure by France, for international release on DVD. See <http://www.columbia.edu/cu/news/03/04/archieRand.html> for more.
5. Amy's sketch from the cover to the Joni Mitchell album *Songs of a Prairie Girl*, 2005, Rhino Records.

Chapter 11

1. Lao Tse, *Tao Te Ching*, The Stephen Mitchell Translation (New York: Harper & Row, 1988), chap. 23.
2. Thanks to Professor John Kahl <www.uwm.edu> for this picture.
3. <http://users.ox.ac.uk/~ouaikido/history.html>
4. <http://www.aikiweb.com/gallery/showphoto.php?photo=873>

Chapter 12

1. Arthur Waley, *The Way and Its Power: A Study of the Tao Te Ching and Its Place in Chinese Thought* (London: Allen & Unwin, 1934), chap. 47.
2. Richard Feynman, *The Feynman Lectures on Physics,* vol. 2 (Reading, Massachusetts: Addison-Wesley, 1963), 18–19. Also see Edwin Taylor and Jon Ogborn, "Quantum Physics Explains Newton's Laws of Motion," *Physics Education* 40 (2005): 1.
3. Feynman, *Feynman Lectures,* chap. 19.
4. Max Planck, *Scientific Autobiography and Other Papers*, trans. Frank Gaynor (New York: Philosophical Library, 1949) quoted by Arthur Young, *The Reflexive Universe* (New York: Delacorte, 1975).
5. The more complete version of Fermat's principle states that the length of optical paths is either a minimum or maximum.
6. Planck, *Scientific Autobiography and Other Papers*, 178.

Chapter 13

1. Lao Tse, *Tao Te Ching*, trans. Gia-fu Feng and Jane English (New York: Vintage Books, 1972), chap. 53.
2. There are many ways of getting to the essence of an experience. We can guess at it, feel it, ask what it was before it was so great, move with it, move more slowly, etc. Each essence approach approximates the big U,

which in principle is the sum of all parallel worlds. The essence of any one of those worlds is, at the same time, the essence or big U of the others.

Chapter 14

1. Lao Tse, *Tao Te Ching*, trans. Gia-fu Feng and Jane English (New York: Vintage Books, 1972), chap. 53.
2. Stephen Hawking, *A Brief History of Time* (New York: Bantam Books, 1988, 1996).
3. Figure 14.3: Thanks to Amy Mindell for the idea of this puppet dialogue.

Chapter 15

1. Carlos Castaneda, *Journey to Ixtlan: The Lessons of Don Juan* (New York: Simon & Schuster, 1972), 13.
2. C. G. Jung, "Psychological Factors in Human Behavior," *The Collected Works of C. G. Jung*, vol. 8, trans. R. F. C. Hull (Princeton, New Jersey: Princeton University Press, 1937, 1969), 114–118.
3. Rebecca Solnit, *A Field Guide to Getting Lost* (New York: Viking, 2005), 17. Solnit speaks about the directional awareness of these people.
4. The material on which my words are based "was collected in the years 1901 to 1906 as part of the work of the Ethnological and Archaeological Survey of California carried on by the University of California's Department of Anthropology." <http://www.sacred-texts.com/nam/ca/scc/scc02. htm>.
5. Dragon painting at Myonshinji Temple, Kyoto, Japan. See <http://www.onmarkproductions.com/html/dragon.shtml>, adapted from the Kyoto National Museum.
6. In Egypt the major weather gods, or field–mood gods, are connected with Shu (goddess of water) and Tefnut (god of dry air). Both gods were children of the sun god.
7. On the top of OM, toward the right, is a dot that represents awareness or cognizance. The cradling crescent moon beneath it reflects this awareness. The symbol beneath the dot and half moon represents the three levels of reality: waking, sleeping, and dreamless sleep. (See <http://en.wikipedia.org/wiki/Nataraja> for more.) To me, these symbols represent basic principles of sentient awareness, reflections, and the resulting deep democracy of levels.
8. Arnold Mindell, *The Shaman's Body: A New Shamanism for Health, Relationships and Community* (San Francisco: HarperCollins, 1993) contains more details about the Nagual.

Chapter 16

1. Carlos Castaneda, *Journey to Ixtlan: The Lessons of Don Juan* (New York: Simon & Schuster, 1972), 266.
2. Amy Sue Kaplan (Amy Mindell), "The Hidden Dance: An Introduction to Process-Oriented Movement Work," master's thesis, Antioch International University (Yellow Springs, Ohio, 1986).
3. Hindus also speak about a Mount Meru, home of the gods at the center of the universe.
4. In physics, spin is an intrinsic angular momentum associated with microscopic particles. It is a quantum mechanical phenomenon; no visible spin can be seen. Whereas angular momentum of large objects comes from their rotation, spin is simply an aspect of the particle's nature.
5. The Ba Kua methods apparently came to China from Mongolia or Siberia. See <http://en.wikipedia.org/wiki/Baguazhang>.
6. Bruce Kumar Frantzis, *The Power of Internal Martial Arts: Combat Secrets of Ba Gua, Tai Chi, and Hsing-I* (Berkeley, California: North Atlantic Books, 1998), chap. 6.
7. Mantak Chia, "Power of Internal Martial Arts," online article, <http://www.universal-tao.com/article/martial_arts.html>.
8. I am thankful to Keido Fukushima, head abbot of the Tofukuji monastery in Kyoto and head of the Rinzai sect, for the idea of the second training. During a conversation with him, he told Amy and me that Zen monks go through their first training in meditation and koan questioning at the monastery. Then they leave the monastery, and life gives them a second training. The Roshi passed or failed monks (so to speak) on their second training only after they came back to the monastery following years in the world. The test occurred by merely drinking tea together. There was no formal method involved for the second training test.

Chapter 17

1. Carlos Castaneda, *A Separate Reality: Further Conversations with Don Juan* (New York: Simon & Schuster, 1972), 191.
2. Arnold Mindell, *The Deep Democracy of Open Forums* (Charlottesville, Virginia: Hampton Roads Publishing, 2004), ix.
3. In *Healers* (New York: Facts on File, 1997), Deanne Durrett writes: "Before the ceremony begins, the medicine man and his helpers work for hours to

create a sand painting. . .. The patient sits or lays on the sand painting during the curing ceremony. Power is thought to be absorbed from the sacred objects depicted in the sand painting. During the chant, the patient relives events in the life of an ancient hero who was cured by the Holy People. Each sand painting must be destroyed before sunset and another painted the next day if needed." This excerpt is also included in the online article "Art and Traditional Healing: Native American Art and the Yei'bi'ci Winter Healing Ceremony" by Subhuti Dharmananda <http://www.itmonline.org/arts/arthealing.htm>.

4. H. S. Poley, *Navajo Sand Paintings I Have Known* (Los Angeles: University of Southern California Press, 1933), 117–118. I found this rare book in the Denver Public Library's department of Western History/Genealogy. Sand paintings shown to the public are not always exact replicas of the originals.

5. Known parallel worlds appear in worldwork as parallel histories and stories, roles and ghost roles (see Part IV of this book). We often see roles switch. They are nonlocal and shared; that means they belong to everyone, though one person or group is usually associated with one role or another at one time or other. For example, because of nonlocality, a "terrorist" is everywhere.

Chapter 18

1. Carlos Castaneda, *The Art of Dreaming* (New York: Harper Perennial, 1994), 260.

2. Waynelle Wilder, "Dream Shifts after Impact: Mild Traumatic Brain Injury (MTBI) and the Nabokov Blues," *Journal of Process-Oriented Psychology* 9 (2004): 77–86.

3. From the website of the Canadian Museum of Nature of Ottawa, Ontario, by permission, <http://www.nature.ca/notebooks/english/blkber.htm>.

4. This drum was given to us by the Haida people for our work there several years ago. The Haida are a First Nations people from Haida Gwai, which now are called the Queen Charlotte Islands, on British Columbia's northern Pacific coast.

5. In that dream, I was polishing my father's car when a bear arrived to chase me around that car!

Chapter 19

1. Jalal Al-din Rumi, *The Illuminated Rumi*, trans. and illuminations Coleman Barks and Michael Green (New York: Bantam, 1997), 127.
2. Arnold Mindell, *The Quantum Mind and Healing: How to Listen and Respond to Your Body's Symptoms* (Charlottesville, Virginia: Hampton Roads Publishing, 2004). Here you will find more about the nonlocality of health issues.
3. C. G. Jung, *The Collected Works of C. G. Jung*, trans. R. F. C. Hull (Princeton, New Jersey: Princeton University Press, 1937, 1969). In volume 16, *The Practice of Psychotherapy*, Jung speaks of the "psychology of transference": an account of the transference phenomena based on the illustrations in the "Rosarium Philosophorum" or "the return of the soul."
4. Jung, *Collected Works*, vol. 16.
5. Gravity is the universe's most pervading field. Yet gravity itself is the weakest of all the forces. Just think of electromagnetic forces. If you think of a paper clip, you can see that it is easy for even a weak magnet to pick up the paper clip. Its weight, or rather the force pulling it down due to the field of gravity, is so weak, even a magnet can pick it up. Yet gravity governs the motion of astronomical bodies. It keeps the moon in orbit around the earth and keeps the earth and the other planets of the solar system in orbit around the sun. On a larger scale, it governs the motion of stars and slows the outward expansion of the entire universe because of the inward attraction of galaxies to other galaxies. (See Appendix 5 for more about that field and its force.)

Chapter 20

1. Lao Tse, *Tao Te Ching*, The James Legge Translation, in *Sacred Books of the East*, vol. 39, ed. F. Max Muller (Oxford, United Kingdom: Oxford University Press, 1891, 2003), chap. 35.
2. The word *community* comes from the Latin *communis*, common. For me, the essence of organizations is their "commons"—that is, the community or U.
3. *Backlight* is a vector description of what I have called the "terrorist" in my *The Year I: Global Process Work with Planetary Tensions* (New York: Penguin-Arkana, 1990). Backlight is also the "most troublesome ghost role" in three of my other books: *The Leader as Martial Artist*, *Sitting in the Fire*, and *The Deep Democracy of Open Forums*.

4. Nicholas Black Elk, as told through John G. Neidhardt, *Black Elk Speaks: Being the Life Story of a Holy Man of the Oglala Sioux* (Lincoln, Nebraska: University of Nebraska Press, 1932, 2000).

5. Arnold Mindell, *The Deep Democracy of Open Forums* (Charlottesville, Virginia: Hampton Roads Publishing, 2004). Worldwork details are given here.

Chapter 21

1. Morihei Ueshiba, *The Art of Peace*, trans. John Stevens (Boston: Shambhala, 2002), 89.

2. The Haida are a First Nations people on the Queen Charlotte Islands, which lie along Canada's northern Pacific coast. For more information about totem poles, visit the Royal British Columbia Museum either online <http://www.royalbcmuseum.bc.ca/totems/totems1b.html> or in Victoria, B.C.

3. From the online story "The First Totem Pole" by Rosa Bell, <http://www.virtualmuseum.ca/Exhibitions/Inuit_Haida/haida/english/language/story3.html>.

4. Illustration by Christian White, in Rosa Bell's online story "The First Totem Pole" <http://www.virtualmuseum.ca/Exhibitions/Inuit_Haida/haida/english/language/story1.html>.

5. We used this big U as a metaskill in all that we did with the Haida. As a result, we are thankful for having learned a great deal from them about the sea, the land, and the sky.

6. Nicholas Black Elk, as told through John G. Neidhardt, *Black Elk Speaks: Being the Life Story of a Holy Man of the Oglala Sioux* (Lincoln, Nebraska: University of Nebraska Press, 1932, 2000).

7. Black Elk, 2.

8. Black Elk, 27, 34, 37, 40, 54, 55, 82, 147, 202.

9. Arnold Mindell, *The Deep Democracy of Open Forums* (Charlottesville, Virginia: Hampton Roads Publishing, 2004).

10. Black Elk, 260.

Chapter 22

1. Ellen M. Chen, *Tao Te Ching, A New Translation with Commentary* (New York: Paragon House, 1989), 116.

Appendix 1

1. Michio Kaku, *Hyperspace: A Scientific Odyssey through Parallel Universes, Time Warps, and the Tenth Dimension* (Oxford University Press, 1995), 262.

Appendix 3

1. B. A. Haisch, A. Rueda, and H. E. Puthoff, "Inertia as a Zero-Point Field Lorenz Force," *Physical Review* A, 49 (1994): 678-694.

Appendix 6

1. William Gilbert, *De Magnete*, trans. P. Fleury Mottelay, republication of the 1893 translation (New York: Dover, 1958).

Appendix 11

1. See Edwin Taylor's excellent summary and annotated bibliography of least action in physics at his website: <http://www.eftaylor.com/pub/BibliogLeastAction12.pdf>. We should also note that a most general formulation of the least-action principle would call it the *principle of stationary action*. See <http://en.wikipedia.org/wiki/Least_action> for more.

BIBLIOGRAPHY

Bell, Rosa. "The First Totem Pole." 2000. http://www.virtualmuseum.ca/Exhibitions/Haida/java/english/totem/

Black Elk, Nicholas, as told through John G. Neidhardt. *Black Elk Speaks: Being the Life Story of a Holy Man of the Oglala Sioux.* Lincoln, Nebraska: University of Nebraska Press, 1932, 2000.

Bray, D. "Protein Molecules as Computational Elements in Living Cells." *Nature* 376 (1995): 307.

Castaneda, Carlos. *The Active Side of Infinity.* New York: HarperCollins, 1998.

———. *The Art of Dreaming.* New York: Harper Perennial, 1994.

———. *The Eagle's Gift.* New York: Simon & Schuster, 1981.

———. *The Fire from Within.* New York: Washington Square Press, 1991.

———. *Journey to Ixtlan: The Lessons of Don Juan.* New York: Simon & Schuster, 1972.

———. *The Power of Silence: Further Lessons of Don Juan.* New York: Simon & Schuster, 1972.

———. *The Second Ring of Power.* New York: Simon & Schuster, 1977.

———. *A Separate Reality: Further Conversations with Don Juan.* New York: Simon & Schuster, 1971.

———. *Tales of Power.* New York: Simon & Schuster, 1974.

———. *The Teachings of Don Juan: A Yaqui Way of Knowledge.* Berkeley, California: University of California Press, 1968, 1995.

———. *The Wheel of Time: The Shamans of Ancient Mexico, Their Thoughts about Life, Death, and the Universe.* New York: Pocket Books, 1998.

Chatwin, Bruce. *Songlines.* New York: Penguin, 1987.

Chen, Ellen. *Tao Te Ching.* New York: Paragon House, 1989.

Clinton, Bill. *My Life*. New York: Knopf, 2004.

Cohen, Brian S. "Being-in-Dreaming: An Introduction to Toltec Sorcery," interview of Florinda Donner. *Magical Blend Magazine*, April 1992, 35.

Diamond, Julie, and Lee Spark Jones. *A Path Made by Walking*. Portland, Oregon: Lao Tse Press, 2004.

Feinstein, David, and Stanley Krippner. *The Mythic Path: Discovering the Guiding Stories of Your Past, Creating a Vision for Your Future*. New York: Tarcher, 1997.

Feynman, Richard. *The Feynman Lectures on Physics* (Vol. 1–3). Reading, Massachusetts: Addison-Wesley, 1963.

———. *QED: The Strange Theory of Light and Matter*. Princeton, New Jersey: Princeton University Press, 1985.

———. *The Theory of Fundamental Processes: A Lecture Note*. New York: Benjamin-Cummings Publishing Co., 1962.

Filkin, David. *Stephen Hawking's Universe*. New York: Basic Books, 1997.

Frantzis, Bruce Kumar. *The Power of Internal Martial Arts: Combat Secrets of Ba Gua, Tai Chi, and Hsing-I*. Berkeley, California: North Atlantic Books, 1998.

Goswami, Amrit, with Richard Reed and Maggie Goswami. *The Self-Aware Universe: How Consciousness Creates the Material World*. New York: Tarcher, 1995.

Gribbon, John. *Q Is for Quantum: An Encyclopedia of Particle Physics*. New York: Simon & Schuster, 1998.

Haisch, B. A., A. Rueda, and H. E. Puthoff. "Inertia as a Zero-Point Field Lorentz Force." *Physical Review A* 49 (1994): 678.

Hameroff, S. "Funda-mentality: Is the Conscious Mind Subtly Linked to a Basic Level of the Universe?" *Trends in Cognitive Science* 2 (1998): 119–124.

Hameroff, S., and R. Penrose. "Orchestrated Reduction of Quantum Coherence in Brain Microtubules: A Model for Consciousness." In *Toward a Science of Consciousness: The First Tucson Discussions and Debates*, ed. S. Hameroff, A. Kaszniak, and A. Scott. Cambridge, Massachusetts: MIT Press, 1996.

Hawking, Stephen. *A Brief History of Time*. New York: Bantam Books, 1988, 1996.

Heisenberg, Werner. *Physics and Philosophy: The Revolution in Modern Science.* New York: Pelican, 1958/1998.

Hillman, James. *The Soul's Code: In Search of Character and Calling.* New York: Warner Books, 1997.

Ione. *Listening in Dreams.* New York: I-Universe, 2005.

James, William. *The Varieties of Religious Experiences.* New York: Random House, 1902, 2002.

Jung, C. G. *The Collected Works of C. G. Jung.* Edited by Herbert Read, Michael Fordham, and Gerhard Adler. Translated by R. F. C. Hull (except Vol. 11). Bollingen Series XX. Princeton, New Jersey: Princeton University Press, 1953.

———. *Memories, Dreams, Reflections.* Edited by Aniela Jaffe. Translated by Clara Winstone and Richard Winston. New York: Vintage Books, 1989.

———. "Psychological Factors in Human Behavior." In *The Collected Works of C. G. Jung*, Vol. 8. Translated by R. F. C. Hull. Princeton, New Jersey: Princeton University Press, 1937, 1969.

Kaplan, Amy Sue (Amy Mindell). "The Hidden Dance: An Introduction to Process-Oriented Movement Work." Master's thesis, Antioch International University (Yellow Springs, Ohio), 1986.

Khan, Hazrat Inayat. *The Mysticism of Sound and Music.* Boston: Shambhala Publications, 1991.

Lao Tse. *The Book of Lao Zi.* Beijing: Foreign Languages Press, 1993.

Lao Tse. *Tao Te Ching.* The James Legge Translation. In *Sacred Books of the East*, Vol. 39, ed. F. Max Muller. Oxford, United Kingdom: Oxford University Press, 1891, 2003.

Lao Tse. *Tao Te Ching.* Translated by Gia-fu Feng and Jane English. New York: Vintage Books, 1972.

Lao Tse. *Tao Te Ching.* The Stephen Mitchell Translation. New York: Harper & Row, 1988.

Lao Tse. *Tao Te Ching: The Book of Meaning and Life.* Translated by Richard Wilhelm (into German) and H. G. Ost-wald (into English). London: Viking-Penguin-Arkana, 1985.

Lessing, F. D., and Alex Wayman. *Introduction to the Buddhist Tantric Systems.* Delhi, India: Motilal Banarsidass, 1993.

Leviton, Richard. *The Galaxy on Earth: A Travelers' Guide to the Planet's Visionary Geography*. Charlottesville, Virginia: Hampton Roads Publishing, 2002.

Maharshi, Ramana. *Talks with Ramana Maharshi*. Carlsbad, California: Inner Directions Publications, 2000.

Maclagan, David. *Creation Myths: Man's Introduction to the World*. London: Thames & Hudson, 1977.

Matthews, Robert. "Inertia: Does Empty Space Put up the Resistance?" *Science* 263 (1994): 613–614.

Microsoft Encarta Premium. CD, DVD. Microsoft Software, 2006.

Mindell, Amy. *The Dreaming Source of Creativity: 30 Simple Ways to Have Fun and Work on Yourself*. Portland, Oregon: Lao Tse Press, 2005.

———. *Metaskills: The Spiritual Art of Therapy*. Portland, Oregon: Lao Tse Press, 1995.

Mindell, Arnold. *City Shadows: Psychological Interventions in Psychiatry*. New York: Penguin, 1988.

———. *Coma: Key to Awakening—Working with the Dreambody near Death*. London: Penguin-Arkana, 1994, 1995.

———. *The Deep Democracy of Open Forums,* Charlottesville, Virginia: Hampton Roads Publishing, 2004.

———. *Dreambody: The Body's Role in Revealing the Self*. Boston: Sigo/Arkana Press, 1982, 1984.

———. *The Dreambody in Relationships*. New York: Penguin, 1987.

———. *Inner Dreambodywork: Working on Yourself Alone*. New York: Penguin, 1990.

———. *The Leader as Martial Artist: An Introduction to Deep Democracy—Techniques and Strategies for Resolving Conflict and Creating Community*. San Francisco: HarperCollins, 1992.

———. *River's Way: The Process Science of the Dreambody*. London: Penguin, 1986.

———. *The Shaman's Body: A New Shamanism for Health, Relationships, and Community*. San Francisco: HarperCollins, 1993.

———. *Sitting in the Fire: Large Group Transformation through Diversity and Conflict*. Portland, Oregon: Lao Tse Press, 1993.

———. *Working with the Dreaming Body*. London: Penguin-Arkana, 1984.

————. *The Year I: Global Process Work with Planetary Tensions*. New York: Penguin-Arkana, 1990.

Mindell, Arnold, and Amy Mindell. *Riding the Horse Backwards: Process Work in Theory and Practice*. New York: Penguin, 1992.

Osborn, Alex F. *Applied Imagination*. New York: Charles Scribner's Sons, 1953.

Penrose, R. *The Large, the Small, and the Human Mind*. Cambridge, United Kingdom: Cambridge University Press, 1996.

————. *The Emperor's New Mind*. Oxford, United Kingdom: Oxford University Press, 1989.

Picasso, Pablo, and Henri-Georges Clouzot. *The Mystery of Picasso*. On video-cassette: Harrington Park, New Jersey: Milestone Films and Video, 2003.

Planck, Max. *Scientific Autobiography and Other Papers*. Translated by Frank Gaynor. New York: Philosophical Library, 1949.

Popper, K., and J. Eccles. *The Self and Its Brain*. New York: Springer-Verlag, 1977.

Puett, Michael J. *To Become a God: Cosmology, Sacrifice, and Self-Divinization in Early China*. Harvard-Yenching Institute Monograph Series. Harvard University Asia Center for the Harvard-Yenching Institute. Cambridge, Massachusetts: Harvard University Press, 2002.

Rawson, Philip, and Legeza Laszlo. *Tao: The Chinese Philosophy of Time and Change*. London: Thames & Hudson, 1973.

Reiss, Gary. *Leap into Living—Moving Beyond Fear to Freedom*. Portland, Oregon: Lao Tse Press, 1998.

————. *Beyond War and Peace in the Arab Israeli Conflict*. Portland, Oregon: Lao Tse Press, 2003.

Rumi. *The Illuminated Rumi*. Translated and illuminated by Coleman Barks and Michael Green. New York: Bantam, 1997.

Schrödinger, E. *Science and Humanism*. Cambridge, United Kingdom: Cambridge University Press, 1951.

Schwartz-Salant, Nathan, ed. *Jung: On Alchemy*. Princeton, New Jersey: Princeton University Press, 1995.

Shermer, Michael. "Three Books Try to Explain Consciousness" [book review]. *Scientific American* (March 2004).

Sloman, A. "The Emperor's Real Mind." *Artificial Intelligence* 56 (1992): 355–396.

Solnit, Rebecca. *A Field Guide to Getting Lost*. New York: Viking, 2005.

Taylor, Edwin. "Computers in Physics." *American Institute of Physics* 12 (1998): 190.

Taylor, Edwin, and Jon Ogborn. "Quantum Physics Explains Newton's Laws of Motion." *Physics Education* 40 (2005): 1.

Taylor, Edwin, and John Wheeler. *Exploring Black Holes: An Introduction to General Relativity*. Rev. ed. New York: Addison Wesley Longman, 2000.

Trungpa, Chögyam. *Crazy Wisdom*. Boston: Shambhala, 1991.

Turing, A.M. "Computing Machinery and Intelligence." *Mind* 49 (1950): 433–460.

Ueshiba, Morihei. *The Art of Peace*. Translated by John Stevens. Boston: Shambhala, 2002.

Von Franz, Marie-Louise. *Number and Time*. Evanston, Illinois: Northwestern University Press, 1974.

Waley, Arthur. *The Way and Its Power: A Study of the Tao Te Ching and Its Place in Chinese Thought*. London: Allen & Unwin, 1934.

Weber, Rene. *Dialogues with Scientists and Sages*. New York: Routledge & Kegan Paul, 1986.

Wilder, Waynelle. "Dream Shifts after Impact: Mild Traumatic Brain Injury (MTBI) and the Nabokov Blues." *Journal of Process Oriented Psychology* 9 (2004): 77–86.

Wolf, Fred Alan. *Parallel Universes, Time Warps, and the Tenth Dimension*. New York: Anchor Books, Doubleday, 1994/1995.

Young, Arthur. *The Reflexive Universe*. New York: Delacorte, 1975.

INDEX

big u, *continued*
  of a relationship,179–180, 182–183
  spontaneous understanding,
    267n11
  vectors, 63, 231
Black Elk, 223–228
black holes, 15
body awareness
  directionality exercise, 13
  Guugu Yimithirr people
    (Australia), 14
  revealing least action, 7–8
  Wintu people (California),
    260n3
body symptoms
  animation exercise, 149–154
  caduceus healing, 140–141
  dis-ease, 137–138
  dreambodies, 138–139
  shamanistic exercise, 141–144
Bohm, David, 80, 83, 263n8
brainstorming, 104–106, 115
Broglie, Louis de, 83
Budo, 118
bugs. *See also* flirts
  aspect of awareness, 247
  catching exercise, 30
  as flirts, 262n13
  immortality, 148–149
  Japanese view, 262n12
  origin of the universe, 29, 262n11
  persistent nature of, 232
  in quantum theory, 35–37
  in relationships, 180
  required for consciousness, 148
  of uncertainty, 81

C
caduceus healing, 140–141
Casimir effect, 237–240
Casimir force, 27–28, 261n9
Casimir, Hendrik, 27–28, 238
Castaneda, Carlos, 3, 58, 59. *See also*
  don Juan
causality, 114–115, 124–126
cavity resonance, 28
chemistry and complexes, 156

Chinese martial arts, 167–169
Chögyam Trungpa, 106–107, 216,
  232
chronic fatigue, 100–101
circle dances, 166–167. *See also*
  spinning
Clinton, Bill, 41
coma recovery, 59–60
communication, 25
community, 213, 273n2 (ch.20).
  See also group wisdom
compassion, 189–191, 227, 266n6
complex numbers
  conjugation of, 265n7 (ch.6)
  described, 63
  in quantum wave function, 262n2,
    264n4
complexes, 156–161
conjugation, 63–65, 263n4, 265n7
  (ch.6)
consciousness
  after sentient awareness, 22
  distinguished from sentient
    awareness, 16–17
  needs bugs, 148
  pervasive awareness, 60
consensus reality
  context of the little u, 124
  defined, 64, 239
  in group work, 214, 216
  interference of, 43–44
  quantum theory represented in,
    75
  in relationships, 176
conservation of energy, 116–117, 256
content and process in group
  problems, 213
Copernican universe, 30–31
Cramer, John, 35–36, 65
crazy wisdom, 106–107, 115
creation in moods and force fields, 91
creation myths
  Abrahamic, 18–20
  Hindu, 160
  Navajo, 18–19, 180–181, 260n8,
    271n3 (ch.17)
  weather systems, 158–161